IN THE
AMERICAN
PROVINCE

IN THE
AMERICAN
PROVINCE

Studies in the History and Historiography of Ideas

David A. Hollinger

THE JOHNS HOPKINS UNIVERSITY PRESS
Baltimore and London

To

Albert Hollinger, Jr.

and

Evelyn Steinmeier Hollinger

". . . for the living of these days."

© 1985 David A. Hollinger
All rights reserved
Printed in the United States of America

Originally published in a hardcover edition in 1985 by
Indiana University Press. Published by arrangement with
Indiana University Press.

Johns Hopkins Paperbacks edition, 1989
The Johns Hopkins University Press
701 West 40th Street
Baltimore, Maryland 21211
The Johns Hopkins Press Ltd., London

Library of Congress Cataloging-in-Publication Data

Hollinger, David A.
   In the American province : studies in the history and
historiography of ideas / David A. Hollinger.
    p.   cm.

  Bibliography: p.
  Includes index.
  ISBN 0-8018-3826-6
  1. United States—Intellectual life—20th century.
2. United States—Intellectual life—Historiography.
3. United States—Historiography.   I. Title.
E169.1.H76   1989
973—dc 19

88-39620
CIP

CONTENTS

PREFACE

THE RECOGNITION THAT one is "in a province" can inspire conflicting sentiments. Some people celebrate the particularity of the province, and advance provincialism as a doctrine. In this view, the virtue of a province is its sustaining homogeneity, its distance from the varied social world beyond provincial borders. Others recoil from this potential confinement, and advance the cause of cosmopolitanism against the imperatives of provincial life. Then, the point of being in a province is to get beyond it, to encounter and absorb a range of experience by means of which one can cease to be "provincial." In between these two abstractions—provincialism and cosmopolitanism—spans a field of concrete possibilities. Somewhere amid these real options most of us try to have it both ways, avoiding at once the constraints of a province too narrowly defined and the discomforting instability of a universe too vast and varied for us to make our own. Having it both ways depends, of course, on finding the right spot along the spectrum from the local to the universal. To be in the American province is good enough for some of us, but for many American intellectuals it has been instead an appalling confinement, a condition to be overcome in the interests of an experience and an identity as great and various as "the West." For yet other Americans, including some intellectuals, this same America has been an expanse so diverse and multitudinous as to render absurd any feeling for it as a "province," a concept better applied to America's regional, ethnic, and religious parts.

Not all of these collected essays bear on the matter of being in the American province, but the notion of "province" looms large enough here to inspire the collection's title. This notion figures somewhat differently in the two sets of studies that make up the volume. In the historiographical essays, the province is a category that I urge be applied in a non-provincial spirit to America itself. The insight that America is a province of a civilization that also embraces the national cultures of Europe is hardly new, but the historiographical implications of this truism have been slow to take hold. Chief among these implications, it seems to me, is that the subdiscipline we call "American intellectual history" ought to recognize as its own a range of problems that have too often been characterized as "European thought," and hence safely ignored by students of American thought. The having of a province for our subject, then, entails not the confining of our attention to uniquely American intellectual developments—vital though these must always remain to the field—but rather the expansion of our scope to include American participation in, and sometimes American leadership of, the intellectual history of the West. The concept of province is a less benign presence in the monographic essays collected here under the heading, "Studies of Intellectuals in Modern America." These essays are primarily devoted to American intellectuals of cosmopolitan inclinations, who often felt themselves surrounded by provincials. Some of these intellectuals did regard America as a viable embodiment of the cosmopolitan ideal, as a world large enough when contrasted to Flatbush or Peoria, but others remained preoccupied with the limitations of life in the American province.

Although real continuities run through this volume, I do not want to exaggerate them and thereby represent this book as anything other than a collection of distinct and self-contained essays. I wrote these eleven pieces for a variety of specific occasions spanning more than a decade. All but one of the eleven has been published previously. I have left them unchanged except for correcting a few editorial errors—mostly my own—made during the process of their first publication. I have written a brief preface for each of the essays, trying to clarify my claims and admitting to some "second thoughts."

Anyone who reads this book straight through, as I was obliged to do while preparing it for the press, will soon weary of certain words. So often have I spoken of "discourse" and "agendas" that I can only ask my reader's indulgence. Such inelegant repetition is not unusual in books of essays, each piece written with a minimum awareness of the stylistic idiosyncrasies of other pieces not intended for back-to-back publication. Yet these particular ruts in my working vocabulary have a significance beyond what they reveal about my own lack of literary imagination. They manifest my concern with making clear the character of my chief subject matter: *arguments*, especially as made by people who "made history" by arguing.

Now, arguments, whatever else they may be, are social acts. As such, they have more in common with other objects of historical study than is sometimes acknowledged. Arguments, like everything else, are generated and sustained by a variety of often shifting conditions, including cultural traditions and the interests of variously constituted social groups. The natural similarities between arguments and other objects of historical study are worth remarking upon only because these similarities have so often been ignored, and even denied, in the professional circles surrounding the study of American intellectual history. The life of the mind has been alternatively mystified and demystified with great fervor. This life, we are sometimes told, is one of singular freedom and purity, fully comprehensible historically if we attend only to the sequential development of autonomous, rational ideas. The unmasking of this extravagant idealism has been performed as an almost sacred duty by others, who have in turn assured us that the life of the mind is a mere function of something else, in which reside whatever powers actually determine the activities of intellectuals.

This is an old disagreement. I allude to it here neither to try to resolve it, nor to dismiss from the historian's responsibility the genuine and enduring issues in social and cultural theory that lie behind the two "straw men" I have just invoked. The simple methodological postulate that "arguments are social acts" does, however, have some appeal in the context of this old disagreement, the terms of which have bedeviled so many efforts to talk sense when addressing the nature of intellectual history. The postulate is not a general theory of any kind (and certainly not of "the role of ideas in history"), but this postulate can help us to cope with the competing claims of any and all social and cultural theories while we study specific cases in the history of ideas. At least this is a hope that informs both the monographic and historiographic studies collected here.

Many colleagues and friends have contributed over the years to the shape of one or more of these essays. Here I will mention only three whose critical advice and encouragement has been of especially great help: Bruce Kuklick, Lewis Perry, and Quentin Skinner. I want also to thank Robert Mandel of the Indiana University Press for suggesting that a book might be made of these essays of mine. I have been helped in many ways by my research assistant, Richard Parmater. Finally, I want to acknowledge the financial assistance of the University of Michigan.

Ann Arbor   D.A.H.
November 1983

I am pleased that The Johns Hopkins University Press is making *In the American Province* available in a softcover edition at a price students can afford. I have taken advantage of this opportunity to correct a few printing errors, but otherwise the text is unchanged from the hardcover edition of 1985.

Ann Arbor   D.A.H.
August 1988

IN THE
AMERICAN
PROVINCE

PART ONE

---

*Studies of Intellectuals
in Modern America*

1

WILLIAM JAMES AND THE

CULTURE OF INQUIRY

The project of interpreting William James is made more worthy and more challenging by the fact that James managed to say so much to so many people about so great a variety of questions. Echoes of his voice have enlivened and helped to shape a multitude of ongoing discussions, the dynamics of which have often led James's readers to reconstruct him in terms of issues rather different from those he was most concerned to address. Hence advocates of this or that currently popular epistemological or metaphysical doctrine will claim James as their own, or set him up as a representative defender of some opposing doctrine. The anachronistic readings of James that sometimes result are not difficult to live with, but a more accurate comprehension of what James himself was doing can make a more authentic James available for use in these contemporary debates. This authentic, historical James is also the one we must have if we wish to get right the intellectual history of the United States.

A truism about James is that he worried over the relation of science to religion. Yet this concern has been distant from the minds of most of the philosophers and scholars of the last fifty years who have drawn inspiration from, and sought to interpret, James's work. The study below insists that an accurate reading of James requires that we not screen out as an irrelevant curiosity the anxiety about the fate of religion in an age of science that James frankly shared with most of the people who heard him lecture and bought his books during his lifetime. By taking this anxiety seriously, we can more easily discern in James's texts what I argue here was James's center of intellectual gravity: A radically secular, naturalistic vision of the process by which knowledge is produced, and a hope that religiously satisfying knowledge might still be forthcoming if only enough people would bring to inquiry—and place at risk in it—their religious commitments. James wished to reform the culture of inquiry by enriching it with exactly those energies that were intimidated by the agnostics and positivists who announced themselves to be the true representatives of "science." He sought to promote this reform exactly while developing the philosophical arguments we know as "radical empiricism," "pluralism," and "pragmatism."

Since "pragmatism" is the topic of an essay following this one in which James is again addressed, I want to indicate here the division of labor between these two essays. "The Problem of Pragmatism in American History" is concerned with a distinctive intellectual tradition in the United States which James helped to create, but which was largely put together by others making use of James's work in the context of the writings of John Dewey. In that essay, I take up James in terms of what the tradition made of him. In "William James and the Culture of Inquiry," however, the preoccupations of later pragmatists are very much beside the point. Here, my aim is to confront James head-on, and to establish what his works said in the context in which he wrote them.

This essay was occasioned by the Harvard University Press's publication of the first seven volumes of a new edition of James's Works *sponsored by the American Council of Learned Societies. Additional volumes have since appeared, but I have not amended the notes to take account of them. The essay was published in* Michigan Quarterly Review XX (1981), 264–283.

WHEN WILLIAM JAMES published *The Will to Believe* in 1897, he explained that his collected "Essays in Popular Philosophy" were not intended for the Salvation Army, nor for "the miscellaneous popular crowd." James was not playing the snob. He was among the least elitist thinkers of his class and generation, and he cared more about the spiritual welfare of nonintellectuals than most academic philosophers ever have. Yet he had a clear sense of his audience, and of the role this audience could play in the enrichment or retardation of civilization. *The Will to Believe, Pragmatism,* and much of James's other work was "popular" in that it was written for intellectuals, only some of whom were philosophers. James believed that decisions about philosophical issues made by the intellectual leaders of his society would have enormous consequences for that society, and he was very much afraid that the wrong choices were being made. Especially did James fear that his contemporary intellectuals were forming a culturally self-destructive idea of what it meant to be "scientific." He believed that these contemporaries, including philosophers, failed to understand the actual, human conditions under which scientific knowledge was created, expanded, and transformed; he believed also that widespread recognition of these conditions could serve to mobilize the intellectual energies of men and women of virtue. These beliefs informed, and largely controlled James's career as a philosopher, the detailed record of which is now being made splendidly available by the Harvard University Press in a new, standard edition under sponsorship of the American Council of Learned Societies.[1]

The editors of *The Works of William James* are not oblivious to James's arguments with his contemporary intellectuals about the culture of inquiry, but they aim primarily to clarify and evaluate James's contributions to discussion of the classical problems of epistemology, metaphysics, and ethics. This clarification and evaluation is performed carefully in the introductions to the seven volumes now in print, although the authors pay only passing attention to ways in which James's formulation and pursuit of philosophical problems served to confront dilemmas felt by a population larger than the philosophical profession. When the editors do nod in the direction of this larger context, they tend to treat all non-philosophers as a vast, undifferentiated mass. Edward H. Madden worries at some length about James's willingness to describe *The Will to Believe* as "popular," and finally attributes this peculiarity to James's awareness that "questions about the ethics of belief, morality, and religion" are close to "every man's heart."[2] Yet James sought to influence an audience both smaller than the universal "mankind" on behalf of which he sometimes spoke, and larger than the professional community whose members now preserve and puzzle over his *Works*. The meaning of what James wrote becomes more fully accessible to us if we read it with this fact in mind.

James's audience consisted of contemporaries who knew what was at issue when the adjective "scientific" was placed within quotation marks. James himself so placed this word frequently, from his earliest writings to his last, and signaled thereby his participation in his generation's uncertainty about the qualities that defined science and its influence on modern society and thought. The terms in which this concern was discussed in James's time, especially during his formative years, were set in the English-speaking world by a particular group of intellectuals who ostensibly *knew* what it meant to be scientific. T. H. Huxley, John Tyndall, W. K. Clifford, and Herbert Spencer were among the most widely quoted of this group of scientists, philosophers, and publicists; they by no means agreed on everything, but their polemical advocacy of science often linked science with either agnosticism, materialism, positivism, or all three.[3] Persons opposed to these outlooks, yet unwilling for whatever reason to be regarded as anti-scientific, commonly referred to these currents of thought as "scientific" rather than scientific.

James's preoccupation with the Cliffords and Huxleys of the world is most pronounced in *The Will to Believe,* where he condemned as unnecessarily stifling the doctrine that one should believe nothing except on the basis of evidence recognized by the sciences. Our lives present us with many issues demanding commitments when evidence of this sort was lacking, James asserted, and our sciences have at their roots certain investments of faith not subject to proof. James's respect for the sciences was nowhere more insistent than in these essays of the 1880s and 1890s; he argued for the expansion and enrichment of the matrix of inquiry in the interests of a knowledge free from the peculiar biases of the likes of Clifford.[4] Yet this preoccupation on James's part went far beyond the collection of essays with which it has always been identified.

The ghost of Clifford hovered over the entirety of *The Varieties of Religious Experience,* and emerged at the very end of this prodigious undertaking in "the science of religion" to receive James's most earnest and withering rebuke.[5] Science was carefully distinguished from "science" in *The Principles of Psychology,* the massive study of the human mind that James climaxed with a brief naturalistic account of science itself: Against those who believed uncritically in the objectivity of science, James grounded in a foundation of human interests both the aspiration to do science, and the particular constructions of science.[6] His refusal to acknowledge as transcendent the authority claimed by the "science" of Clifford was expressed throughout his *oeuvre,* from his early book reviews through the last volumes he was to write, *A Pluralistic Universe* and *Some Problems of Philosophy.*[7]

This refusal was expressed with unusual cogency in *Pragmatism.* Here, in lectures written in 1906 and 1907, James brought into a single, integrated argument his basic answer to both of the two movements against which his career was the most persistently directed: the party of "science" noted above, and the frankly religious, "idealistic" movement professing faith in an eternal world-order existing prior to human participation. Both struck James as obstacles to the development, within his society, of a satisfactory moral and intellectual life. The seriousness of the second obstacle became apparent to James at mid-career, when he confronted the absolute idealism of his formidable colleague at Harvard, Josiah Royce. James's objections to all varieties of monistic idealism took form against the backdrop of his dissent from the "scientific" tendency to treat the world as a hard object gradually being discovered by means of the suppression of human subjectivity. In *Pragmatism,* James responded to both of these faiths in a completed universe by outlining his own understanding of how our knowledge of that universe actually grows. In *Pragmatism,* moreover, James was explicit about the larger intellectual setting in which he carried out his work as a philosopher. James packed into this little book more of what he had to say than he managed to get into any of his other works.

James leaves not the slightest doubt that *Pragmatism* is written for people worried about the fate of religion in the wake of the advance of "science." The text opens with a construction of "The Present Dilemma of Philosophy," according to which the concerned soul, turning to philosophers for guidance, is faced with an obviously unacceptable choice between "toughminded" empiricist-skeptics and "tender-minded" religious idealists. James then claims to offer a solution: *Pragmatism* proceeds to lay out a middle way between "crude naturalism" and "transcendental absolutism," and indeed concludes with a chapter on "Pragmatism and Religion" in which is spelled out the superior appeal of "pragmatism" to persons too tender to give up religion but too tough to give up science.[8]

These striking features of the text are incidentally acknowledged by H. S. Thayer. "Evidently," speculates Thayer midway through his introduction to this volume of the *Works,* James's main purpose in this book was the "application of pragmatism to religious and metaphysical problems." To support this, Thayer quotes two statements of James's. The first is James's observation that pragmatism is "primarily a method of settling metaphysical disputes that might otherwise be interminable." The second is James's reminder that in the lecture of 1898 in which he first pulled "pragmatism" from the obscurity of Charles S. Peirce's neglected writings, he had applied it to religion.[9] Thayer, instead of analyzing the text's structure, has looked for straightforward statements of purpose. The latter are of course relevant, but one would hope that the traditions of literary scholarship practiced by the Modern Language Association could have at least a heuristic effect on readings of texts that bear the stamp of the Association's Center for Editions of American Authors. The editorial apparatus in this volume is considerably longer than James's text, but Thayer has read this text primarily as a container of statements and theories, not *as a text*.

James depicted the "tough" and "tender" styles of philosophy as temperaments, but he acknowledged that these temperaments had historically specific constituencies. "Never were as many men of a decidedly empiricist proclivity in existence as there are at the present day," he declared. "Our children," he added, "are almost born scientific."[10] It was in this situation that James wanted to defend the possibility, at least, of taking up one form or another of religious belief while remaining in touch with science. James did not vindicate Islam or Christianity as such. The religion he defended was no more than what he took to be the common denominator of religious life: The primal "religious" belief that the universe contains an element responsive to human strivings.[11] Thayer is correct to identify James with the Christian "modernism" of his milieu, according to which religion was a fine thing but specific theological doctrines were felt to be something of a distraction. Thayer is correct, also, to attribute to James the view of God as a hypothesis "that in the nature of things there are conditions responsive to the highest moral and esthetic aspirations."[12]

The refusal of Clifford and the other "toughs" on the block to entertain even this hypothesis upset James, but he had little use for the ways in which the hypothesis was pursued by his more "tender" neighbors. He found the philosophies of Royce, T. H. Green, and other idealists too "remote and vacuous" to sustain the "old confidence in human values." They failed, in James's view, to show how religion was connected to the "concrete facts and joys and sorrows" of a practical, human existence. Specifically, these idealistic philosophies bought the reassurance of a religious universe at the expense of any recognition of the uncertainties, risks, disappointments, and obligations that any sentient being knows are part of the world's destiny; these philosophies invited us to "just give up, fall on our father's neck, and be absorbed into the absolute life as a drop of water melts into the river or sea."[13] James, by contrast, invited people to invest their energies in a struggle of indefinite outcome in which individuals—acting alone and in cooperation with others—seek to make the universe respond to their faith in that universe's best possibilities. That the concluding chapter of *Pragmatism* is devoted to an impassioned, even evangelical formulation of this invitation indicates how explicitly this book was intended to enlist its audience in the intellectual and moral enterprise described in the bulk of the text.

That enterprise was the creation and maintenance of the corpus of beliefs about the world which at any given time we take to be true. *Pragmatism*'s account of this enterprise stressed the dependence of true beliefs upon man-made traditions, and thereby reminded people that the content of culture—including scientific knowledge—depends in part upon exactly what human energies are invested in it. James in *Pragmatism*, no less than in *The Will to Believe,* was calling upon his audience to invest, in inquiry, a range of resources which the "toughs" wanted to prevent from entering the field and which the "tender-minded" were inclined to keep sequestered in trust funds.

Pragmatism's account of the natural history of beliefs began with the experience of individuals. The process by which any of us settles into new opinions is always the same, James insisted. "The individual has a stock of old opinions already, but he meets a new experience that puts them to a strain." The result of this challenge is an effort to modify the "previous mass of opinions," saving as much of it as possible; "at last some new idea comes up which he can graft upon the ancient stock with a minimum of disturbance of the latter, some idea that mediates between the stock and new experience and runs them into one another most felicitously and expediently." The body of truth, then, "grows much as a tree grows by the activity of a new layer of cambium."[14] This much James said in his second, and eventually most famous chapter, "What Pragmatism Means," but one of *Pragmatism*'s most striking features as a text is the frequency and conviction with which James returns to, and develops, this theme. In so doing, James makes clear that the account he has introduced with reference to an *individual's* stock of opinions takes for granted the place of this individual in a cooperative, *social* process.

It is to "a social scheme of cooperative work genuinely to be done" that James calls his audience at the homiletic peak of the book, and it is to the traditions with which society presents every individual that James points whenever he discusses the conditions for holding and changing one's beliefs. "We trade on each other's truth" both as contemporaries and as participants in an ongoing process the history of which has endowed us with the "funded truths" that inevitably make up nearly all of what we believe. James, far from asserting that the individual could make knowledge in his or her own image, was at pains to emphasize the power of socially possessed, traditional beliefs; he was, moreover, adamant about the obligation to integrate one's new experiences with the harvest of history. [15]

This harvest, and all future harvests depended in part on what was committed to the investigations of the world by the aggregate of human beings. While James depicted the individual as "pent in" between "the whole body of funded truths squeezed from the past" and "the coercions of the world of sense about him,"[16] he saw the mobilized humanity of his civilization—dead, living, and unborn—as the creator and supervisor of the beliefs housed in that civilization. These beliefs and whatever might come to take their place were not, James insisted, mirrors reflecting with varying degrees of accuracy given sections of an eternal and absolute reality that carries its own meaning; rather, these beliefs had to be maintained and altered in the course of our contact with a stream of sensations and relationships between sensations that were, in themselves, "dumb":

> . . . they say absolutely nothing about themselves. We it is who have to speak for them. . . . A sensation is rather like a client who has given his case to a lawyer and then has passively to listen in the courtroom to whatever account of his affairs, pleasant or unpleasant, the lawyer finds it more expedient to give.[17]

This perspective reversed the attitude of Huxley, who had asked that people sit passively before "Fact" like children, and follow it wherever it may lead. The world we experience directly comes to us like a "block of marble," said James; we "carve the statue ourselves." James did not deny that "reality" offered more resistance to some human suggestions than others; his point was rather that "the human touch" affected virtually every aspect of reality accessible to us. Even our immediately experienced sensations and the relations between them were instantly "humanized in the sense of being squared, assimilated, or in some way adapted, to the humanized mass" of beliefs already funded. This "humanized mass," moreover, was just that: It was not a fragment of the Absolute.[18]

What most needs to be emphasized about *Pragmatism*'s account of the natural history of beliefs is that it included, explicitly, the beliefs that make up the content of the sciences. Huxley, Clifford, and their allies predicated science's claims to lead society on science's radical distinctness, on the immunity of verified knowledge from the impulses and idiosyncrasies of human beings. So deeply, indeed, did this notion of science's transcendent objectivity take root that much of recent work in the sociology, philosophy, and history of science has remained preoccupied with overcoming this quaint conceit in the interests of a fuller understanding of the social and cultural foundations of knowledge.[19] The "toughs" were covertly tender when it came to science; they made it exempt from their hard-nosed naturalism. The nature in which James was willing to ground science was not, to be sure, as materialistic as theirs, nor was it as spiritual as the divine idea in which the idealists so confidently absorbed the workings of all minds, including scientific ones. James was willing to acknowledge his own tender aspects, but when he was attacked by heirs of Huxley and Clifford, it was often a matter of the pansy calling the marshmallow soft.

It was specifically to an understanding of the history *of science,* indeed, that James attributed his recognition of the contingent character of true beliefs. Before 1850, people took for granted that "the sciences expressed truths that were exact copies of a definite code of non-human realities," but the "enormously rapid multiplication of theories" since that time had inspired "the notion that even the truest formula may be a human device."[20] James said this in a paper of 1904, while defending the ideas of John Dewey, F. C. S. Schiller, and himself for the elaboration of which he then wrote *Pragmatisim.* In *Pragmatism* itself, James presented his account of the natural history of belief *as the basis for* the philosophy of "pragmatism." What "Messrs. Dewey, Schiller and their allies" have done, insisted James, was merely to generalize into a theory of truth the process by which people settle into new opinions.[21]

The extent to which any description of how people arrive at truth could serve as an adequate "theory of truth" was of course the most hotly debated issue between James and *Pragmatism*'s critics among philosophers. It was primarily to defend what he had said about "truth" in *Pragmatism* that James wrote the essays collected in 1909 as *The Meaning of Truth.* That James notoriously failed in this famous controversy to persuade most of his fellow philosophers of the correctness of his position should not deflect us from understanding that position, nor from grasping its importance to James's entire program. Misunderstandings are especially easy to come by at this point in reading James; this is because James, as Thayer cogently points out, was not offering at all what philosophers generally count as a "theory of truth."

Theories of truth, explains Thayer, ordinarily consist of "an explanatory analysis and definition of the notion of 'truth,'" and will seek to define this notion by representing "all or most of the cases in which the word 'truth' characterizes beliefs, statements, or knowledge in some significant way." James was not trying to get philosophers to give up other theories of truth and accept another one, Thayer continues; James was trying to clarify what these theories actually *meant*.[22] For example, the notion that truth is "agreement with reality" James would accept, but James claims to provide a meaning for this notion when he argues, for example, as follows:

> *ideas . . . become true just in so far as they help us to get into satisfactory relation with other parts of our experience. . . .* Any idea upon which we can ride, so to speak; any idea that will carry us prosperously from any one part of our experience to any other part, linking things satisfactorily, working securely, simplifying, saving labor; is true for just so much, true in so far forth, true *instrumentally*.[23]

Agreement with reality is not, then, a "stagnant property inherent in" an idea; rather the truth of an idea is something that happens to it: "It *becomes* true, it is *made* true by events.[24] When other philosophers complained that such talk really did not carry one very far toward clarifying the essence of truth, James replied that he was not trying to speak about the "essence" of truth. There simply was not, he insisted, very much to be said about that subject. Richard Rorty, in a recent address, has caught James's message exactly: "it is in the vocabulary of practice rather than of theory, of action rather than contemplation, in which one can say something useful about truth."[25]

At stake for James in the controversy over "the pragmatist theory of truth" was the release, for fuller involvement in the enterprise of creating and maintaining beliefs, of the intellectual resources intimidated by the "toughs." If truth were mistakenly believed to be always what it was, regardless of the investments made and actions taken by its pursuers, how could one expect people to commit their best energies to the struggle? The tender-minded thinkers sometimes claimed to inspire strenuous moral striving, and they certainly opposed materialism, agnosticism, and positivism, yet when they came to talk about "truth" they placed themselves so far away from the fray that they became, to James, part of the problem rather than part of the solution. The matrix of scientific investigation was the central location for creating and maintaining beliefs, yet the exclusion from that matrix of tender-minded hopes and subjective desires made all the more sense if the world's truth were mistakenly thought to be standing absolute and whole, waiting for the veils of human fantasy to be cut away. James believed that this "cutting," moreover, was being done by animated razors unaware that they, themselves, embodied a particular human sensibility that was needlessly restricting the character of the knowledge being produced. Shortly after *Pragmatism* appeared, James responded to one critic with this clarification of his purpose:

> I was primarily concerned in my lectures with contrasting the belief that the world is still in process of making with the belief that there is an "eternal" edition of it ready made and complete. The former, or "pluralistic" belief was the one that my pragmatism favored. Both beliefs confirm our strenuous moods. Pluralism actually demands them, since it makes the world's salvation depend upon the energizing of its several parts, among which we are.[26]

This energizing of the world's human parts in the interests of the world's salvation was also the ultimate aim behind James's "radical empiricism," although the latter served this aim less directly than "pragmatism" did. James sometimes encouraged people to approach these two dimensions of his program separately, but he more often alluded to their partnership. Our understanding of this partnership has not been advanced by the decision of the editors of the *Works* to include *Essays in Radical Empiricism,* a volume that obscures this relationship. In 1912, Ralph Barton Perry edited under this title a volume of James's essays. Perry justified this step on the basis of the fact that the recently deceased James had, at one point, contemplated getting out such a collection. But James put aside the idea, and in 1909 placed some of his "radical empiricist" papers in *The Meaning of Truth.* Perry published his own selection of James's papers; this collection then became so firmly established "in the James canon," we are told by the editors of the *Works,* "that the present edition follows Perry's selection and order" with one exception.[27] The editors do provide an exhaustive and meticulous account of the history of each of the texts collected by Perry, but their decision to reaffirm the conventions of James scholarship shows a lamentable lack of nerve. A wiser course would have been to add these essays to the volume of the *Works* entitled *Essays in Philosophy,* a chronological edition of the most distinctly philosophical papers James had not included in any of the collections he, himself, designed. If "pragmatism" was a text of that name as well as an idea, "radical empiricism" was only an idea.

The idea James originally asked "radical empiricism" to be was a very general one. He introduced this term as a label for the "attitude" of relentless anti-dogmatism he believed characterized *The Will to Believe.* The empirical attitude, he explained in the preface to that volume, regards "its most assured conclusions concerning matters of fact as hypotheses liable to modification in the course of future experience." A "radical" empiricism differed from fashionable "half-way empiricism," he added, in its willingness to go all the way: to treat as a hypothesis even "monism," the doctrine that the world is a single system. This attitude always fit James's sense of himself; his reference to it could easily fit among the prefatory remarks to any of his works, especially *Pragmatism.* Moreover, he attributed "half-way empiricism" to the same "scientific" cadres who keep popping up in *Pragmatism:* thinkers who "dogmatically affirm monism" in the name of "positivism or agnosticism or scientific naturalism."[28]

A year after he introduced himself as a "radical empiricist," James began also to call himself a "pragmatist."[29] Once this second tag was firmly affixed to the philosophical freight James was most eager to get moved about, he began to use the former label to refer to a specific part of his program directed more exclusively to philosophers than "pragmatism" was. Conventional empiricist philosophers had left the "relations" between things less authentic than what they relate, James complained in *The Journal of Philosophy* in 1904. As a result of this omission, philosophy had been rendered vulnerable to "the addition of trans-experiential agents of unification, substances, intellectual categories and powers, or selves." This calamity might have been avoided had empiricists been more radical, and taken as real "everything that comes . . . conjunction as well as separation, each at its face value." This concern for a fuller notion of experience was anything but new to James in 1904, but his previous efforts to reform empiricism had been in work that he called "practical and psychological."[30] In the *Principles of Psychology,* for example, James had argued that relations as well as particulars come to us as part of a single "stream," and that how we apprehend them depends in part upon what we bring to the experience. Yet in making this argument James had stopped short of drawing explicit conclusions for philosophy; he had grudgingly acquiesced in the implication of the idealists that his argument made no philosophical sense in the absence of "an inclusive mind."[31] James was now ready, in the last half-dozen years of his life, to assert in the name of "radical empiricism" that this overarching consciousness could be dispensed with in metaphysics and epistemology.

This part of James's program entailed a critique of idealism's technical achievements not attempted in the more arm-waving, foot-stomping attack on the idealists he carried out simultaneously under the rubric of "pragmatism." There, James was focusing directly on idealism's deficiencies as a source of inspiration for strenuous and virtuous labor in the intellectual world. In order to more thoroughly undercut what he saw as the complacency generated by the idealists, however, James had to speak directly to the consideration that kept philosophers themselves loyal to idealism. This was idealism's answer to a problem that had been handled awkwardly by the classical empiricist tradition of Hume and Mill: How do the particular bits and pieces of experience cohere for us, and become intelligibly related? If the most aggressive partisans of "science" rarely paused to ponder this question, it was the business of professional philosophers to worry about it. While the classical empiricists had tried to show how these particulars of experience became "associated" within minds to which they were said to be external, the triumphant idealists had a neater solution: They attributed coherence to a huge, single consciousness of which individual minds and their objects partook. To them James now replied that "pure experience" was enough.

"Pure experience" for James was not so much a substance as a substitute for the notion that the world is made up of any particular substance. He pleaded with philosophers to recognize, first, that the realm of experience is the only realm about which it made sense to philosophize, and second, that this realm is, in itself, devoid of the "mental" and "physical" components that metaphysicians were forever trying to find in the structure of the world. Above all, experience as it is contains the relations between things as well as the things themselves; the entities in our world become constituted in the course of experience. Although James sometimes spoke as if "pure experience" were a single, primal "stuff," his message was clearly that any such "stuff" was merely an expanse occupied by temporality, diversity, and contingency:

> . . . experience as a whole is a process in time, whereby innumerable particular terms lapse and are superseded by others that follow upon them by transitions which, whether disjunctive or conjunctive in context, are themselves experiences, and must in general be accounted at least as real as the terms which they relate. . . .

> The only function that one experience can perform is to lead into another experience; and the only fulfillment we can speak of is the reaching of a certain experienced end . . . the whole system of experiences as they are immediately given presents itself as a quasi-chaos through which one can pass out of an initial term in many directions and yet end in the same terminus, moving from next to next by a great many possible paths.[32]

James's effort to press the philosophical adequacy of this outlook upon his fellow philosophers soon became intertwined with his defense of pragmatism. Philosophers singled out from the text of *Pragmatism* James's statements about truth, and thereby created a professional discussion of "pragmatism" considerably narrower than the discussion James had sought to inaugurate with his book. So it was that *The Meaning of Truth* contained both James's defense of *Pragmatism* against its critics, and several of the pieces that he had originally had in mind for a collection on "radical empiricism." James's most-quoted summary of "radical empiricism" is found in the preface to *The Meaning of Truth,* where it flows into, and firmly bonds with, his summary of the pragmatist view of truth.[33] This coming together of "pragmatism" and "radical empiricism" strikingly confirms the partnership of the two, yet John J. McDermott regards the clarification of this relationship as an enormous undertaking beyond the scope of his introduction to *Essays in Radical Empiricism.*

"By benefit of hindsight and responding to this century's philosophical controversies surrounding the meaning of pragmatism," McDermott notes humbly, "I would submit my own opinion that the acceptance of a radically empirical doctrine of relations is necessary if the pragmatic method is to prevail."[34] No doubt this is true, but to grasp the meaning of James's work we are not obliged to establish the grounds on which we might now judge James's philosophy a success. McDermott begins to properly compare the relevant texts as texts, but pulls away from the task because he is stymied by James's own observation of 1906 that no "logical connection" exists between "pragmatism" and "radical empiricism." Had McDermott been willing to carry on an analysis of the texts, he might have addressed helpfully the striking hand-in-glove fit of two things: the account of the natural history of belief offered in *Pragmatism,* and the account of the process of experience in "radical empiricism."

Experience itself, James declared, grows at its edges; it lives "like the thin line of flame advancing across the dry autumnal field which the farmer proceeds to burn." Life on this line is retrospective as well as prospective: "It is 'of' the past, inasmuch as it comes expressly as the past's continuation; it is 'of' the future in so far as the future, when it comes, will have continued *it*."[35] What is carried into this line of experience, of course, is the "stock of opinions" the discussion of which dominates *Pragmatism*. It is on this line that adjustments are made in these beliefs; it is exactly there that old truths are discarded, new ones adopted, and the bulk of our beliefs carried onward in the absence of challenge from what we encounter. "Pragmatism" stressed the grounding of our belief in a field of changing experience interpreted by tradition; "radical empiricism" went on to explain that this experience, in turn, lacked definite boundaries and principles of definition.

This is to put negatively part of what James sought to put positively in his "pluralism." While James was in the midst of defending *Pragmatism,* and of integrating this defense with his papers in "radical empiricism," he was invited to deliver the Hibbert Lectures at Oxford University in the spring of 1908. These lectures became *A Pluralistic Universe,* James's most systematic attempt to show what metaphysics could contribute to the cause of a more effectively defined and acted-upon world. Since this book was an effort to reform what we, today, would call the "professional culture" of English-speaking idealist metaphysics as it then existed, James took for granted a "tender-minded" setting for discussion; he began by contrasting the cynical-materialist style of philosophy with the sympathetic-spiritual, and disposed of the former "as not calling for treatment before this present audience."[36]

Much of what James prescribed was no surprise: Philosophers were to envision the universe as a "distribution" rather than a "collection" of experience, were to overcome the ancient bias according to which only the unchanging could be "real," and were to "thicken up" their work by taking into account more of the particulars of life that the sciences were making it their business to study in detail.[37] Richard J. Bernstein recognizes the harmony between *A Pluralistic Universe* and James's earlier work, and properly disagrees, in his introduction, with philosophers who have dismissed this volume as a casual afterthought to James's career. The book has often been felt to be hopelessly "irrational" and "anti-intellectual." Whether or not these adjectives are appropriate, *A Pluralistic Universe* did register two salient shifts in James's center of gravity.

One of these shifts was James's greater sympathy for ways of creating and maintaining beliefs that were ostensibly irreconcilable with the ways of science. Even when the matrix of inquiry is fully enriched, and freed of the peculiarities that distinguish the "scientific" world view from the comprehensive science he wished to promote, there remained outside of its scope, James implied, aspects of experience with which metaphysics must deal. These aspects constituted the "inner" life of the flux of experience as a whole, and they could only be apprehended by a leap of sympathy in which our "concepts" and "logic" were of no service. "We of course need a staple scheme of concepts, stably related with one another, to lay hold of our experiences and to co-ordinate them withal," James granted, but his reading of Henri Bergson had convinced him that metaphysics should address "the change itself" that goes on between the "states" that we analyze conceptually.[38] James had frequently paid his respects to experiences outside of intellect, as when he so vividly contrasted the benefits of religious experience to the benefits of the science of religion in *The Varieties of Religious Experience*,[39] but the life he had always sought to influence was the life lived with concepts and logic. This was still largely the case at the end of his career, but in *A Pluralistic Universe* he acknowledged an additional enterprise in which investments were worth making.

James's second shift was toward the panpsychism of the idealists. He was as caustic as ever about "the Absolute," but he accommodated, in *A Pluralistic Universe,* a notion of consciousness apparently purged of the singularity, abstractness, and permanence of structure for which he had always faulted idealists. James had also suspected the idealists of complacency, and he tried to mitigate this in his "pluralistic" idealism by placing God in the thick of the struggle, cheek-and-jowl with the rest of the world's parts:

> . . . because God is not the absolute, but is himself a part when the system is conceived pluralistically, his functions can be taken as not wholly dissimilar to those of the other smaller parts. . . . Having an environment, being in time, and working out a history just like ourselves, he escapes from the foreignness from all that is human, of the static timeless perfect absolute.[40]

James did not cease to call upon his audience to commit themselves in the struggle to make the world right. The "pluralistic" universe is "self-reparative through us," he explained, and gets "its disconnections remedied in part by our behavior." Philosophies were important because they helped to define the thoughts that "determine our acts," which in turn help make the world what it is. James's purpose in *A Pluralistic Universe* was still to strengthen and animate exactly those human resources rebuffed or patronized by the "scientific" outlook that was riding like a parasite on the back of an expanding science; if these resources could be released from inhibitions of the "dusty-minded professors" by the agency of Bergson, James was delighted.[41]

It was emblematic of James's entire career that his most "far-out" philosophical reflections should have been articulated in the particular book of his designed to speak the most specifically to a constituency that was anything but far-out: the intellectually and socially conservative professional culture of English-speaking idealism, bastion of an uplifting, enlightened, liberalized Protestant faith. It was inhabitants of this locale, not a group of Buddhists or anarchists, whom James urged to "dive," with Bergson, into the "flux."[42] Similarly, when James in 1896 had urged people to exercise the "will to believe" in the face of the challenge by Clifford and Huxley, he was not prescribing this exercise for Russian nihilists or Bible-thumping evangelists: "Here in this room," he dared his audience of Yale and Brown students to acknowledge, "we all of us believe" without "reasons worthy of the name" in "molecules and the conservation of energy, in democracy and necessary progress, in Protestant Christianity and the duty of fighting for 'the doctrine of the immortal Monroe.' "[43] There was a touch of self-mocking in this, but such beliefs were characteristic of the kinds of people James was most concerned to inspire. James condemned the holding of such beliefs dogmatically; he opposed just as actively the scuttling of them on grounds that they were based on "insufficient evidence."

It is even further back in James's career, however, that we find the most forthright expression of his loyalties, his sense of what threatened them, and his strategy for defending them. In 1881, James carried out before a gathering of Unitarian ministers what we can now recognize as the act of prophecy he was to perform throughout the following three decades:

> . . . if the religion of exclusive scientificism should ever succeed in suffocating all other appetites out of a nation's mind, and imbuing a whole race with the persuasion that simplicity and consistency demand a *tabula rasa* to be made of every notion that does not form part of the *soidisant* scientific synthesis, that nation, that race, will just as surely go to ruin, and fall a prey to their more richly constituted neighbors, as the beasts of the field, as a whole, have fallen a prey to man.[44]

Here the stakes were weighed, and the issues encapsuled. Then James went on to express hope, and to identify the sorts of people he expected to vindicate this hope in the face of a challenge he now described in terms of a growing population of hostile intellectuals:

> I have myself little fear for our Anglo-Saxon race. Its moral, aesthetic, and practical wants form too dense a stubble to be mown by any scientific Occam's razor that has yet been forged. The knights of the razor will never form among us more than a sect: but when I see their fraternity increasing in numbers, and, what is worse, when I see their negations acquiring almost as much prestige and authority as their affirmations legitimately claim over the minds of a docile public, I feel as if the influences working in the direction of our mental barbarization were beginning to be rather strong, and needed some positive counteraction. And when I ask myself from what quarter the invasion may best be checked, I can find no answer as good as the one suggested by casting my eyes around this room. For this needful task, no fitter body of men than the Unitarian clergy exists.

The cause for which James was enlisting the Unitarians was not the defense of religious orthodoxy, but the use of the Unitarian practice to help perpetuate and expand the larger inquiry betrayed by the repressive "scientific" invaders:

> As, then, you burst the bonds of a narrow ecclesiastical tradition, by insisting that no fact of sense or result of science must be left out of account in the religious synthesis, so may you still be the champions of mental completeness and all-sidedness. May you, with equal success, avert the formation of a narrow scientific tradition, and burst the bonds of any synthesis which would pretend to leave out of account those forms of being, those relations of reality, to which at present our active and emotional tendencies are our only avenues of approach.

Nothing is more essential to an understanding of James than recognition of his commitment to the critical revision of *existing traditions,* especially those of the milieu he shared with Royce and other "tender-minded" intellectuals. He was less interested in establishing timeless and universal rules for the justification of true belief than he was in acknowledging the contingency of all beliefs, and in seeking to make the most out of the beliefs to which he and his contemporaries were heir. His expressions of pride in the "Anglo-Saxon race" make us want to remind ourselves of the truth that James was among the least racist and ethnocentric of the New England aristocrats of his time,[45] but the sense of community and of tradition in these passages are vital to their meaning. Damned as he often was as someone who would have the world float on a wish, James was profoundly and consistently aware of the indispensability as well as of the contingency of starting points. No American intellectual of James's generation with a comparable public following was more cosmopolitan than James, yet none was more cognizant than he of the power of time, place, and tradition.

To grasp the function performed in James's career by the positions he took on philosophical issues, then, is to become conscious of the centrality, to James, of the sense that the practices in which people find themselves constitute the controlling facts of intellectual life. This sense had no place in either the "tough" or "tender" syndromes whose virtues James sought to combine through his own witness on its behalf. The centrality of this sense to James's work has long been underestimated; assessments of James as a whole have continued, even in recent years, to focus on the anachronistic issue of whether James was not really more tough—or tender—than this or that other scholar has claimed.[46] Where James differed from most of his contemporaries—and, for that matter, from most of his philosophical successors—was in the intensity of his commitment to what Richard Rorty has called "the conversation of the West."[47] The interlocking set of traditions that make up this conversation, James was saying, was *it*; whatever we may discover outside of this conversation will depend on what we invest in it, because there is no guarantee that nature holds in store for us anything in particular.

This conviction is not hard to find in James's texts unless one is aloof from James's relation to his audience. To prescribe sensitivity to this relation would seem a truistic methodological point,[48] but interpretations of James have in fact been dominated by two other considerations: the structure of James's personality, and the problems of philosophy. These two sets of determinants are conventionally invoked to explain James's work; it has been pointed out, for example, how James's personal needs were satisfied by voluntaristic answers to the issues presented to the philosophers of his time by the dynamics of philosophical argument. All this is fine, as far as it goes. But it pays insufficient attention to the actual setting of the action: the extensive realm of discourse between James's individual temperament and the technical content of the discipline he practiced. It was there, amid the preoccupations and anxieties of James's contemporary intellectuals, that James's personality and the problems of philosophy found each other. James's insistence that life was "a real fight" in which one's all must be given[49] was obviously a reflection of the psychological pattern for which his "Moral Equivalent of War" has become the most legendary expression, but so, too, was this insistence part of James's call to his contemporaries to commit themselves to a cultural struggle about the authenticity of which he had no doubt.

It is not enough to see James as a "trimmer," trying to restore balance by getting any lop-sided ship of thought to throw overboard ideas he did not like, or to at least move them across the deck where their weight would function differently in the maintenance of the craft. James was concerned with the seaworthiness of certain fleets: Those sailing from the most cosmopolitan ports in the West, laden with cargoes of traditions he regarded as the most promising resources for the further exploration and enrichment of the world. The mariners he most wanted to encourage were those with at least some appreciation for these traditions, but he found many of them slouching in their cabins, taking their destiny for granted. The mariners, on the other hand, of whom James was most suspicious were those so infatuated with the newly designed vessels of science that they were willing to sail without the ballast that sustained even science itself. The proper manning and equipping of these fleets was the chief business of James's career.

2

THE PROBLEM OF PRAGMATISM

IN AMERICAN HISTORY

Pragmatism is a "problem" in two senses of the term, one monographic and the other historiographic. Monographically, pragmatism is something to be studied: It is just another item on the agenda, along with why America became an imperial power in 1898, and the truth about Alger Hiss. What has made pragmatism a historiographical problem, too, is the fact that in recent years historians have virtually drawn a blank on it as a monographic problem. "What am I to say about pragmatism," teachers of lecture courses and writers of textbooks sometimes ask one another? "That's a real problem," is often the response. Scholarly communities do change their agendas now and then, and pragmatism may well drop out of the list of monographic problems addressed by historians of the United States. It will then cease also to be a historiographic problem, for no historian will be troubled by having nothing to say on the subject. One way to solve the historiographical problem, then, is to become convinced that pragmatism need not be a monographic problem at all. The essay reprinted below takes the opposite approach: It tries to solve the historiographic problem by treating the monographic problem seriously, by making an argument about pragmatism.

Basic to the argument is a distinctive cluster of hopes and aspirations about a culture based on science. I try to identify these ideas, and to demonstrate their animating role in the most widely disseminated writings of the leading pragmatist philosophers, as well as in the work of intellectuals who popularized and defended pragmatism from the 1910s through the 1940s. This cluster contained three assertions: That inquiry itself was a discipline that could stabilize and sustain a modern, "scientific" culture for which truths could be only tentative and plural; that the social and physical world was responsive to human purpose; and that inquiry was an activity open to the rank-and-file membership of an educated, democratic society. These ideas bonded very easily with the two phenomena most often said to constitute "pragmatism": (a) the theories of meaning, truth, and goodness contributed to philosophy by Peirce, James, and Dewey; and (b) the impatience with principles, privilege, stasis, and tradition stereotypically attributed to Americans in general. I argue that the widespread affirmation of the philosophy of pragmatism on the part of American intellectuals during the first half of the twentieth century derived from the understanding that pragmatism's theories of meaning, truth, and goodness entailed a distinctive and reassuring vision of a "scientific" culture in the making. *Pragmatism, in this view, was more than a response in peculiarly American terms to some of the classical issues in philosophy; pragmatism was also a specific response to contemporary uncertainties and yearnings about science's cultural capabilities.*

In my eagerness to clarify the dynamics of pragmatism as a historical episode, I invoked what I now am obliged to acknowledge was premature closure on pragmatism's life as a philosophy. I suggested that the term "pragmatism" would probably not survive to denote whatever philosophical inspiration might be derived from the work of Peirce, James, and Dewey. Even Dewey's admirer Richard Rorty, I implied, would come to be known by some other label. Yet in the few short years since I wrote, Rorty has become one of America's most widely discussed philosophers while repeatedly identifying himself as "pragmatist."

I believe I also slighted the most obvious, enduring legacy of the pragmatist movement. This is the fixing of the meaning of the words "pragmatic" and "pragmatism" as we use them in common speech and apply them to American cultural heroes. Not always has it been taken for granted that these words refer to a "see-if-it-works" suspicion of dogma, of doctrine, and of the rigid adherence to abstract principles and theories. This sense of what it meant to be pragmatic was far from dominant amid the welter of notions mentioned by the editors of the Oxford English Dictionary *during the very earliest years of this century. As the primary meaning of "pragmatist," the editors selected "busybody," a definition that certainly had to be replaced before Benjamin Franklin, Thomas Edison, and Franklin D. Roosevelt could be appreciated as "pragmatists."*

This essay was published in the Journal of American History LXVII (1980), 88–107.

In 1950 HENRY STEELE COMMAGER saw no reason to doubt that "pragmatism" was a central theme in American life, flowing naturally out of American experience and becoming, in the twentieth century, "almost the official philosophy of America."[1] Being pragmatic was so essential to being American, observed the Amherst pamphlet on "Pragmatism and American Culture" in the same year, that to debate the merits of pragmatism was to place "American civilization itself . . . on trial."[2] Indeed, people seeking to identify what was wrong with America—or what was so splendid about it—had been dissecting the writings of pragmatists for years.[3] The indispensability of the concept of pragmatism for the study of American history was implied across the board, from the narrowest of scholarly monographs to the most sweeping assessments of the American character, from the gushiest patriotic tract to the most embittered denunciation of American shortcomings.

In 1980, "pragmatism" is a concept most American historians have proved they can get along without. Some nonhistorians may continue to believe that pragmatism is a distinctive contribution of America to modern civilization and somehow emblematic of America, but few scholarly energies are devoted to the exploration or even the assertion of this belief. The space devoted to pragmatism in textbooks has diminished markedly; the authors of the "survey text" generally felt to be the most intellectually demanding and up-to-date find few occasions to employ the concept or even to note the historical reality of its use by some Americans of earlier generations.[4] The concept of pragmatism has not entirely disappeared from monographic and synthetic writing about American history and culture, but the decline in its popularity has been abrupt, has issued from no concerted attack upon it, and has gone virtually without comment.

Scrutiny of the ideas of Charles Peirce, William James, and John Dewey goes forward as industriously as ever,[5] to be sure, but this scrutiny is increasingly the business of philosophers addressing other philosophers, and is increasingly isolated—even when carried out by historians—from the study of the rest of American history. What has all but disappeared is a particular sense of the significance of pragmatism: That the works of Peirce, James, and Dewey manifest an important episode not only in the development of Western philosophy, but in American history, and that these thinkers were somehow representative of the life of the mind in the United States.

If the case of the vanishing pragmatist has gone generally unreported and unexplained, it is partly because this case is entailed by a larger one that has been widely applauded and can be easily explained: the case of the vanishing American. A holistic approach to American historical and cultural studies had been taken for granted by the relevant literature on pragmatism; when the "American character," the "American mind," and the "American" came into scholarly disrepute in the 1960s and 1970s, gone by implication were the traditional bases for claims concerning the importance of pragmatism. The belief that students of America were addressing a single entity had also been common to writings on such other standard topics as Puritanism and democracy. Studies of these topics, too, were changed in striking ways by the decline of holism; yet pragmatism's fate was different in the extent to which it came to be seen as a thing apart. Studies of Puritanism and of the political culture of democracy have reconstituted themselves in keeping with the insight—currently the leitmotif of prescriptive historiography—that Americans of different classes, ethnic backgrounds, or educations create and experience very differently the themes that still serve, somewhat lamely, to unify "American history."

That pragmatism should become so extreme an instance of compartmentalization follows partly from the fact that it, of the several concepts favored by the scholarship of a generation ago, was most exclusively the property of intellectual historians. Puritanism and democracy could be dealt with by social and political historians as well as by intellectual historians, but pragmatism required some of the skills of precisely those historians most identified with, and consequently most fearful of, the discredited holism of the recent academic past. In intellectual history's search for exactness and particularity during the 1960s and 1970s, topics became more circumscribed and tended to be defined in terms of specific individuals, groups, organizations, or institutions.[6] It was only natural that pragmatism should come to be regarded as a more strictly philosophical episode, as a distinctive theory of meaning and truth possessed and developed by an easily identified community of practitioners of a technical discipline. In this view, pragmatism's historical significance is assigned primarily according to its role in Western philosophy, and the issues in pragmatism's history that require attention concern chiefly its origins and the steps by which it was articulated and defended in debates with other philosophers.[7] America is relevant only because the leading pragmatists happened to be Americans; scholars can then argue over whether this or that aspect of American life—in connection with this or that aspect of the inherited Western philosophical tradition—promoted the contribution of pragmatism to western and worldwide philosophical discourse. Such studies, at their most sophisticated, analyze pragmatism in terms of two philosophical traditions, one developing at Harvard in the works of Peirce, James, Josiah Royce, and C. I. Lewis, the other developing through the work of Dewey and his followers at Chicago and Columbia.[8]

Just how far such studies have taken pragmatism from the "America" of older scholarship is dramatically illustrated by one of the most rigorously historical and Americocentric of recent books related to pragmatism, Bruce Kuklick's *Rise of American Philosophy: Cambridge, Massachusetts, 1860–1930.* Kuklick treats extensively the institutional matrix of Harvard University and looks carefully at the anxieties about science and religion that animated the educated public during the era of pragmatism's growth; yet the pragmatism one encounters in his book derives less from the unique, supposedly practical exigencies of American life than from a text of Immanuel Kant, the most cloistered of eighteenth-century German philosophers. This pragmatism, moreover, serves not as the official philosophy of America, but as one of several bases for the radical academicization of philosophy by superprofessionals Ralph Barton Perry and C. I. Lewis.[9]

The achievement during recent years of an impressively richer literature on the pragmatist philosophers is certainly no cause for complaint. Nor is there point to insisting on the reintegration of pragmatism into American history in the absence of a specific set of terms on which the place of pragmatism in American history can be clarified. Reintegration in itself is a worthy goal only for those with a prior commitment to the wholeness of the American past. But something that was persistently called "pragmatism" implanted itself deeply in the intellect of many educated Americans during the early decades of the twentieth century; one wonders how this could come about if pragmatism were no more than what we can now see of it in histories of philosophy and what we once saw of it in the older American Studies scholarship. Perhaps an uncritical reassertion of the historiographical commitments of a generation ago is not the only alternative to abandoning pragmatism as a problem broader than the study of a small branch of a single American academic discipline.

If our understanding of American history can be enriched by the study of pragmatism, that enrichment can scarcely be expected to come about so long as pragmatism is either stretched to cover all of America or confined to those of its formulations sufficiently fruitful philosophically to have found places in the history of Western philosophy. In the first instance, the tradition of Peirce, James, and Dewey is flattened into a style of thought characterized by voluntarism, practicality, moralism, relativism, an eye toward the future, a preference for action over contemplation, and other traits of the same degree of generality. Each of the traits commonly attributed to pragmatism can indeed be found at some level in the writings of one or more of the leading pragmatists. And, even if we now gasp ritualistically at the thought of attributing these traits to Americans "in general," there is no reason to doubt that these traits were among the intellectual ideals of a good many of the rank-and-file Yankees with whom scholars once tried to link James and his cerebral colleagues. Yet the obligation to characterize the pragmatists as representatives of America inhibits exploration of the relationship between the pragmatist philosophers and the more specific segments—chronological and social— of America in which the writings of the pragmatists appeared and demonstrably functioned. In the second instance—the confining of pragmatism to its philosophic contributions—the tradition is sharpened into a highly distinctive theory of meaning and truth to which the writings of other modern philosophers can be contrasted. Often this theory is projected as an ideal type toward which the pragmatists strived, but which they failed to fully articulate. In this view, the task of the scholar is to fill in the holes in the formulations of the pragmatists in order to complete and clarify their arguments. Even when the pragmatic theory of meaning and truth is made the subject of more authentically historical studies, in which the actual development of the ideas of one or more of the pragmatists is reconstructed, the mission of the scholar can be achieved with little attention to the constituency won among Americans by the work of the pragmatists.

The historiographical terrain between these two approaches to pragmatism is not altogether unoccupied, but the studies found there are most often designed to illuminate something other than pragmatism's basic nature and role in American life. A recent example is James B. Gilbert's *Work without Salvation,* which shows James's pragmatism to entail an uncommonly sensitive response to a crisis in vocation experienced by

James's generation.[10] Another is Robert Booth Fowler's *Believing Skeptics*, which sketches the "pragmatic attitude" proudly defended by a number of political commentators during the Cold War.[11] The pragmatism of academic intellectuals outside of philosophy is more directly addressed in Darnell Rucker's 1969 study of Dewey's followers at the University of Chicago and in what remains after more than thirty years the best book in this genre, Morton White's *Social Thought in America: The Revolt against Formalism*.[12] White depicts Dewey's pragmatism as one of a series of affirmations of the world's historicity, particularity, social interdependence, and, above all, its susceptibility to experimental manipulation. White comes the closest to confronting the pragmatist tradition head on, but his book makes no attempt to discuss Peirce or James. Moreover, White's focus on the highly abstract issue of "formalism" versus "antiformalism" has served to obscure his strongest contribution: an account of the hopes pinned on the somewhat more concrete ideal of "scientific method" by Dewey and some of his most prominent allies among historians and social scientists.

The recognition that the intellectuals who rallied to pragmatism were preoccupied with the place of science in modern life is indeed the point at which to begin an assessment of pragmatism's role in the lives of Americans who cared about it. The writings on meaning, truth, goodness, and other basic philosophical issues on account of which Peirce, James, and Dewey became known as pragmatists were the apex of a larger intellectual edifice constructed by these three men and their followers in response not only to the great epistemological and metaphysical questions of post-Kantian thought, but also to the desire for a way of life consistent with what they and their contemporaries variously perceived as the implications of modern science. Peirce, James, and Dewey were conspicuous leaders, among Americans, in the efforts of Western intellectuals to find and articulate such a way of life. That these efforts were so widespread as to constitute the framework for much of European and American intellectual history in the late nineteenth and early twentieth centuries is well known, as are the facts that ways of life as well as epistemologies were felt to be at issue and that the pragmatists were among America's most listened-to participants in this enterprise. Yet these aspects of the scene deserve more attention in the interpretation of pragmatism than historians have accorded them, for they largely define the specific setting in which

Peirce, James, and Dewey gained constituencies beyond philosophy, were perceived as part of a single tradition, and thus functioned as related presences in the history of the United States.

Viewed in this setting, the pragmatists emerge as reflectors of, and powerful agents for, a distinctive cluster of assertions and hopes about how modern culture could be integrated and energized. The particular elements in this cluster were often articulated singly and in relation to other ideas by other moralists of the period, including some critical of pragmatism, but the combination of elements found in the writings of the pragmatists and their popularizers was nowhere else advanced more persistently and with more notice from educated Americans. Since the basic texts of Peirce, James, and Dewey were the raw materials out of which the pragmatic tradition was forged, I will use these texts as the basis of my account of the combination of elements peculiar to the pragmatists.

One element in this combination was a sense of the role of scientific method in a universe of change and uncertainty. The pragmatists were more concerned than were many of their contemporaries with the integrity and durability of *inquiry,* on the one hand, and the tentativeness, fallibility, and incompleteness of *knowledge* on the other. While they sometimes compared the body of existing knowledge favorably to the smaller amount available in the past, and while they often noted the superior reliability of empirically supported propositions over other propositions, the pragmatists were never among the leading celebrants of knowledge's solidity, vastness, and stability. It was rather to what they called the "spirit" of science, or its "method" and "attitude" that they looked for a foundation stable enough to support a modern culture. Knowledge was transient, and as such was another aspect of the universe of change through the experience of which the attitude of inquiry was, in itself, the most reliable single guide. Some of the pragmatists were more eager than others to see the knowledge available at a given historical moment applied vigorously to social, religious, and political life, but the priority of method as a cultural commitment was projected vividly in the works of Peirce, James, Dewey, and a host of followers.

This projection is easiest to illustrate in the case of Dewey, who was forever insisting that if only people could become scientific in the way they went about things, the potential for human fulfillment would be liberated from the bondage of a sterile, repressive, outrageously long-lived antiquity. "The future of our civilization depends upon the widening spread and deepening hold of the scientific habit of mind."[13] This assertion of Dewey's became a favorite epigram among his admirers[14] and expressed accurately, if blandly, the methodological emphasis of his thought. This emphasis was so tightly bound up with skepticism about the adequacy of existing and yet-to-be-discovered knowledge that Dewey's prescribed "scientific attitude" was defined *in terms of* a principled openness toward, and an enthusiastic search for, new and temporarily valid knowledge in a universe of constant change.[15] Willingness to accept and act upon the facts at hand would not satisfy Dewey as it had satisfied the many Victorian moralists eager to make people obey facts; Dewey's devotion was to the process of investigation itself.

So, too, was James's. The claim of some scientists to have virtually completed their task inspired James's proudest scorn; "our ignorance," he said, is "a sea."[16] His legendary assaults on the pretensions of science turned the supposed ideals of the scientific endeavor against the arrogance of contemporary scientists: James piously and passionately reminded them of the "scientific" imperative to inquire farther, to remain critical of past findings, to remain free from dogmatism.[17] If T. H. Huxley, as has often been observed, turned the tables on established Christianity by claiming for Darwinian science a Protestant morality more strict than that of the church, so, too, did James turn the tables on the established science of Huxley's generation by claiming for psychical research an ideal of free inquiry more unflinching and open-minded than that of Huxley and W. K. Clifford. Scholars have made much of James's defense of religiously conventional and scientifically unorthodox beliefs, such as the conceivable reality of spirits; what needs more emphasis is what James did and did not do with such beliefs. He supported no movement to protect such beliefs from science; instead, he instituted what he regarded as a scientific investigation of the evidence on which these beliefs were supposedly founded.[18] While James developed a reputation as a hostile critic of the world views of many contemporary apologists for science, he also gained a reputation as a striking exemplar of the ideals of scientific inquiry.[19]

Peirce was more inclined than either James or Dewey to suspect that the object of knowledge was, technically speaking, finite,[20] but he too depicted inquiry as virtually endless and its results as unavoidably fallible. He could be as eloquent as James on "the paucity of scientific knowledge"[21] and on the sentiment expressed in his own, often quoted injunction, "Do not block the way of inquiry."[22] Peirce was unusual—even in an age of extravagant "scientism"—in the extremity and singularity with which he identified goodness and progress with science, and he was among the first admirers of science to focus this adulation explicitly on the community of investigators and on the common methodological commitments that enabled members of this community to correct both each other and the stock of propositions they took to be true.[23] It was in direct response to Peirce's vision of an eternally self-correcting community of inquiry that Royce "solved" *The Problem of Christianity* by urging the church to model itself on the scientific community.[24]

Yet it would be misleading to imply that Peirce's vision of the scientific community and its moral functions was widely noted beyond a few departments of philosophy; he was, by virtue of his great creativity and prolonged neglect, the Melville of American philosophy. The aspects of his work that did function decisively in the discourse of his generation and of the one immediately following his death in 1914 were those singled out by James and Dewey, particularly the aspect James in 1898 dubbed the "principle" of pragmatism.[25] This principle—to the much disputed substance of which we must now attend—connoted in all its formulations a willingness to treat knowledge as temporal and to treat method as both primary and enduring.

To take account of the practical consequences an object might have is the way to form a clear idea of it, Peirce had said in 1878 in "How to Make Our Ideas Clear." In what was to become the classic illustration of the pragmatic theory of meaning, Peirce analyzed in terms of this maxim the calling of a thing "hard." To be hard, a thing must be able to resist scratching by other substances; such "effects" constitute the "whole conception" of hardness. "There is absolutely no difference between a hard thing and a soft thing so long as they are not brought to the test," said Peirce, insisting, in effect, that the "qualities" often said to inhere in objects be translated into the behavior the objects manifest in relation to other objects.[26] The uncertainty of Peirce specialists even today about just what Peirce was trying to say[27]—what consequences were "practical," for example, and was the maxim a general one or designed only for science?—need not deflect us from identifying the essential freight that this proposal of Peirce's was made to carry in the development of the pragmatist movement once James launched it in 1898.[28]

To that movement no paper was more central than James's "What Pragmatism Means," in which he presented "Peirce's principle" as the basis for an entire philosophy. That philosophy was to be more scientific in outlook, James alleged, than philosophies, as a class of intellectual constructions, tended to be. Pragmatism's predecessors and rivals were too committed to one particular set or another of "results" of inquiry, such as the conclusion that the world is made up of "Energy" or that it is all contained within "the Absolute." Such philosophies employed merely "verbal solutions," reasoned from "fixed principles," built "closed systems," and fell victim to "dogma, artificiality, and the pretence of finality in truth." Pragmatism stood for less and was capable of doing more; it carried less baggage, was more autonomous, and was open to more possibilities. The pragmatic method of tracing the consequences of ideas operated in the manner of a hotel corridor—a metaphor James adopted from his Italian follower, Giovanni Papini—through which one might pass in order to get in and out of rooms representing a virtual infinity of intellectual activities.[29]

When James moved to the explicit statement of a theory of truth, he began with the observation that to modern science "laws" were at best "approximations," too numerous and too subject to "rival formulations" to enable us to view any of them as "absolutely a transcript of reality." Theories "may from some point of view be useful" by summarizing old facts and leading us to new ones. It was to this analysis of scientific knowledge that James connected the theory of truth he attributed to himself, to the British pragmatist F. C. S. Schiller, and to Dewey and his Chicago disciples. Truth in any realm was an "idea that will carry us prosperously from any one part of our experience to any other part, linking things satisfactorily, working securely, simplifying, saving labor; [it] is true for just so much, true in so far forth, true *instrumentally*." Such sentences put James on the defensive with other philosophers, so he spent much time during his last years trying to elaborate and defend "this pragmatist talk about truths in the plural, about their utility and satisfactoriness, about the success with which they 'work,' etc."[30] Yet in all these disputes, including those involving Dewey and other pragmatists after James's death in 1910, one thing was never in doubt: Whatever else the pragmatist theory of truth entailed, it carried with it the sense that truth was a condition that happened to an idea through the course of events as experienced and analyzed by human beings. This temporality of truth was basic even to the less publicized depiction by Peirce of truth as a "fated" opinion, as something that a community of investigators would eventually agree upon.[31] What was rejected everywhere in the movement was the notion of truth as "a stagnant property inherent in" an idea, apart from the process of its emergence in history and from its possession by human beings interacting contingently with each other and with the larger natural world.[32]

That this social and physical world was responsive to human purpose was a second conviction advanced by the pragmatist tradition. If one basic element in this tradition was a belief that inquiry itself could stabilize and sustain a culture for which truths could be only tentative and plural, another was the sense that inquiry could change the world. Not that the world altogether lacked resistance to human imagination and will; but neither was the world's structure so hard-and-fast as to force human purpose into headlong retreat with each new discovery of science. In contrast to the moralists who hailed or lamented the scientific enterprise as the exploration of a one-way street, down which orders for belief and conduct came from "nature," the pragmatic tradition carried a faith in inquiry's reconstructive capabilities in the most rigorous of the sciences and in everyday life.

This faith is consistent with the pragmatic approach to truth as a form of utility, but is not entailed by it. Ideas, in this view, are instruments that not only can become true by doing their job in inquiry, but can also transform the environment to which they are applied. This effect takes place most obviously in the improvement of medical and industrial techniques, but the effect was held by Dewey and his followers to operate throughout experience even at the cognitive level, in the knowing relation itself. For Dewey, the entire knowing process is a manipulative one in which inquirers seek to rearrange to their satisfaction whatever components of a given situation stimulated inquiry.[33] Peirce's account of inquiry as a response to doubt has sometimes been taken to imply a transformative role for inquiry, but Peirce drew back from such implications, and he was in any event no agent of their popularization. Dewey did the most to identify this reconstructive vision with pragmatism, while trying over a period of several decades to clarify what he meant by it.

In precisely what sense does inquiry "change" the various "situations" it is led to confront? How do we evaluate the claims to utility that may be advanced on behalf of various reconstructive solutions? It is a striking feature of the history of pragmatism that Dewey's most detailed answer to these questions appeared only in 1938, long after his more vague and

question-begging pronouncements had helped win for his reconstruction-
ist vision a following greater than it has enjoyed during the more than
forty years since he did his best to justify it philosophically.[34] Persons
attracted to the vision were all along held in tow by a few prominent,
easily apprehended assertions of Dewey's; the world, Dewey reassured his
public, has been proven by the growth of science and invention to be
sufficiently amenable to human ends to warrant yet more experimentation
with it, particularly its previously neglected social and moral dimensions.
Here the connection between pragmatism and early-twentieth-century
reform[35] was at its closest, but Dewey's social engineering was only one
example of pragmatism's confidence in the responsiveness of nature to
human purpose. This confidence was equally hard to miss in James's
"voluntarism."

James focused on the vitality of will versus outside forces in determin-
ing the life of the individual, but he also addressed the effect of human
purpose on the universe outside the self. Not only did his formidable work
in psychology assist vitally in the demolition of the passive mind of the
British empirical tradition;[36] James's most popular essays continually asserted that "will" was an authentic force in the world. James was particularly reassuring about the role of purpose in the inquiries carried out by
scientists; the phenomena of nature would ultimately decide an issue, but
all the more decisively if scientists brought to their investigation—
critically, to be sure—their own most intense hopes for a given outcome.[37]

The advancement of human purpose in the world through inquiry was
not to be limited to professional scientists or even to philosophers. It was a
mission and a fulfillment open to virtually anyone. The pragmatist tradition consisted also in this third basic element: the sense that inquiry was
accessible on meaningful levels by the rank-and-file membership of an
educated, democratic society. The pragmatists did not insist that all
forms of inquiry were accessible to everyone, nor did they deny that
inquiry was subject to a division of labor according to which people were
sometimes dependent upon the expertise of others. Inquiry was a continuum of investigatory, reconstructive endeavors exemplified above all by
the work of Galileo and his scientific successors, but available for practice
in appropriate contexts by any citizen capable of assimilating its spirit.

Dewey translated so many of life's activities—humble and exalted—
into the terms of inquiry that Bertrand Russell once accused him of being
unable to distinguish between the work of a scientist and that of a brick-

layer.[38] Dewey did seek to distinguish between the controlled, reflective, experimental inquiry characteristic of specialists and the common sense thinking of everyman, but even then he insisted on their similarity and urged a program of public education to render common sense more effective by closing the gap between it and experimental science. James, too, emphasized the continuity between the intellectual life of the average soul, on the one hand, and James's own vocation as a scientist and philosopher on the other. Always an acerbic critic of the elitist pretensions of academic professionals, James urged the laity to take on the most demanding intellectual problems it could, and to adopt in their pursuit the pragmatic method long practiced without hoopla in the laboratory and now characteristic of the best philosophers.[39]

No index of the accessibility of inquiry was more dramatic than its availability to people wanting answers to ethical questions. Not only were social scientists encouraged to extend to the social realm the search for facts pioneered by practitioners of the physical sciences; persons of any station confronting issues in politics and morals were encouraged to face them "scientifically." The continuum of inquiry as depicted by Dewey, and less explicitly by James, included ethical choices as well as the explanation of physical and social phenomena;[40] the pragmatic tradition was proverbially reluctant to make what were, to other philosophic traditions, all-too-clear distinctions between the good and the true, between value and fact. This reluctance stimulated a vast polemical literature, in which critics generally insisted that the formulations of pragmatists begged the standard philosophical questions while the pragmatists, especially Dewey, argued that these questions, as traditionally conceived, were simply outdated. Although Dewey made a determined, and increasingly technical, effort to perform his own philosophical analysis of ethical judgment in terms of "inquiry," his work also served to reinforce a feeling James had first inspired in admirers of pragmatism that many of philosophy's standard questions were irrelevant. These admirers might cheer Dewey along as he fought his learned opposition, but they knew that a *little* philosophy—provided it was, like their own, the right philosophy—was enough. The active life of inquiry, it was clear, needed to wait upon no guidelines from the cloistered men who sat and talked about "is" and "ought."

The pragmatists' combination of senses of what the possibilities were for a modern, scientific culture seems at first glance very general indeed. Yet it was specific enough to distinguish pragmatism from a number of other, highly visible signposts even within the intellectual neighborhood populated by enthusiasts about science and its cultural contributions. Pragmatism's anti-elitist bias distinguished it, for example, from the program for behaviorist research and social reorganization popularized by John B. Watson,[41] whose understanding of how the human mind worked was both similar to Dewey's and loudly applauded by many followers of both James and Dewey. Socialism, too, was offered frequently in the name of science, and it attracted some pragmatists when the latter were led to think of socialism as appropriately experimental and democratic,[42] but the pragmatist tradition's emphasis on the continuity of inquiry cut against the grain of class-based, revolutionary socialism. Russell's "A Free Man's Worship"—one of the most widely cited testaments of the 1910s and 1920s—celebrated an ascetic's renunciation of human hope in the face of a hard, hostile, science-discovered world.[43] Sinclair Lewis's *Arrowsmith* was built around the precious unattainability, by any but the most superhuman of heroes, of the scientific ideal.[44] Nobel physicist Robert A. Millikan's *Science and the New Civilization* assured the nation's Babbitts that their conservative social values were in no way threatened by scientific knowledge or inquiry.[45] Innumerable industrialists, engineers, and medical professionals filled popular and learned magazines with adulation of past and future technological progress, without hinting that the imperatives of inquiry itself might come to occupy the spiritual landscape once supervised by the Christian church.[46] The imposing bulk and permanence of existing knowledge was incandescently hailed, and mastery of its detailed contents earnestly prescribed, by a multitude of publicists and spokesmen for scientific societies.[47] Oliver Wendell Holmes, Jr., linked adulation of scientific method with serene acquiescence in the often cruel operations of an unresponsive world.[48]

The pragmatist tradition that distinguished itself in this context, and that was yet more distinctive when contrasted to outlooks skeptical of science, was constituted by more than the careers of Peirce, James, and Dewey. Until now I have made attributions to this tradition exclusively on the basis of the most extensively absorbed texts of these three men because these texts provided the adhesive to make pragmatism a tradition: From these texts the less original pragmatists drew inspiration, and to these texts educated Americans went when they wanted to confront "pragmatism." But the tradition is manifest not exclusively in these classical texts; it is found also in the writings of those who sought to summarize, elaborate upon, defend, and sympathetically analyze the contributions of the three masters. Such writings, indeed, were instrumental in establishing the canon of pragmatist classics and in sustaining a particular sense of what was common to thinkers as diverse as Peirce, James, and Dewey.[49] Attention to such writings can confirm or correct an impression of where pragmatism's center of gravity was located as pragmatism went beyond its great texts and as it transcended departments of philosophy.

If, for example, Joseph Ratner's introduction to the Modern Library Giant of 1939, *Intelligence in the Modern World: John Dewey's Philosophy,* were difficult to assimilate into what is here characterized as the pragmatist tradition, one would want to quickly revise that characterization. Ratner's 241-page introduction serves as both an attempted summary of Dewey's thought and a polemical assertion of that thought's correctness. The essay has never been taken seriously as a contribution to the philosophical refinement of pragmatism, as have the works of C. I. Lewis and George Herbert Mead, for example.[50] Nor should it so be taken. Yet it is a crucial historical document as a representative reading of Dewey and as, in turn, an agent of this reading's dissemination. So widely circulated was this book that yellowing, pencil-annotated copies can be found today in used bookstores far from Chicago and Columbia in some of the remotest areas of the United States.

Galileo's discovery of a "*general* method, available and adaptable for use by all . . . no matter what the area," is for Ratner, as for Dewey, the central moment in history. For three centuries this discovery was taken advantage of only by a handful of people, mostly those practicing the physical sciences. Resistance by philosophers to the Galilean general method of experimental inquiry is "as bad a case of cultural lag as one could ever hope to come across." At last, Dewey has come along to lay out the implications of Galileo's breakthrough for "philosophy" in the most comprehensive sense of the term, including our understanding of and prescriptions for everyday life. In so doing, Dewey has performed for the modern world the tasks performed for the ancient world by the great Athenian philosophers, explains Ratner, taking it as obvious that the more complete adoption of the Galilean method is the chief problem for modern philosophy and for the larger culture philosophers must help to reconstruct. Much of Ratner's time, therefore, goes into demonstrating how "the two greatest of Dewey's contemporaries," Russell and Alfred North Whitehead, despite their eagerness to take account of scientific knowledge and method, remain mired in prescientific ways of thinking: They have not fully substituted the Galilean experimental attitude for the ancient "quest for certainty." They have even failed to see how fleeting a presence our current knowledge is: Russell, for example, took Newtonian physics as given in 1914 and in 1927 took Einsteinian physics as given.[51]

Ratner's Dewey is fully consistent with the outlook of the two most prolific and popularly read interpreters of pragmatism, Horace M. Kallen and Sidney Hook.[52] Kallen and Hook have long been recognized as elaborators, respectively, of James's more individualistic, unsystematic approach to the vocation of inquiry and of Dewey's more social and organized approach. Yet the careers of Kallen and Hook illustrate how different the problem of pragmatism looks when it is addressed in American history rather than in Western philosophy. Both of these writers were trained as philosophers by their respective masters, and both addressed some of the same technical questions involving "truth" and "meaning" that their mentors did. Yet what Kallen and Hook wrote about these questions did not make a lasting mark on the course of philosophical argument; hence, their writings are not, as are C. I. Lewis's and Mead's, given detailed and sober treatment in philosophers' histories of pragmatism. One need find no fault whatever with these histories to observe that Kallen and Hook, in their exceptionally long careers as self-defined "pragmatists," are fundamentally constitutive of pragmatism as a presence in America. The ideas attributed above to the founders of pragmatism are easily found in the writings of Kallen and Hook, often offered from forums of culturally strategic importance. Kallen wrote the article on pragmatism for the *Encyclopaedia of the Social Sciences*—a monument in so many ways to the ideals of pragmatists—where he performed the standard equation of pragmatism with science and democracy.[53]

No one has ever mistaken Herbert Croly for a philosopher, nor the *New Republic* for a journal of philosophy. Yet Croly and his magazine have been routinely denoted as "pragmatist" for years, as have been Croly's *New Republic* associates, Walter Weyl and Walter Lippmann. The sense in which these three men were pragmatists is left implicit in Charles Forcey's meticulous and extremely helpful monograph on the trio, *the Crossroads of Liberalism,* in which the appellation is regularly applied.[54] Yet the intellectual portraits that Forcey constructs do, indeed, make Croly, Lippmann, and Weyl unambiguous participants in the pragmatist tradition as I have characterized it. The writings of the three confirm the impression left by Forcey. Lippmann's influential *Drift and Mastery,* for example, was a vehicle for precisely the combination of hopes and aspirations found in the classic texts of the pragmatist philosophers.[55]

Lippmann later soured on all three themes in this combination, but the tradition was carried on by other publicists and academics of various affiliations, including historians Frederick Barry and James Harvey Robinson, Senator Paul H. Douglas, and the popular radio personality and lecturer Lyman Bryson.[56] Bryson, who wrote a number of *Drift-and-Mastery*-like books of cultural criticism, taught at Columbia Teachers College, where colleagues of his had institutionalized the pragmatist tradition in the early 1920s. There some 35,000 teachers were trained by William Heard Kilpatrick, a devoted if vulgarizing disciple of Dewey who relentlessly emphasized "method over content."[57]

The pragmatist tradition, then, was considerably more concentrated in structure and constituency than have been the general tendencies—practicality, voluntarism, moralism, flexibility, openness—one or more of which have often been used to characterize James Madison, Benjamin Franklin, or John Winthrop as pragmatists. If the tradition was amorphous compared to the clearly defined philosophical work that forms the tradition's most easily identified core, this larger tradition was nevertheless more specific and concrete than the stereotypical American traits that informed some of the work of the pragmatists and motivated some Americans to identify themselves with pragmatism. Pragmatism became a tradition in the discourse of American intellectuals as the work of James, initially, then of Dewey and to some extent of Peirce, was perceived to constitute a rudimentary "philosophy of life" providing a coherent orientation toward the ill-defined but undoubtedly massive and consequential entity these intellectuals called "science."

So considered, pragmatism had a lot to offer, including the supremely important fact that it did not try to offer too much. It was so spare that one could believe in it while entertaining a whole range of other beliefs, ancient and modern, idiosyncratic and conventional. Hadn't Papini said pragmatism was not so much a philosophy as a way of doing without one?[58] There was something to this, even if only because people sympathetic to pragmatism so much enjoyed quoting it. Critics also quoted it, voicing thereby what was eventually to become the standard critique of pragmatism: that pragmatism was too shallow to accomplish anything and that its adherents had mistaken vacancy for liberation. But liberating it undoubtedly did feel to many American intellectuals. Pragmatism demanded very few commitments at a time when the need to have "a philosophy" was still felt by people who were sensitive to the risk of being burned by too large and too long a hold on beliefs of greater scope. Hadn't the Darwinian revolution shown how rapidly our assumptions about the world could change? And hadn't the increasingly discredited efforts of some thinkers to build out of "evolution" a comprehensive system now confirmed the danger of taking a philosophy too far? Wasn't the urban, industrial order of 1910 more different from American life in 1860 than the latter had been from life in 1810? Pragmatism promised a small but versatile supply of insights with which to prepare oneself for an existence in which more changes were no doubt on the way.

If the inevitability of change were to be successfully faced by society as a whole, a philosophy of limited scope was surely needed by the class of managers and bureaucrats assigned the task of supervising American public affairs. It can scarcely be a coincidence that the age in which pragmatism became popular was also the age in which American intellectuals were unprecedentedly engaged by the managerial ideal.[59] Fully consistent with this ideal was the elevation of "bold, persistent experimention" to the level of a principle in the rhetoric of the New Deal.[60] Spare as pragmatism was, it was fleshy enough to support this much admired principle, to sustain an optimistic perspective on science, and to reinforce certain of the least contested, most familiar, and most security-providing ideals in American culture.

One such ideal concerned "action." By closing the gap between thinking and doing, pragmatism preferred action to passivity wherever the choice presented itself. Method was emphasized over bodies of knowledge, and whatever potential for stasis knowledge might have was undercut by repeated reminders of its temporality. Humanity's relation to the universe was depicted in terms of the purposive action people might employ to affect their fate. The activity of inquiry was something confined not to a few—with the rest of the world passively looking on—but opened to as many persons as could meet the challenge of performing it.

Pragmatism was also "democratic." Not only was its method announced as widely accessible and as an engine of improvement; the very practice of that method was supposed to be open, undogmatic, tolerant, self-corrective, and thus an easily recognized extension of the standard liberal ideology articulated by Mill and cherished by so many late-nineteenth-century Americans. Pragmatism was also "moralistic," "voluntaristic," and "practical." It is no great trick to go on down the list, finding these dispositions in the writings of the pragmatists and their popularizers *as these writings specifically advance* the cluster of ideas by means of which pragmatism became a presence in American intellectual life. What needs to be emphasized is that these dispositions had a function in pragmatism other than to provide the terms for supererogatory rhetoric and to be crudely mirrored in a theory of meaning and truth: These dispositions were focused and put to use by pragmatism's capabilities as an orientation toward science at the level of "philosophy of life."

This emphasis need not prevent the recognition that theories of meaning and of truth can be important to large numbers of people and that the pragmatic theory was indeed a source of pragmatism's appeal. When James said that truth was no "stagnant property," but something that happened to ideas in the course of a particular sequence of events, one did not have to be a philosopher to take an interest in the issue. That meanings, truths, and goods were somehow functions of relationships, and not absolutes written into the structure of being, was of course an arresting concept. But the power of such concepts to obtain and keep widespread attention derived in part from the context in which they were advanced. This is to say that pragmatism's answers to philosophical questions, in the narrow sense of the term, gained interest and plausibility among nonphilosophers because these answers were, like "democracy" and "action," built into a "philosophy" in the broad, Emersonian sense, and one that was equipped with an apparently viable orientation toward science.

Pragmatism as a presence in the discourse of American intellectuals consisted essentially of three interpenetrating layers: a theory of meaning and truth that served to flag the movement, a cluster of assertions and hopes about the basis for culture in an age of science, and a range of general images stereotypical of American life. Pragmatism no doubt meant many things to different people, and enabled people to cope with a variety of concerns; yet it is of this three-layered structure that we are justified in thinking when we refer to the pragmatist tradition as manifest in the first half of the twentieth century.

To so regard pragmatism is not to insist that the historical significance of Peirce, James, or Dewey is exhausted by each's participation in pragmatism. Much of what Peirce wrote about "signs" and what James wrote about the psychology of religion, for example, has flourished well outside of this tradition and can claim attention philosophically as well as historically. Nor does this view of pragmatism insist that, with its decline in popularity during the 1940s and after, the pragmatic themes in the writings of "the three" were rendered so anachronistic as to mock the efforts of more recent thinkers to learn something from them. Few American philosophers can claim to be more vividly contemporary than Richard Rorty, for example, who addresses and appreciates Dewey from a perspective that Croly would find hard to recognize.[61] If pragmatism has a future, it will probably look very different from its past, and the two may not even share a name.

To bring the problem of pragmatism in American history down to a question of what pragmatism did for two generations of intellectuals may seem a narrow construction of the problem. Yet this modesty enables a more authentic pragmatism to come more clearly into view. The relations between this pragmatism and both the history of philosophy and the history of the United States are then more easily identified. If "pragmatic" ideas about meaning, truth, and goodness were latent in those parts of American culture discovered by Alexis de Tocqueville and explored by Louis Hartz and Daniel J. Boorstin,[62] these ideas remained mute and inglorious until explicitly developed by certain members of a particular, science-preoccupied generation of intellectuals. These ideas, moreover, did not become part of the public culture of the United States until spread by these same intellectuals and their immediate successors. The pragmatic theory of meaning and truth could not come into being until it was rendered in specific language, and it could not become a cultural possession until that language was taught to people with a will to use it. Since this language was worked out and popularized by late-nineteenth and early-twentieth-century American intellectuals, it is in the discourse of these intellectuals that the problem of pragmatism primarily resides. The pragmatism found in that discourse performed a number of political, philosophic, and religious acts that historians have only begun to assess. Not the least of these acts was the persuading of a great many people that pragmatism was an emblem for America.

3

SCIENCE AND ANARCHY:

WALTER LIPPMANN'S

DRIFT AND MASTERY

An entity called "progressive social thought" has long bedeviled historians. Efforts to define it have failed to win agreement, yet a persistent sense of its singularity has retarded what is normally the next step in our professional routine: The triumphant announcement that younger, more empirical historians have discovered a number of little entities where the previous generation of mushheads had been able to see only one. Walter Lippmann's Drift and Mastery *is, in any event, right in the middle of "progressive social thought" by almost everyone's reckoning. It is one of the documents that has to be confronted, whether progressivism has one or many intellectual histories. This book of 1914 figures so large in studies of progressivism because it can be quoted to illustrate most of the many ideas that have ever been termed "progressive."*

Yet for all its range of complaints and enthusiasms, Drift and Mastery *is a well-integrated essay sustained by confidence in what Lippmann called "the discipline of science." I have tried to show what this concept meant to Lippmann, and how it functioned in the text to transform a host of political, economic, and cultural observations into a single and consistent statement. Although this book is often cited as an example of progressive faith in "experts," who could be expected to manage society rationally and efficiently, I argue here that Lippmann's notion of "scientific method" was far less technocratic than is often implied. Whatever we may conclude about the progressivism of which Lippmann was an intellectual leader, Lippmann himself aspired to something grander than bureaucracy: He sought a culture organized around science.*

This essay was published in American Quarterly XXIX (1977), 463– 475.

OF THE MANY YOUNG Americans still moved by "Dover Beach" in the early twentieth century, none was more adamantly and publicly opposed to the nostalgia and traditionalism of Matthew Arnold than was Walter Lippmann. In *Drift and Mastery,* Lippmann condescendingly declared the inherited culture so moribund that additional attacks on it would be arcane. Yet even in this book of 1914 Lippmann soberly endorsed Arnold's vision of "ignorant armies," and his lament for lost certitude. The tradition-affirming remedies proposed by Arnold and by his more fanatically neoclassical American followers, Irving Babbitt and Paul Elmer More, were "altogether academic," Lippmann believed, but "their diagnosis does locate the spiritual problem": the loss of "authority" (111, 119).[1] Lippmann's answer, the "mastery" he prescribed, was adherence to the most thoroughly modern yet potentially authoritative thing he could think of: "the discipline of science."

To recognize that Lippmann meant by "drift" many of the same things Arnold denounced as "anarchy," and that he saw in science many of the same capabilities Arnold assigned to "culture," is to suspect immediately that Lippmann, like so many other "progressives," partook of historians' favorite syndrome from the period, the conservative use of an allegedly liberal program in seeking social control and the consolidation of American civilization. Yet the comparison suggests something much more particular—and more worthy of exploration—about Lippmann and about the multitudes of educated Americans who responded to *Drift and Mastery* with instant enthusiasm. If recent historiography has shown how eager middle-class Americans were to maintain a unified, national culture,[2] we need to be reminded that this drive for solidification coexisted with a conviction of the nation's evolutionary destiny and with a devotion to its revolutionary heritage. Growth, even diversification, was a positive good, as was the extension into modern social and economic circumstances of the liberties wrested from English autocrats in 1215 and 1776. *Drift and Mastery* spoke eloquently to this tension between expansion and consolidation by seeking to recast in technocratic and evolutionary terms the Arnoldian tradition of cultural criticism. Lippmann's sense of what "science" was, taken together with the social and spiritual ends he articulated, helps us to see how the scientific ideal promised to resolve the conflicting desires for authority and order, on the one hand, and for liberation and flexibility on the other.

The explicit argument of *Drift and Mastery* is simply stated. The contemporary epoch was an age of transition like no other, for the terms on which human life was to proceed had been altered with unprecedented completeness and finality by "scientific invention and blind social currents" (16), and by "iconoclasts" (112) who responded to modernizing forces by subjecting the inherited moral ideas to a destructive critique. Hence a new generation, confronted with circumstances infinitely more complex than those experienced by all previous generations, was obliged to fight against the "chaos" (17) of freedom. The problem was no longer the oppressive strength of Tradition, but the appalling vacuum left after the Rock of Ages had been smashed. The danger was that people would merely drift, that they would bury their heads in the sands of outmoded, formalistic philosophies incapable of addressing and influencing the swirling realities of the new age. In political affairs, for example, a salient instance of pathetically antiquated thinking was Woodrow Wilson's "New Freedom," with its naive emphasis on small entrepreneurs. Still, as one cast about for hints of understanding and stability, one could discern the first promptings of a hearty and truly sophisticated civilization. The centralization urged by Theodore Roosevelt's New Nationalism, the craftsmanship and efficiency of the new ostensibly nonprofiteering managerial class, and the increasing application of "the scientific spirit to daily life" (87) all implied that modern America might indeed master its own complicated fate. In any case, whatever vitality the new generation possessed would "fritter itself away" unless it came "under the scientific discipline" (150, 174).

Implicit throughout the execution of this argument was a definite vision of the healthy and the good—a set of positive values—that informed Lippmann's disdain for the dying civilization, his critique of contemporary thinkers, and his sketch of the new, "scientific" order. If Lippmann insisted in an abstract idiom that external authority be replaced by authoritative human choice, that "purpose" be substituted for tradition (116, 147), he was at the same time committed to choices and purposes of *certain* kinds, particularly those guided by "frank worldliness" (143, 174) and by enthusiasm for the "variety of life" (161, 163). Lippmann scorned asceticism and parochialism as marks of weakness and psychological immaturity; he challenged his readers to "love variety" and "rejoice in change," and to thereby prove their own "strength" and "health" (115). Dogmatic religions and nondemocratic governments may have provided humanity with a measure of stability, but they inhibited the fulfillment of man's spiritual and social potential; the Catholic Church represented what was most hateful in the past, for it had "tried to make weakness permanent" by fostering the false virtues of "poverty, chastity, [and] obedience" (115, 140).

It was a pinched, backward fear of diversity and worldliness that Lippmann held responsible for keeping most contemporary Americans under the influence of old folkways, and for preventing Americans from accepting the dignity of new and wider responsibilities. In a polemical chapter entitled, "A Nation of Villagers," Lippmann denounced Wilson's brand of Progressivism as provincial, as a continuation of the defense William Jennings Bryan had made of "the old and simple life" (81) of prairie traders and farmers. This was "an unworthy dream," proclaimed Lippmann; "the intelligent men of my generation can find a better outlet for their energies than in making themselves masters of little businesses" (85). Wilson's freedom was for the small-time profiteer; he said nothing of the need for freedom from the "narrowness" and "limited vision" of petty competitors (84). As a counter to the Wilsonian attachment to "local rights" and "village patriotism" (86), Lippmann offered a cosmopolitan vision: "communication is blotting out village culture, and opening up national and international thought" (87). That this more complete, total perspective on human affairs was being resisted, even by so many leaders of liberal thought, inflamed Lippmann just as Arnold had been angered by the dogged particularism of British Nonconformism, which threatened, in Arnold's phrase, "to provincialise us all around."[3]

Arnold had wanted to "extirpate" the "narrowness, one-sidedness, and incompleteness" of British Dissent by bringing the latter into "contact with the main current of national life."[4] Certainly, Lippmann could not have sympathized with Arnold's attempt to use the established church as a means toward this end, but Lippmann shared Arnold's contempt for the "liberalism" that would justify wearing blinders, however freely chosen. "Doing what one likes"[5] was no more viable a social ideal for Lippmann than for Arnold. Like Arnold, Lippmann was engaged in an effort to elevate a whole society spiritually and to integrate it socially around a common discipline. The "study of perfection" proposed by Arnold entailed the replacement of "provinciality" by "totality," which meant "getting to know, on all the matters which most concern us, the best which has been thought and said in the world; and through this knowledge, turning a stream of fresh and free thought upon our stock notions and habits. . . ."[6] This was exactly Lippmann's general aim, even if Lippmann's sense of "the best" included more contributions of scientists than did Arnold's, and was more receptive than Arnold's to future revision. Arnold's notorious opposition to the Dead Wife's Sister Bill[7] may make it difficult, from a late twentieth-century standpoint, to see him as even a halting promoter of Lippmann's "frank worldliness," but the "Hellenism" Arnold urged upon the strict and dour England of Herbert Spencer[8] entailed a pagan "spontaneity" that was to become a proverbial article of faith for the young intellectuals of Lippmann's circle in the New York of 1914.[9] Arnold, moreover, was more friendly to science and to change than critics like T. H. Huxley led many to believe.[10] Of all the English-speaking moralists of the generation prior to Lippmann's, Arnold had most commandingly practiced the genre of criticism to which *Drift and Mastery* belongs, and had most intently and subtly employed that genre to balance the claims of discipline and stability against those of emotional romanticism.

Lippmann's belief in the power of science to institutionalize his vision of the healthy and the good depended, obviously, on a particular set of perceptions of science. Above all, science was to Lippmann a method and a spirit, rather than a body of knowledge, and was hence easily transferable from physical and biological inquiry to other human activities. Lippmann attributed to science several specific properties which, while far from original with him, were crucial to the credibility of his program for "mastery." Lippmann's clever and seemingly effortless exposition made them appear naturally related to one another. Chief among these properties was intersubjectivity.

Only in science, explained Lippmann, can we be sure that "from the same set of facts men will come approximately to the same conclusions" (155). Against the "scattered anarchy of individual temperaments" (156) one can pit the international, transpersonal order fostered by science: Cooperation shall bind the world together, just as scientists advance each other's work "whether they live in Calcutta or in San Francisco" (154, 156). The intersubjectivity of science might not fully "wipe out the older cleavages" of race and nationality, but it could provide the "common discipline," the "binding passion" (154) needed to unite civilization and to inspire the energies of diverse individuals.

The intersubjective character of science did not imply, Lippmann insisted, any of the passivity, bloodless abstraction, and antiseptic stoicism so often mistakenly felt to attend upon the "impersonal" outlook of science. Such an implication would make a mockery of Lippmann's spiritual aims. Crucial to the plausibility of Lippmann's program for mastery, then, was a second property he attributed to science: the concrete interests and dreams of the individual human beings who participated in it. Far from abnegating man's emotional needs, science is grounded in them: science matures as it recognizes the "role that fantasy plays in all its work" (165). Science is "a very human thing . . . it springs from a need, is directed by curiosity to choose an interesting field of study, and in that field seeks results that concern men" (165). In science, "the imagination comes into its own" (165). How sad it was that "most people" believed that there was "something inhuman about the scientific attitude" (158):

> They think at once of a world grown over-precise, of love regulated by galvanometers and sphygmographs, of table talk abolished because nutrition is confined to capsules prepared in the laboratory, of babies brought up in incubators. Instead of desire, statistical abstracts; a chilly, measured, weighed, and labeled existence. . . . Science as it comes through the newspapers announces that kissing is unhygienic and that love is a form of lunacy.

This image of science Lippmann was determined to undermine, not only through sarcasm, but through his examples of true scientific activity. His archetypal scientist was not the reticent Darwin, sitting quiet and alone at Down House with his white barnacles, but the robust and omnivorous William James, who sought out spiritualists while searching for evidence that ghosts might exist (161). Indeed, Lippmann's favorable depiction of science followed very much the same pattern as James's celebrated critique of the "scientific" naturalism of W. K. Clifford. The difference was that James, who manifested no need to identify his own position with true science, casts his remarks about physicalism and positivism in the form of an attack on the apparent imperialism of science,[11] while Lippmann, who was more expansionist regarding science than even Clifford, portrayed science as the embodiment of James's mode of thought and feeling.

Closely tied to this emphasis on the positive role of imagination and interest in the process of science was the third crucial property Lippmann attributed to science, an intense determination to "treat life not as something given but as something to be shaped" (151). This was the most amorphous yet the most important of the three—Lippmann's discursive style did not, of course, permit their systematic enumeration in his text—and was expressed primarily in a prophetic rather than a descriptive voice.

The hope that science could bring about the "domination of nature" was a prominent theme in the ideology of science since the time of Bacon, at least; Lippmann employed this idea to reassure his readers that the march of science was the triumph of human purpose, not the retreat of that purpose in the face of "hard realities" discovered by pulling back the veils of human illusion. If science were only the latter, the authority it could impose on civilization would be as repressive and potentially narrow as that provided by the traditions now forsaken. Science was of course a means of distinguishing what was true from what was illusory, but Lippmann was preoccupied with getting beyond this truism to what he believed was the actual experience of science: "the yielding of fact to intelligent desire" (170). He did not seek to defend this view with a detailed epistemology or sociology of science, but he did explore, aphoristically, the paradox of wish-fulfillment through diligent attention to facts.

"If thinking didn't serve desire, it would be the most useless occupation in the world," Lippmann insisted, while explaining that desires are to be subjected to criticism in the light of what we learn about the world while seeking to fulfill those desires. We must "obtain a delicate adjustment of our own desires to what is possible" in order that desires will be *intelligent*. We must "know fact from fancy, search out . . . prejudice . . . learn from failures," and engage in "close observation," but this liberation from blind desire enables us to interact directly with the world and impose our critically revised will upon that world (169–170). "Science," ultimately, "is the unfrightened, masterful, and humble approach to reality . . . its promise is the shaping of fact to a chastened and honest dream" (151).

If Lippmann dodged and obscured the hard question—to what extent did critical revision of one's desires entail the covert surrender of them to "reality"?—he certainly left his readers with the vision of a plastic world and Promethean promise for mankind. On this issue, *Drift and Mastery's* tradition was that of Emerson's belief in the ability of the human mind to make reality, not the skeptical tradition of Emerson's critic, Melville; there was no White Whale in the young Lippmann's cosmos, waiting for a chance to bring human hopes down to size.

No wonder the book had such appeal: few authors had so smoothly integrated apparently conflicting aspirations of the age. Lippmann encouraged people to believe that they would be organized, efficient, functional, and under firm control without sacrificing impulse, choice, fantasy, and liberty; and this happy combination, he led them to hope, could be effected by welcoming rather than resisting the "impact of science" that was felt by many to be inevitable. Correct as historians have been to call the book "the classic statement of the managerial idea,"[12] this classical status owed much to Lippmann's ability to depict managerialism as a triumph of spirituality. Readers who were accustomed to disagreeing with each other shared an excitement about *Drift and Mastery*. Theodore Roosevelt loved the book, and Randolph Bourne said he would have given his soul to have written it.[13] The uncritical enthusiasm of the revolutionary *Masses* was matched by reviews in "established" daily and weekly newspapers throughout the country.[14] Reviewers missed neither Lippmann's emphasis on science nor his mission of bringing contrasting drives into cooperation.[15] The sense that everything could be gained, and nothing lost, was welcomed by one especially engaged commentator:

> Drift all you must. Master all you can. Master all you must. Drift all you can. I want to be in the stream. I want the big stream to be in me. I want to take account of everything. I want everything to take account of me. I want life so orbic I can put my arms around it in an embrace of revelation. Yet I also want life so atmospherically liberated I couldn't include it in any finite definitions. . . . I want reason. But I don't want too much logic. I want order. But I don't want too much system.[16]

Not everyone liked *Drift and Mastery*. Its commitment to the future and its relentlessly secular vision of the healthy and good were not always accepted. For example, the *American Hebrew* complained of Lippmann's glib rejection of traditional authorities and insisted that the "Rock of Ages" was as firm as ever.[17] The Jesuit response was markedly more bitter. Lippmann had arrogantly ignored the achievements of the past and the vitality of contemporary religion, said *America;* his performance brought to mind Hilaire Belloc's description of the self-important pragmatist, who, oblivious to his own barbarism, "struts like a nigger in evening clothes."[18]

A different objection to *Drift and Mastery* held that the book failed to identify and criticize a new tyrannical authority: the expert. At least one reviewer accused Lippmann of "dogmatism" in his defense of this usurpation of the authority of "the People" by an elite of specialists.[19] But the infrequency of this charge serves to remind us of another source of Lippmann's appeal. *Drift and Mastery,* for all its celebration of "administrative science," implied that the scientific spirit could be learned and practiced by *anyone*. Lippmann's case for experts differed from that of L. L. Bernard[20] and many other contemporary advocates of a scientifically managed society in that Lippmann presented science as the fulfillment of democracy. From Lippmann there issued no patronizing remarks about the capabilities of the masses; *Drift and Mastery* did not announce the replacement of democracy by an oligarchy of technicians. When Lippmann asked that everyone's daily work be saturated with the "spirit of science" (152), the latter phrase was no euphemism for "obedience."

If Lippmann was dogmatic about anything, it was the status of science as the "discipline of democracy." Whatever actual or potential links other thinkers might detect between authoritarianism and the earnest mimicry of scientists by political agents, Lippmann's faith was pure: ". . . when the impulse which overthrows kings and priests and unquestioned creeds becomes self-conscious we call it science," for science ultimately "*is* self-government" (151). The consistency and sheer conviction of Lippmann's preachments in this vein may have diminished whatever fears readers might have had about a new autocracy of privileged knowledge, but Lippmann provided another, more programmatic kind of reassurance: the theme in *Drift and Mastery* that is often called Lippmann's "pluralism."[21]

"The world is so complex," Lippmann explained, "that no official government can be devised to deal with it." There were limits to what even the most centralized, efficient, farsighted, and fully scientific state could accomplish. Therefore, "voluntary groupings based on common interests," particularly labor unions and organized consumers, were essential to the achievement of a stable and equitable social order (96). The "democracy" that meshed so well with science was not the antiquated individualism, according to which an infinity of autonomous persons interacted with the state, but rather the democracy of collective action by diverse groups of similarly disposed individuals. And the scientific role was not exclusively that of the state official, "planning" on the basis of the inputs by metascientific, myopically self-regarding constituencies; rather Lippmann saw each of these groups as potential possessors of the scientific spirit. The rational refinement of purposes, the heroic criticism of one's own traditions, the reaching out to a more comprehensive grasp on contemporary reality, the expansion of opportunities for cooperation—all of these were legitimate aims for particular interest groups as well as for the "administrative scientists" of government and industry (e.g., 175).

It was the "common discipline" of science, then, that saved Lippmann's pluralism from becoming, in spite of his wishes, a justifier of the competing provincialisms against which Lippmann's program for mastery was directed. Lippmann's sense of the variety and contingency of social life was as authentic as his belief in organization and consolidation; he believed the tension between the two could be made dynamic through science, "the culture under which people can live forward in the midst of complexity" (151).

In addition to his "pluralistic philosophy" (115), Lippmann had another, more subtle means of distinguishing his version of scientific civilization from the dictatorship of experts. *Drift and Mastery* itself, a highly accessible and seemingly unpretentious act of intelligence, was presented as an example of operation of the scientific spirit. The very structure of the book supported this impression: It began concretely with a treatment of muckraking as a kind of datum, then proceeded to extract from muckraking and from other passionate, ostensibly diverse tendencies of the day consistent patterns of behavior and aspiration. The book built from these patterns to its climactic prescription of scientific mastery as a means to strengthen the healthy and to renounce the reactionary. Throughout, Lippmann's own desires frankly operated to single out salient "facts," and his program sought to shape the world revealed by those facts. Lippmann demystified the scientific role and made it seem more congruent with jargon-free cultural criticism than with the mystic arts of surgery and physics. That Lippmann was of almost no help in distinguishing science from non-science was noticed by a few,[22] but this analytical failing was easily overlooked by an American generation peculiarly determined to affirm the compatibility of science with just about everything else held to be of value, especially democracy.

In identifying criticism so closely with science, Lippmann was expressing a faith in the power of public discussion that antedated *Drift and Mastery*,[23] and that he expressed in other terms during the many decades in which he had ceased to think of criticism and science as aspects of the same metier.[24] Yet this faith in the efficacy of critical discourse received the most insistent articulation and justification in *Drift and Mastery*. Here, at the high point of his infatuation with science, did Lippmann assign least modestly to critics like himself the pivotal role of creating a consciousness necessary to social reorganization (e.g., 175). It is not surprising, therefore, that *Drift and Mastery* has been remembered as a benchmark in the growth of criticism as a social role in the United States.[25]

Lippmann's confidence in the centralized state was also at its strongest when he was enamored of the scientific ideal. Lippmann was later to gain fame criticizing New Deal efforts to act in keeping with his earlier political vision,[26] but his advocacy in 1914 of the "New Nationalism" needs to be remembered in connection with his then impassioned commitment to science. William E. Leuchtenburg has cautioned against viewing *Drift and Mastery* as a strictly political document; what needs to be underlined yet more boldly is the scientific imagery of what Leuchtenburg correctly calls Lippmann's "program of spiritual and artistic liberation."[27] The most salient context out of which *Drift and Mastery* comes, therefore, is neither the "New Nationalism" of progressive politics, nor the search of young intellectuals for a social role, nor even the Greenwich Village rebellion in which Lippmann was so illustrious a participant.[28] All of these helped give form and life to the text, but none integrated it and provided the aegis under which these other forces in Lippmann's intellectual world found free expression. This integration was performed by Lippmann's conviction that potentially anarchic impulses could be transformed into orderly growth through the discipline of science. This conviction was not unique to *Drift and Mastery,* but few books of the late nineteenth or early twentieth centuries were at once so fully defined by it and so popular among educated Americans.

This is not to insist that a historical reading of *Drift and Mastery* is the only appropriate response to the text. Indeed, the book's status as a "classic" derives partly from its ability to transcend its own aims and speak to successive generations of American intellectuals, including those not strikingly in sympathy with Lippmann's faith in science. Even Leuchtenburg, whose discussion of the text is as historically sensitive as any, declared that "much of the excitement" of reading the book in 1961 was the sense that Lippmann was "facing really for the first time . . . much the same questions we face today."[29]

And Leuchtenburg was able to feel this even while gently mocking as "chimerical" Lippmann's hopes for consumer organization and while ignoring altogether the seriousness with which Lippmann took feminism.[30] That both feminism and consumerism could become strong enough in the brief period since Leuchtenburg wrote to provide a basis for yet another generation's interest in *Drift and Mastery* is perhaps the most dramatic testimony of all to the prescience of the young Lippmann.

To look away from *Drift and Mastery's* still engaging extremities in order to concentrate on its less prescient core, as this study does, is more than an exercise in antiquarianism. It is to enter the terrain on which the "revolt against formalism" and the "search for order" compete for the attention of historians. These often-quoted phrases—contributed originally by Morton White and Robert Wiebe[31]—are not necessarily exclusive of one another, but the relation between the drives denoted by these phrases has not always been clear. It is arresting that in a single text should be found so determined an articulation of both. Nowhere is the antagonism toward stasis, doctrine, and absolutism more intense than in *Drift and Mastery,* and nowhere is the yearning for control and organization more real. The ease with which Lippmann fulfilled each of these impulses through an expression of the other reinforces the sense that the two are compatible; yet it also feeds the suspicion that very little of the intellectual history of the period can be described and explained in the inclusive terms of either.

A close analysis of the text of *Drift and Mastery* discourages emphasis on the more or less timeless, highly abstract ideals that may dominate a society's imagination; what matters is not whether "order" or "liberty," for example, define the spirit of an age. Nor it is enough to grant that "formalism" and "anti-formalism" always exist in a state of tension, and to chart the shifting strengths of each. Instead, our attention is demanded by the precise mechanisms that embody and reconcile these abstractions, and that create *historically specific* intellectual phenomena. One such mechanism is the concept of scientific method, as formulated and applied by *Drift and Mastery;* and one such phenomenon is the effort, toward which this book was a signal contribution, to revise the public culture of the United States in keeping with what participants in the effort took to be the implications of science. To insist on this measure of concreteness in assigning historical significance to texts is neither to forsake breadth of generalization nor to abandon the degree of abstraction needed to facilitate comparisons between particular phenomena. It is, however, to seek the most authentic points of contact between a text and the historical moments that produced and absorbed it.

4

ETHNIC DIVERSITY, COSMOPOLITANISM, AND THE EMERGENCE OF THE AMERICAN LIBERAL INTELLIGENTSIA

The absorption of many persons of Jewish origin into an American intellectual life that had once been overwhelmingly Protestant is surely an event of some consequence, but few historians have recognized it as a problem for research. Interest in the topic has increased and sharpened since this essay was first published in 1975, and I am pleased that the piece has played a role in this process of scholarly mobilization. I believe the essay helps to put in place a basis for overcoming what has been a persistent inhibition felt by potential explorers of this particular segment of American history. The inhibition stems from a legitimate suspicion of ethnically over-determined and potentially invidious interpretations of ideas: The fear is that one will be led to characterize as "Jewish" this or that preoccupation of American sociology or literary criticism or political theory. Down the road of such characterizations lies the "booster-bigot trap": the choice between the booster's uncritical celebration of "Jewish contributions" and the bigot's malevolent complaint about "Jewish influence." One way to avoid this trap, and to overcome the historiographical inhibition attendant upon it, is to recognize how historically specific and contingent were the concerns and preferences that Jewish and non-Jewish intellectuals brought to one another, and how dependent upon reciprocal, dialectical interchanges was the new cultural matrix created by these intellectuals for themselves and their successors. This is to insist that it is a mistake to look for an unmediated "Jewish impact," according to which an allegedly distinctive and timeless set of dispositions are found to have been imposed here and there by an ostensibly monolithic population of Jewish intellectuals.

This essay identifies the cosmopolitan ideal as the most powerful ideological agent in the integration of a single but scattered community of American intellectuals. Although the essay takes for granted that values and interests more specific than cosmopolitanism inevitably informed senses of what was or was not "cosmopolitan," I wish I had more explicitly acknowledged that one person's expanded horizons can be another's confinement. Just how the cosmopolitan ideal was interpreted, and how it was then translated into concrete undergraduate curriculums, ideological persuasions, agendas for disciplines, and the like, is the substance of much of the unwritten history of American intellectuals during the mid-century decades.

For all its susceptibility to different interpretations, the cosmopolitan ideal is definite enough to be distinguished from the cultural pluralism associated with the name of Horace Kallen. I was so certain of this when I wrote that I sketched the distinction quite casually, only to learn from others after publication that the distinction had often been missed, and that my point was thus more important than I had realized. What distinguishes cultural pluralism from cosmopolitanism is the commitment of the former to the survival and nurturing of the ethnic group as such. While cosmopolitanism is inherently suspicious of ethnic particularism, cultural pluralism actually prescribes it and envisions a society full of particular groups, each respecting one another. Adherents of the cosmopolitan ideal have often made supportive references to cultural pluralism in the interests of promoting the common cause of "tolerance." But such support has generally been offered when society as a whole, rather than an intellectual elite, is being discussed. Full-blown cosmopolitanism, as defined in the essay below, was understood to be a realistic ideal primarily for intellectuals. Not every citizen could be expected to become as multitudinous as Margaret Mead or Lionel Trilling, but all Americans needed to be protected from the hated ethnocentrism of the long-dominant Anglo-Saxons. Cultural pluralism was understood as a potential brake on this uniquely threatening variety of provincialism.

To denote my subject as an "intelligentsia" did not seem an especially striking step when I took it, but I have since encountered a strange form of passive resistance to my use of the term. Citations to the essay sometimes get wrong the last word of the title: for "intelligentsia" one will write "intelligence," and another will write "intellectual." There may be a lesson for me in these little mistakes of scholars friendly to the essay. Perhaps "intelligentsia" is too lofty, and "community of liberal intellectuals" would have been easier to swallow? However awkward, the title of the essay here remains what it was when published in American Quarterly XXVII (1975), 133–151.

IN 1916 RANDOLPH BOURNE expressed the hope that ethnic diversity would enable the United States to develop a style of life and thought more fulfilling than that of any of the single, national cultures of Europe and America. Exactly at the point in history when the majority of native-born Americans were the most anxious about the cultural effects of massive immigration from Eastern and Central Europe, Bourne depicted this immigration as a unique opportunity for Americans to liberate themselves from "parochialism," and to develop in themselves a truly "cosmopolitan spirit."[1] His denunciation of contemporary chauvinism was of virtually no importance in a national political context; public policy was influenced rather by those who wanted to assimilate immigrants into a preexisting American norm, and to drastically limit additional immigration.[2] Yet Bourne's articulation of the cosmopolitan ideal was with, rather than against, the drift of history when his efforts are viewed in another context: the emergence of a national, secular, ethnically diverse, left-of-center intelligentsia.

This intelligentsia had become a prominent feature in American life by the end of the 1940s.[3] Its most obvious leaders included Edmund Wilson, Lionel Trilling, and Dwight Macdonald, among men of letters; David Riesman and Daniel Bell among social scientists; and Reinhold Niebuhr and Sidney Hook among philosophical essayists. The discourse of this intelligentsia was largely institutionalized in the liberal arts divisions of several major universities and in such journals of opinion as the *New Republic*, the *Partisan Review*, *Commentary*, the *Nation*, and, more recently, the *New York Review of Books* and the *New York Times Book Review*. So influential was this intelligentsia during the 1940s, 1950s, and 1960s that most Americans who thought of themselves as "intellectuals" were either members of it, or part of its audience.[4] Although the precise extent of this community of discourse can be a matter for argument,[5] persons who identify with it recognize one another so readily that some sociologists have described "intellectuals" as virtually an "ethnic group."[6] The analogy is ironic in view of the diversity of the actual ethnic origins of these intellectuals. In Bourne's time, leaders of American "high culture" were predominantly Anglo-Saxon and Protestant, not only in origin but in their sense of what it meant to be an American; by mid-century, this leadership was approximately half Jewish and half "WASP,"[7] and its two halves worked in concert to serve values that were distinctly aloof from conventional ethnic particularism of any species. Indeed, the potentially obvious, but rarely spelled-out cosmopolitanism of the mid-century intelligentsia is a key to the latter's historical development.

The "cosmopolitanism" to which I refer is the desire to transcend the limitations of any and all particularisms in order to achieve a more complete human experience and a more complete understanding of that experience. The ideal is decidedly counter to the eradication of cultural differences, but counter also to their preservation in parochial form. Rather, particular cultures and subcultures are viewed as repositories for insights and experiences that can be drawn upon in the interests of a more comprehensive outlook on the world. Insofar as a particular ethnic heritage or philosophical tradition is an inhibition to experience, it is to be disarmed; insofar as that heritage or tradition is an avenue toward the expansion of experience and understanding, access to it is to be preserved.

Bourne believed that a process of cultural cross-fertilization was underway, especially among young people: "It is not uncommon for the eager Anglo-Saxon" in college to "find his true friends not among his own race but among the acclimatized German . . . Austrian . . . Jew . . . Scandinavian or Italian," for such persons "are oblivious to the repressions of that tight little society in which the Anglo-Saxon so provincially grew up." These immigrants, in turn, were experiencing a transformation, for contact with Anglo-Saxons expanded their own cultural horizons. This process seemed especially productive when young Jewish intellectuals were involved; Bourne specifically praised the contributions of Felix Frankfurter, Horace Kallen, Morris R. Cohen, and Walter Lippmann.[8]

Bourne was far from alone in espousing cosmopolitanism and in believing that Jews were more useful to the cause than were other immigrants. Floyd Dell was grateful that Davenport, Iowa, had so many descendants of the immigration of 1848, especially Jews, for it created a more liberated, intellectual environment. A pivotal influence on Dell was a heretical rabbi who ministered mostly to "Gentiles, Socialists and Atheists."[9] The Nebraskan Alvin Johnson, who prided himself on his "prosemitism," was excited by the opportunities afforded by Columbia University for meeting and learning from "unlike types."[10] Lincoln Steffens rejoiced in the expanded horizons he and his journalistic colleagues obtained by keeping tabs on Abraham Cahan and the cultural life of the Lower East Side.[11] Hutchins Hapgood's *Spirit of the Ghetto* explored in detail the intuition that what made the East European Jews remarkable was their passionate intellectuality, their determination to pursue abstract ideas about art, metaphysics, and political economy to ultimate and universal conclusions.[12] And the young Edmund Wilson was inspired by what he identified as the "cosmopolitanism" of Paul Rosenfeld, who was, according to Wilson, never defensive about his "catholic interest in art and life," and who introduced Wilson to "a whole fascinating world, united though international, of personality, poetics, texture, mood."[13]

Perhaps it is no surprise to learn that an ideal of cosmopolitanism was somehow involved in the legendary efforts of the 1910s and 1920s to transcend the limitations of Victorian literary tastes, commercial civilization, superpatriotism, and "Puritanism." Yet "cosmopolitanism," unlike "alienation," is not a central concept in the very works that have made the history of these revolts against American conventions so familiar.[14] Alienation may have been real enough as a *condition,* but those who experienced it and those who have since written about it have sometimes depicted it, misleadingly, as an ideal, or value, or doctrine. Attention to the proverbial alienation of people like Bourne, Dell, Van Wyck Brooks, John Reed, Harold Stearns, Max Eastman, and Ezra Pound has tended to obscure their actual values, especially their cosmopolitanism.

What is often termed the "alienation" of the literary radicals and expatriates of the 1910s and 1920s is their antiprovincialism, the obverse side of the coin of cosmopolitanism. The heart of the matter was expressed in "Provincialism the Enemy," an essay of 1917 by the greatest expatriate of all, Ezra Pound. "The bulk of the work of Henry James's novels is precisely an analysis of, and thence a protest against all sorts of petty tyrannies and petty coercions," explained Pound, who linked James with Flaubert and Turgenev in the great "struggle against provincialism." Whatever these authors protest about "artistic detachment or any theories of writing," warned Pound, their work has ultimately been in the fight against provincialism, and their weapon "has largely been the presentation of human variety." Insofar as this literary tradition has a social counterpart, it is found, Pound explained, in the nations that most recognize "diversity," especially France and England, with their great capitals of Paris and London. What defects France has can be traced to its provinces; Napoleon, for example, was the "incarnation" of the "ever damned spirit of provincialism," and "only a backwoods hell like Corsica would have produced him." The ideal circumstance for the advancement of culture would be a tunnel from London to Paris; this would "make for a richer civilization, for a completer human life." In the process, the differences between the two cities would be attractively accentuated, and "nothing," concluded Pound "is more valuable than just this amicable accentuation of difference, and of complementary values."[15]

It was appropriate that the iconoclast Pound should refer to Henry James, for the latter represented a tradition that the young intellectuals of the 1910s and 1920s were reasserting and radically enlarging. The standard "literary culture" of nineteenth-century America included a guarded, genteel cosmopolitanism that attributed to upper-class Europeans a life more complicated, expansive, and fulfilling than James, for example, believed could be generated by purely American experience.[16] Although James himself was unnerved and offended by the actual working-class immigrants he encountered in New York, many native-born Americans of his generation had trusted that out of the diversity of European races and cultures a unified, superior society could be created in the United States. This older "cosmopolitan nationalism" was virtually eclipsed by resurgent nativism in America at large, just when the young intellectuals were taking up the tradition among themselves.[17]

If antiprovincialism pushed Pound toward expatriation, it led others to the apparently opposite strategy of "cultural nationalism." The latter outlook, as formulated by Van Wyck Brooks, Lewis Mumford, and Harold Stearns, was less a criticism of non-American art and letters than it was an attempt to bring to their own national culture an intensity and scope comparable to that of European civilization. They looked to a new intelligentsia to manifest a more diverse, more broadly based emotional and intellectual existence, and they were eager for this cause to be advanced by persons of any ethnic origin.[18]

H. L. Mencken's onslaughts against American chauvinism did not spare even the newest of Ellis Island arrivals, but his scorn for them derived from values very similar to Bourne's. Mencken condemned the immigrants for the speed with which they dropped their heritage and transformed themselves into the average American boob.[19] What to Bourne was a robust hope—that immigrants would retain enough of their own past to enrich American life—was to the more cynical Mencken a lamentably unlikely prospect.

If the concept of alienation has tended to obscure the reality of the cosmopolitan ideal as held by cultural critics in America, especially those of Anglo-Saxon stock who became prominent before 1930, then the concept of "assimilation" has tended, analogously, to obscure the cosmopoli-

tan ideal as held by intellectuals of Jewish origin.[20] Certainly, this ideal
has been more widely attributed to Jews than to others,[21] but more
emphasis needs to be given to the fact that when Jewish immigrants and
their children responded avidly to classics of American literature, this
response was part of a larger discovery of modern and Western culture
generally. The so-called "Americanization" of the East European Jews, in
particular, was an extension, indeed an explosive flowering of the *haskalah,* the "romantic enlightenment" already underway within the Pale of
Settlement in the nineteenth century. Memoirs of intellectual life on the
Lower East Side establish beyond doubt that newly liberated Jews grasped
simultaneously for Marx and Horatio Alger, George Eliot and Washington Irving, Voltaire and Benjamin Franklin.[22] True, the settlement houses
did tend to present Western civilization as filtered through the genteel
tradition, but the most self-consciously intellectual of the immigrants
were not interested in substituting a new parochialism for the one left
behind; instead, they aimed to "possess" for themselves, as Morris R.
Cohen put it in 1902, all the benefits of "the Age of Reason," of modern
life generally.[23]

Cohen was the first Russian-born Jew to become a member of the
American Philosophical Association, a regular contributor to the *New
Republic,* and a prominent secular moralist. To a generation of immigrant's sons at the City College of New York, he was a cultural hero, the
preeminent exemplar of success as an American intellectual. Typed
though he was by his admirers and his critics as "the Paul Bunyan of the
Jewish Intellectuals,"[24] Cohen was determined to be a thinker, not a
"Jewish thinker" nor even an "American thinker"; he opposed both Zion-
ists and the killers of Sacco and Vanzetti as parochial tribalists. It was this
insistent cosmopolitanism that defined the terms on which Cohen was
"assimilated": Not only was he first introduced to American intellectual
life and then inducted into it by patrons who were, themselves, critics of
American parochialism—Thomas Davidson, William James, and two
German Jews of Cohen's generation, Felix Frankfurter and Walter Lippmann—but he soon became a symbol of cosmopolitanism for Anglo-
Saxons such as Bourne, Oliver Wendell Holmes, Jr., and John Herman
Randall, Jr.[25]

To emphasize "cosmopolitanism" as opposed to "alienation" or "assimilation" is therefore not merely a semantical gesture. This change in
emphasis gets us closer to the dynamics of the process whereby the intel-

ligentsia comes into being. It would not be enough even to say that persons alienated from one heritage were assimilated into a group alienated from another heritage; it was the affirmative dimension, the cosmopolitan ideal, that made rapport between the two ethnic types possible. In this view, the intelligentsia that came fully into its own in the 1940s was formed primarily by the merger of two, originally autonomous revolts against two distinctive provincialisms, and what mattered most about the Jewish immigrants was not their ethnicity, nor even their inherited devotion to learning, but their impatience with the limitations of ethnic particularism. Certainly, the ethnicity of the Jews appealed to some Anglo-Saxons in search of counter models to the apparent deficiencies in their own upbringings,[26] but this function could often be performed by the ethnicity of Italians, Slavs, and other immigrant groups. What made the young Jewish intellectuals so pivotal in the development of the intelligentsia was the depth and authenticity of their revolt against the constraints of the East European Ashkenazim, and the universalist tone of that revolt. The "American" discourse of the sons of Harvard—and of Davenport, Iowa—into which the heirs of the *haskalah* were "assimilated" was a discourse with cosmopolitan aspirations of its own, aspirations that were in turn reinforced and intensified by liberated Jews.

Among the most liberated of the Jews was Joseph Freeman. Bewildered by the dissolution of traditional Jewish culture and unpersuaded by the claims of its religion, the adolescent Freeman tried to find an identity for himself in the tradition of Western, secular literature, especially that of the Enlightenment and of the English romantics. Hostile to the commercialism of his father, he yearned for a means to distance himself from the ethos of the Jewish businessman. His life began to fit together at the age of sixteen, when he discovered *The Masses:* somewhere in "mysterious Greenwich Village" there were "native Americans who had integrated the conflicting values of the world." At the center of the *Masses* group was Max Eastman, himself married to a Jewish woman, as Freeman was quick to note. When Freeman and his Jewish friends gazed at Eastman, they "at last . . . saw Shelley plain." Here was the embodiment, "in sensuous outline," of the "New Spirit of the Intelligentsia": the prematurely white-haired Eastman "looked Beauty and spoke Justice." Freeman followed *The Masses* in its flight "from Moses and Jesus to Venus and Apollo," and found in that flight other "souls," like himself, "in rebellion against puritan bondage." And when Freeman actually joined the staff of the *Liberator,* the postwar successor of *The Masses,* he rejoiced that "Nordic Americans" like Eastman and Floyd Dell did not make him suffer for his Jewish origins: "I felt that on a small scale the *Liberator* group represented that ideal society which we all wanted, that society in which no racial barriers could possibly exist." By the time he worked for the *Liberator,* Freeman had come to feel that he and his friends were "no longer, culturally, Jews"; rather, they were "Westerners initiated into and part of a culture which merged the values of Jerusalem, Egypt, Greece and ancient Rome with the Catholic culture of the Middle Ages, the humanistic culture of the Renaissance, the equalitarian ideals of the French Revolution, and the scientific concepts of the nineteenth century." To this they added "socialism," which seemed to them "the apex" of Western culture.[27]

While in sheer numbers it was East European Jews like Freeman and Cohen who would eventually make up the "Jewish half" of the intelligentsia, the early stages of the accommodation were facilitated by a small but influential group of Jews of German origin, whose families had immigrated, in most cases, two or three generations before. An index of their importance is the fact that about half of the earliest editors of the *New Republic* and *Seven Arts*—perhaps the two most influential journals in the early development of the intelligentsia—were German Jews: Walter Lippmann, Walter Weyl, James Oppenheim, Waldo Frank, and Paul Rosenfeld. Even Bourne and Brooks, whose names are always associated with *Seven Arts,* were comparative latecomers to the enterprise; and only when they joined the magazine was it relieved, as Oppenheim put it, "of the onus of being non-Anglo-Saxon."[28]

The German Jews were more assimilated and generally well-off than their East European counterparts; many had grown up on the Upper West Side and had spent their summers in Atlantic City. Rosenfeld and Frank were graduates of Yale, Lippmann of Harvard; Rosenfeld had even gone to a military academy in the Hudson Valley.[29] Yet Bourne and Edmund Wilson were aware of, and pleased by, cultural capacities that seemed to distinguish such Ivy League Hebrews from Gentile peers. And when Rosenfeld spoke of Bourne, he praised him as one Anglo-Saxon American "not yet ready to renounce the Elizabethan heritage of liberty," and a person whose "multitudinous interests" made him a "salon" in and of himself.[30] Brooks appealed to Rosenfeld as a mixture of "Harvard blandness" with the critical ideal of Taine and Herder; Brooks was, Rosenfeld observed, a truly "cosmopolitan" critic.[31]

Horace Kallen, too, was German-born, and it was his earliest formulation of the theory of "cultural pluralism" that helped inspire Bourne's manifesto of 1915.[32] Kallen was a leading critic of the "100 per cent Americanism" that would use the "melting pot" not to create a new national mixture, but to melt down immigrant stock into a substance malleable enough to be molded into a traditional Anglo-Saxon American.[33] Kallen contributed in some ways to the growth of the cosmopolitan ideal, but his outlook differed importantly from the vision of Bourne and of most of the members of the nascent intelligentsia. Kallen, a Zionist, tended to favor the retention of parochial loyalties almost for their own sake; he was not so much for cross-fertilization as for the harmonious cooperation and mutual enrichment of clearly defined, contrasting, durable ethnic units.[34] Bourne shared some of Kallen's hope that a plurality of particularistic interests could function as countervailing forces in the social order in general, yet Bourne's scope was more limited: Bourne was moved by the idea of a community of intellectuals, a complex, yet unified, single discourse to which a variety of contingent particularisms would make their distinctive contributions. He was more willing than Kallen to see the immigrants themselves undergo cultural changes. Moreover, Kallen's attempt to speak about the ethnic composition of American society as a whole gave his program a more broadly political character than was characteristic of the ethnic attitudes of most intellectuals, a few of whom defended continued, massive immigration but most of whom expressed their cosmopolitanism more locally and quietly, in the social relationships of a community in-the-making. And in this more private sphere Kallen, like other German Jews, was active in the growth of the community; it was in Kallen's Wisconsin living room, for example, that New Yorkers Bourne and Eastman first met each other.

Hence by the late 1920s and 1930s, sons of East European immigrants had the opportunity of following the lead not only of former *Landsleuter* like Cohen and Freeman or of halfway figures like Lippmann and Rosenfeld, but of Anglo-Saxons whose own outlook had been influenced by the presence in America of Jewish intellectuals. By the time Alfred Kazin and Lionel Trilling were growing up, they could take as their "American" model Edmund Wilson, who had himself learned so much from Rosenfeld. Kazin and Trilling were attracted by Wilson's wide-lensed surveys of modernism and of Marxism, but they were most fascinated by Wilson as the incarnation of the great tradition of Greenwich Village. Kazin in the 1930s identified explicitly with Bourne, Brooks, and the New York of 1912;[35] Trilling consciously "signalized" his own "solidarity with the intellectual life" itself by taking an apartment in the Village just across the way from where Wilson himself could be seen each evening, working at his desk. Trilling saw Wilson as the embodiment of the least provincial aspects of the Village; from Wilson one got a "whiff of Lessing at Hamburg, of Sainte-Beuve at Paris."[36]

The young Kazin saw himself as simultaneously an American studying American literature and a Jew fulfilling, through his criticism, a vaguely Jewish "mission to humanity." He attributed his drive to create to his ethnic heritage, yet felt he had emancipated himself from the cultural content of that heritage; he had been most influenced by "Blake, Melville, Emerson, the seventeenth-century English religious poets, and the Russian novelists," none of whom, he said in 1944, had any "direct associations" with Jewish culture. As for the latter entity, he believed it indistinguishable, in its contemporary form, from middle-class chauvinism of any sort.[37]

As a graduate student in the late 1920s Trilling had contributed to the *Menorah Journal,* but by the end of the 1930s had come to lament as "provincial and parochial" all such efforts at "realizing one's Jewishness." The issue was not that of "escaping" Jewish origins, Trilling explained, but of taking one's life for what it was. "I cannot discover anything in my professional intellectual life" traceable to a specifically Jewish background, said Trilling, and "I should resent it if a critic of my work were to discover in it either faults or virtues which he called Jewish."[38]

Educated Americans in general received Kazin's *On Native Grounds* and Trilling's *The Liberal Imagination* as helpful analyses of the American social imagination, as works that made available to all a more enlightened perspective on the intellectual experience of the previous half century. Opinion on these books today is somewhat more divided,[39] but the attention they commanded in the 1940s and 1950s is an important episode in what Leslie Fiedler has hyperbolically called "the great take-over by Jewish-American writers" of a task "inherited from certain Gentile predecessors, urban Anglo-Saxons and midwestern provincials of North European origin," the task of "dreaming aloud the dreams of the whole American people."[40] The lives of Kazin and Trilling were caught up in the dialectic of ethnic diversity and cosmopolitanism; in the course of working out their own relation to the life of the mind in America, they achieved a critical ambience that persons far removed from Morningside and St. Nicholas Heights responded to as eagerly as Kazin and Trilling had once responded to the example of Edmund Wilson. But when Kazin and Trilling had read *Axel's Castle,* they were, by their own testimony, acutely aware that they were Jews and that Wilson was not. To the Americans of various backgrounds later inspired by *The Liberal Imagination* and *On Native Grounds* such distinctions were far less important, when they were noticed at all. Among the reasons for this change was the more complete integration, in the intervening years, of the intelligentsia.

It was partly on account of Joseph Stalin that this integration proceeded as quickly as it did. The issues of the 1930s were new and immediate to Malcolm Cowley as well as to Alfred Kazin, to Dwight Macdonald as well as to Sidney Hook.[41] However one resolved one's own attitude toward Stalin, the act of doing it was the first traumatic intellectual and moral experience that the old Ivy Leaguers and the New York Jews went through together. The struggle against each other and against the non-Leftist world over issues that seemed frighteningly important created bonds of antagonism and of friendship that cemented together the community of discourse of the 1940s, 1950s, and 1960s. Trilling probably exaggerated only very slightly when he observed in 1967 that the experience of participating in, or responding to Stalinism "created the American intellectual class as we know it."[42]

To a remarkable extent, the argument over Stalinism was carried out within the terms of the cosmopolitan ideal. Was or was not Marxism the most fully comprehensive, the least culture-bound analysis of society? Was the Soviet Union fulfilling or betraying the universalism of the Marxist vision? Was the enlistment of artists "on the side of the worker" a step beyond the conceptual prison of individual idiosyncracy, a step into a truly international movement that would eventually open up all of life's opportunities to all human beings; or, was such enlistment a callow enslavement to a new parochialism in which the freedom to grow and to experiment at will was repressed? Did the Popular Front Against Fascism afford an opportunity for the expansion of experience through rapport with folk and bourgeois cultures, or was the Popular Front, by virtue of its uncritical support for potential allies of the Soviet Union, a program for the stagnation of the intellect and for the covert preservation of unregenerate nationalism?

The most influential answers to the questions of the 1930s were those offered by the *Partisan Review*. Indeed, the story of how the anti-Stalinist writers gathered around the *Partisan Review* after 1937 and used it to perform a job of intellectual demolition on the Popular Front has assumed the proportions of a legend comparable to that associated with Bourne's attacks on John Dewey during World War I.[43] Although the *Partisan Review* group came together on the immediate basis of attitudes toward politics and literature, not attitudes toward ethnicity, the composition of the editorial board was an index of how the ethnic foundation of the intellectual community had shifted since the days of *Seven Arts*. The old Ivy League tradition was still represented, this time by Yale men Dwight Macdonald, F. W. Dupee, and George L. K. Morris, but the editors of Jewish origin—Philip Rahv and William Phillips—were products of the East European immigration, Rahv having actually been born in Russia. The other founding editor, Mary McCarthy, was a lapsed Catholic from Seattle. The opposing "Stalinists" were similarly constituted ethnically, but it was the *Partisan Review* that won the argument, and so decisively that its writers virtually established their own outlook as the ideological basis for the cultural criticism done by the intelligentsia for the subsequent two or three decades. It was in a context of anti-Stalinism and anti-Fascism, therefore, that the *Partisan Review* writers drew upon the cosmopolitan ideal, as in Harold Rosenberg's classical formulation of it in 1940.

In "The Fall of Paris," Rosenberg commented on the loss of "the laboratory of the twentieth century," first to the Popular Front and then to the Nazis. Before anti-Fascist unity had filled Paris with sympathy for "the conventional, the sententious, the undaring, the morally lax," and before Hitler had shut things down completely, this "cultural Klondike" had been the home of "the searchers of every nation."

> Released in this aged and bottomless metropolis from national folklore, national politics, national careers; detached from the family and the corporate taste; the lone individual, stripped, yet supported on every side by the vitality of other outcasts with whom it was necessary to form no permanent ties, could experiment with everything that man has within him of health or monstrousness. . . .

Its hospitality created by "a tense balance of historical forces, preventing any one class from imposing . . . its own restricted forms and aims," Paris was the "only spot where necessary blendings could be made and mellowed." In Paris, "no folk lost its integrity: on the contrary, artists of every region renewed by this magnanimous milieu discovered in the depths of themselves what was most alive in the communities from which they had come." Only this "international of Culture" could enable "American speech to find its measure of poetry and eloquence," only ideas spreading from here "could teach a native of St. Louis, T. S. Eliot, how to deplore in European tones the disappearance of centralized European culture—and a modern rhetoric in which to assault Modernism." And while the capital of the international culture is now gone, modernity in the arts survives "as solid evidence that a creative communion sweeping across all boundaries is not out of the reach of our time."[44]

Although it would be an exaggeration to say that New York took the place of Paris as the cultural capital,[45] the temporary ascendancy of Hitler in Europe suddenly transformed America, as Kazin put it in 1942, into "a repository of Western Culture" in a world overrun by its enemies.[46] This impression was not simply a general one; it had the specific reinforcement of the new intellectual migration. However parochial and nativist American society remained in the 1930s and early 1940s, it at least managed to accept a number of the prominent political dissenters and non-Aryan physicists, philosophers, and psychoanalysts driven out of Central Europe.[47] The presence in America of spirits like Thomas Mann, Jacques Maritain, and Albert Einstein, noted Kazin, intensified one's pride in trying to create here "a new cosmopolitan culture."[48] Values once associated with Europe, especially Paris, now had no physical, geographical, social foundation more solid than that provided by the United States. Suddenly, America did not seem so outrageously provincial. This is the context in which we must see the legendary patriotism of the intelligentsia in the Cold War era.

With varying degrees of certainty and enthusiasm, the intelligentsia of the 1940s and 1950s believed that the United States had become a viable, if imperfect embodiment of the cosmopolitan ideal. This "nationalism" triumphed only when it was felt to be distinct from the sensibility of the same name that had been so firmly rejected by the likes of Bourne, Cohen, and Rosenberg. The superiority of America to the Soviet Union was partially described in terms of the greater freedom and diversity that seemed to characterize American society. One needs neither to quarrel with nor to affirm the appropriateness of this assessment to understand that much of its persuasiveness derived from the actual social circumstances of the intelligentsia at the time: Its members had come out of their various "exiles"—expatriation, the Diaspora, displacement from contemporary Europe—to find not simply "America," but to find each other. Feeling, in each other's presence, that cosmopolitanism was substantially a fact, they could not only choose sides in the Cold War, but could even show selective appreciation for American provincialism. The life depicted in *Let Us Now Praise Famous Men* was in no way a threat and could be drawn upon as a source of insight, in accordance with the cosmopolitan ideal.[49] The same could be felt about even Brooklyn or the Lower East Side: *A Walker in the City* could scarcely have been written until its author was utterly secure not simply as an American, but as a cosmopolitan.[50]

If the intelligentsia as a whole found it easier by the 1940s to accept American identity, so, too, did many of its Jewish members find themselves moved to assert their ethnic identity after 1945, when the full dimensions of the European holocaust became known. For some, this assertion amounted to a qualified, if not open, affirmation of parochialism. Ben Hecht, for example, underwent an intensive "conversion" to a religious and ethnic tradition that had played almost no part—even privately—in the first forty-nine years of his life.[51] Yet the "Jewishness" more commonly acknowledged was of a sort that could, like the patriotism of the period, be made compatible with the cosmopolitan ideal. Norman Podhoretz, for example, appreciated the liberation achieved by Trilling's generation, but was troubled by the absence of any representatives of Judaism in the international "Republic of Letters" to which his Columbia education of the 1940s had introduced him. Yet in 1954, when two highly respected, nonsectarian critics seriously proposed the admission of the Yiddish classics to this Republic, Podhoretz was ambivalent: While reading the texts offered by Irving Howe and Eleazer Greenberg, Podhoretz was "oppressed more powerfully than ever before by the feeling that very little of this has anything to do with that part of me which reads English, French, and Russian fiction, and everything to do with that part of me which still broods on the mystery of my own Jewishness." The pleasure of reading Yiddish literature was not, Podhoretz reluctantly concluded, that of reading "good fiction," it was rather "the pleasure of Old World charm and quaintness, titillating but not challenging, and therefore not to be taken too seriously." What irony, he exclaimed, "that this should be the effect of a literature which more than any other demands to be taken with the most apocalyptic seriousness!"[52] Podhoretz, by "accepting" (instead of rejecting) Yiddish literature as parochial, participated in no simple "return" to a clearly delineated, but dormant entity called the Jewish tradition. Associations with Jewish life that had once been impediments to growth were now avenues to expansion. Once it appeared possible to delve into an aspect of sensibility associated with Jews, without thereby cutting off other experiences, such explorations became more attractive.

To say that the mid-twentieth-century intelligentsia had managed to absorb a certain amount of patriotism and an ambiguous element of ethnic identification into its system of values is not, of course, to make a judgment about the viability of this integration. One could, perhaps, object that the intelligentsia was not "really" cosmopolitan, but was merely another intellectual province, blind to issues that it should be confronting and oblivious to values that a larger view of life would compel it to recognize. Yet this is merely to carry on the argument within the intelligentsia's own terms, to criticize its members for a "parochial" failure to live up to the cosmopolitan ideal.[53] Quarrels of this sort over the practical meaning of commonly held, abstract ideals are endemic to any community of discourse and are to be distinguished from disagreements over the validity of fundamental values, such as the cosmopolitan ideal. Disagreements of the latter variety did appear in the mid-1960s.

The intelligentsia could not avoid being affected by a series of abrupt changes in its political environment, beginning with the expulsion of whites from civil rights organizations by black separatists. This was followed quickly by an upsurge of vehement ethnic particularism among "white ethnics," whose festering resentment at the attention blacks had been given during the civil rights era was now intensified by the specter of "black power." In the meantime, Israel's Six-Day War against its Arab enemies inspired a greater number of American Jews to take an active interest in the fortunes of Israel and to take their own "Jewish ethnicity" more seriously. These pressures impinged upon the intelligentsia, moreover, exactly at a time when it was being divided—often violently— over the Vietnam War and the growth of the New Left, divisions that were not directly related to the rise of particularism, but which sharpened the general feeling that the intellectual community was experiencing a shake-up.

Simultaneously, the cosmopolitan ideal was put on the defensive in an episode internal to the intelligentsia: the controversy over Hannah Arendt's *Eichmann in Jerusalem.* In this book Arendt—herself a refugee from Hitler's Europe—criticized the response Jewish leaders had made when confronted with persecution and genocide.[54] Arendt was accused of making the victims of Nazi terror look worse than the terrorists. Dwight Macdonald, one of the most determined defenders of the cosmopolitan ideal, complained that some Jewish writers were pulling their punches when it came to assessing the behavior of Jewish leadership; Daniel Bell was guilty of a "cop-out," insisted Macdonald, when Bell invoked a special standard for the evaluation of Jews.[55]

By the early 1970s it was clear that *Commentary,* under the leadership of a much-changed Norman Podhoretz, had moved decisively toward both Jewish particularism and political conservatism, while the *New York Review of Books* resisted both of these trends.[56] The relative merits of parochialism and cosmopolitanism, as competing ideals, were now openly debated within the intelligentsia.[57] Irving Howe, whose cosmopolitanism had once been as principled as Dwight Macdonald's, admitted that the cause of Israel had led him to modify his outlook.[58] Meanwhile, the upswing of ethnic patriotism was promoted in other contexts by Michael Novak, a Catholic writer of Slavic origin, and by Harold Cruse's influential *The Crisis of the Negro Intellectual.*[59]

Whatever the eventual fate of the cosmopolitan ideal among American intellectuals, the ascendancy of that ideal from the mid-1910s through the mid-1960s entailed certain beliefs about the spiritual capacities of individuals and of subcultures. The opportunities presented by life were felt to be broader than a choice between various particularisms (whether in the form of ideologies, religious traditions, or folkways). It was believed possible for human beings of diverse experience to put together a perspective on the world more authentic, reliable, and satisfying than any perspective generated by the intensification of a narrowly constricted range of experience. There was no reason in principle, it was assumed, why an individual could not have Whitman's "multitudes" within him or her and yet be able to achieve the stability required to enjoy those multitudes and to set priorities among them; similarly, it was hoped that a subculture could be complex and variegated without losing its integrity. In other words, the cosmopolitan ideal implicitly attributed to people the ability to confront, absorb, and profit from experience not only qualitatively different from, but *quantitatively greater* than, that of any given provincial existence.

It makes sense, therefore, that the ascendancy of the cosmopolitan ideal should correspond so neatly to the era in which American intellectuals were the most conscious of the difference between "intellectuals" and other people, and that the epoch should be flanked on either end by periods in which "elitism" was suspect even among intellectuals. The point is not that either of these two conditions of early- and mid-twentieth-century America was the "cause" of the other, but that cosmopolitanism, as opposed to mere pluralism, is difficult to maintain as a prescription for society at large unless one is willing—as most American intellectuals have not been—to attribute to the general population a prodigious capacity for growth. The cosmopolitan ideal commanded the widest allegiance from American intellectuals when it was implicitly understood to be their peculiar possession, when members of the intelligentsia did not feel obliged—as many of them did after the mid-1960s—to adopt values that could be justified in the wider context of general social theory.[60]

The recognition of the nature and role of the cosmopolitan ideal has been impeded, ironically, by a preoccupation with this very distinction between intellectuals and other Americans. The concepts of "alienation" and "assimilation" cannot help but entail, as a starting point, the "given" world of the official, majority culture of the United States. Studies of the history of intellectuals are thereby inclined to revolve around a single, needlessly narrow question: To what extent, and for what reasons, have intellectuals of various descriptions been estranged from, integrated into, or apologists for the established moral and political order of the society?[61] Commentaries on this question are destined, it would seem, to become variations on the Odyssean theme of withdrawal and return that has defined the autobiographies of so many intellectuals themselves, especially Malcolm Cowley's *Exile's Return.*[62] This theme is far from unimportant, but so, too, is the system of values that made the intelligentsia not simply a collectivity of persons with similar experiences but an interacting community of discourse.[63]

5

THE CANON AND ITS KEEPERS: MODERNISM

AND MID-TWENTIETH-CENTURY

AMERICAN INTELLECTUALS

Specialists in American intellectual history have been slow to count cultural modernism among the major problems of their field. Yet the importance of modernism in the "high culture" of the United States during much of the twentieth century is being taken increasingly for granted by almost everyone except historians of the United States. In the recent writings of Daniel Bell, for example, modernism functions in much the same way that puritanism did in the cultural criticism of the 1920s: it was an emblem, and to a large extent the cause, of America's spiritual ills. Although students of the arts and of literature have written extensively about American involvement in modernism, their scholarship has not been effectively exploited by historians of the United States. So fine a book as Hugh Kenner's A Homemade World: The American Modernist Writers *(1975) has been virtually ignored.*

Nor have American historians shown much initiative themselves in clarifying and pursuing the issues in the history of North Atlantic civilization encompassed by the rather indefinite term, "modernism." This lack of initiative would make sense if modernism and America had been marginal to one another. But wasn't T. S. Eliot from Missouri? Wasn't Ezra Pound a native of Idaho? Didn't the American Gertrude Stein insist that modernism and America were made for each other? °ince the essay below was written, Malcolm Bradbury has argued that Stein was correct: "Struggling Westward: America & the Coming of Modernism," En-counter, January 1983, 55–60, and February 1983, 57–65. There have been other recent, promising signs of historiographical change, including the appearance of Daniel J. Singal's The War Within: From Victorian to Modernist Thought in the South, 1919–1945 *(1982). The study below is offered in support of the movement that I believe is now underway to explore the role of modernism in American intellectual history, and the role of America in the history of modernism.*

This particular study enters the topic from what might be described as its tail end. I am concerned here with the literature of modernism in its most established, canonical, academic stage. This is the stage at which the texts we now call "modern" came to be widely recognized as products of a single literary movement of that name, with analogues in the arts. Especially in the history of literature is this stage to be sharply distinguished from the creative stage of "modernism," when the items in the canon were actually produced. The texts that found their way into the canon of the 1940s and 1950s were written in the 1920s, and before.

While studying this canonical stage of literary modernism, I have had in mind a loosely comparable episode in late-nineteenth and very early-twentieth-century America: the literary canon of the "genteel" tradition. That canon—which included Longfellow and Lowell; Emerson and Whittier; Tennyson and Thackeray—was a more intimate possession of a larger segment of the educated public than was the modern canon. What this Victorian canon meant to its public was clarified a quarter century ago by Henry F. May, in The End of American Innocence *(1959). In the Victorian case as well as in the modern, enormous spiritual authority was assigned to a distinctive set of secular texts, and the social role of the literary critic was assigned a significance and gravity that leading intellectuals in any number of other times and places might find peculiar.*

The mystique of modern literature during the 1940s and 1950s was sustained, in part, by the need then felt by many American intellectuals to reassess liberalism and its philosophical underpinnings. This reassessment itself has properly caught the attention of historians, who often associate it with the name of the theologian and political theorist Reinhold Niebuhr. I argue here that a function of the modern canon was to provide for illiberal and anti-liberal ideas a temporary shelter, a "literary" domicile outside the realm of prosaic argument. Within this privileged space, intellectuals could explore ideas considerably more distant from liberalism than Niebuhr's, yet could do so free from the obligation to specify these ideas and evaluate them in relation to other commitments and interests.

This essay is the only one in the volume not previously published. It is a revised version of a paper read in Los Angeles on December 28, 1981, at the ninety-sixth

Annual Meeting of the American Historical Association. The essay has been strengthened by the suggestions of Thomas Bender, George Bornstein, Charles Capper, William Chace, Daniel W. Howe, Henry F. May, and Peter Slater.

WHEN AUGUSTINE TRIED to make sense in Christian terms of the fate of Rome, he had a great deal of explaining to do. He was obliged to show that the Scriptures did indeed give meaning to the shocking events of the fifth century, including the death of the eternal city. This task required of Augustine a reverent, imaginative, and technical commentary on the ancient texts. *The City of God* was destined to long serve the West as a model for the act of interpretation, as an example of a heroic intellect using available tools to fashion a credible order out of cultural chaos. Among those who eventually remembered Augustine in this way was the American man of letters R. P. Blackmur. Blackmur believed that the shocks of twentieth-century life demanded a critical response almost Augustinian in scope. Western civilization was simply dissolving before one's eyes. But "unlike Augustine," Blackmur observed in 1948, "we lack a special revelation." Casting about for insights, for fragments from which to build a culture, Blackmur and his contemporaries would have to make do with what Blackmur called "the masterpieces of our time":

> . . . the poetry of Eliot, Yeats, Valery, Rilke; the novels of Joyce, Gide, Heming-way, Proust, Mann, Kafka; the plays of Shaw, Pirandello, O'Neill; the music of Stravinsky, Bloch, Bartok, Ravel, Satie, Schoenberg; the paintings of Matisse, Picasso, Rouault, Marin, Hartley; the sculpture of Maillol, Brancusi, Faggi, LaChaise, Zorach, Archpenko, Moore.[1]

It was thus to the *modern literary canon* and its analogues in the arts that Blackmur directed the attention of contemporary intellectuals. In the difficult, often austere works of modern art could be found the beginnings of whatever sense was to be made of the age. "*Ulysses* is the direct aesthetic experience of the breakdown of the whole Graeco-Christian world," Blackmur allowed, while *The Magic Mountain* is "the projected aesthetic experience of both that world and the sickness which is breaking it down." These voices of Joyce and Mann were human, not divine, but at least they did speak, and about the most momentous, bewildering, and important experiences at hand. The artifacts of the modern imagination deserve patient, respectful, even technical scrutiny; one is justified in treating them, Blackmur insisted, in much the same fashion that "Augustine treated the scriptures in the Fifth Century." Yet, to so treat modern art was not to offer oneself as the father of a new church. Blackmur professed to speak from a "secular point of view" confronting a "secular world which is not well understood." God was either nonexistent or silent, but men and women had voices, and by listening to the most sensitive and creative of these voices, we can "discover what our culture is."[2]

Blackmur's "A Burden for Critics," from which I have been quoting, was an extreme formulation of ideas about modern literature, and about the mission of criticism, that were shared by many American literary critics during the 1940s and 1950s. It was a time of sober resolve for Americans, when the much-discussed "burden of world power" was being accepted by their government, and when the step into "the awful responsibility of Time" was taken by Jack Burden, the carefully named hero of one of the period's most celebrated novels.[3] Literary critics, too, proved able to take themselves and their responsibilities very seriously indeed. None of these responsibilities was more serious than the presentation to contemporary intellectuals of a distinctly modern literature. This devotion to the modern canon has been less interesting to scholars than has another dimension of the critical enterprise at the same moment: the innovations and controversies carried out in the name of the "New Criticism" and its methodological rivals. Our enormous scholarly literature on these methodological goings-on has paid only passing attention to the more general enthusiasm for modernism shared by many of the New Critics and their disputatious opponents.[4] That enthusiasm was especially manifest in the willingness to endow with great spiritual authority the texts said to embody the elusive but portentous quality called "modern." This vesting of authority implied a remarkable fit between a body of texts and a body of readers, between the canon and its keepers. To explore that "fit" is the aim of this essay.

I introduce the problem with Blackmur not only because his pronouncements about both modern literature and the vocation of the critic are unusually forthright, but also on account of his social identity. Blackmur was neither a Southerner nor a Christian; nor was he a New Yorker of Jewish origin; nor was he a regionalist; nor had he been a Marxist during the 1930s. He was not a graduate of Vanderbilt, nor of Harvard, nor of

Columbia. These things that Blackmur was not are worth mentioning here because what little discussion there has been of the appeal of the modern canon has addressed that appeal in the context of the needs and interests of intellectuals who were one or more of the things that Blackmur was not. Blackmur's background was New England WASP; he was secular in his spiritual orientation and was inconspicuous about politics. He did not complete a college degree. Yet he was one of the most listened-to critics in the United States until his death in 1965, and was in direct and sustained intellectual contact with the men and women whose lives are the basis for our stereotypes of the period. He can serve to remind us that the problem of "the canon and its keepers" is a broad one.[5]

The problem gains interest from the success with which critics of the mid-century decades advanced the cause of modernism in the intellectual life of educated Americans. The curriculum of undergraduate studies at many educational institutions was very much affected by the views of these critics. Literary discussion outside as well as inside the learned quarterlies took account of what these critics thought concerning what were the truly great works of literature. To be moved by Eliot and Kafka, rather than by Longfellow, or by the middlebrow best-sellers of Lloyd C. Douglas and Thomas B. Costain, was one of the things it meant to be an "intellectual" in the United States in 1950 or 1960.

In order to address the fit between the canon and its keepers, one must distinguish sharply between the history of modern literature and the history of what has been done with that literature by its most articulate and loquacious readers. It would not do to replace the study of the great texts with the study of the differential reception and use of those texts by different groups of readers, but the two kinds of inquiry can draw upon one another, and can go forward without getting in each other's way. "Literary Modernism" is a problem in *authorship,* even when it is understood that the modern movement that ended about 1930 was largely constituted after the fact, by critics, the people who decided what was and was not part of the movement.[6] The formation and criticism of the canon is preeminently a problem in *readership*.

The sharpness of the line between authorship and readership is underlined by the consistency with which the American critics of the mid-century decades accorded special status to authors whose major work had appeared in the 1920s, or before. Rarely were the contemporary works of "new" authors added to the canon. Rather, the canon was expanded either by adding new works of Eliot, Mann, and other pioneers still active, or by discovering or upwardly reevaluating the pre-1930 work of previously unrecognized or undervalued authors. During the 1940s more and more space on the honored shelves was made for Kafka, Conrad, Pound, and Dostoevsky, and by 1950 room was made for Nietzsche. Yet of these five writers, four were long dead. Pound was still writing, but he, too, was a giant from the past, an enigmatic survivor from the days when he had served as master to even so founding a father of modernism as Eliot. Distance between Pound and his readers also derived from the fact that Pound spent the first half of the 1940s as a bona fide fascist, and was, during the second half, understood to be insane.[7]

In 1947, Morton Dauwen Zabel played the role of advocate for Conrad in his introduction to *The Viking Portable Conrad*. This major document from the campaign to consolidate Conrad's position in the canon illustrates the authority of the canon, the arguments by which expansion of the canon was justified, and the sense of confident possession of that canon enjoyed by critics. "The plight of the man on whom life closes down inexorably, divesting him of the supports and illusory protection of friendship, social privilege, or love" was a theme of Conrad's, Zabel explained, as it was a theme in the work of "Ibsen, James, Mann, Gide, and Kafka," and to some extent of Joyce and Hemingway. The "hero of modern fiction," Zabel added, "is the man marked by apartness and alienation," the man encountered in Conrad and, yes, in James, Mann, Joyce, and Kafka. Zabel systematically bolstered his basic points about Conrad with comparisons to other previously canonized modern authors. Conrad, as a co-worker with the established artists of the tradition, is thus a figure with whom the reader is to identify: Conrad, concluded Zabel, was permanently and securely "one of us."[8]

The logic of this argument had the effect of completing a mythical social circle. The "new" author is brought into a community with the old, and with the enlightened reader, whose enlightenment is revealed by the intimacy he is capable of feeling with the authors, old and new. This style of argument has had a long tenure in the discourse of modernism, and is still employed when a given critic wants to establish the modernist credentials of a favored author. In one of the most arresting of the essays in this genre, Marshall Berman argued in 1978 that Marx, too, was modern. Modernism, notes Berman, "has come to denote a family of artistic and intellectual movements that have been radically experimental, spiritually turbulent and militant, iconoclastic to the point of nihilism, apocalyptic in their hopes and fantasies, savagely destructive to one another—and often to themselves as well—yet capable of recurrent self-renewal." A proper reading of *The Communist Manifesto* shows Marx to be "the first and greatest of modernists," a "kindred spirit of Eliot and Kafka and Gertrude Stein."[9]

The authors invoked with such portent by Zabel and Berman had won their positions gradually, through a process of survival by critical selection in which the operative forces had been the opinions of F. R. Leavis, T. S. Eliot, Edmund Wilson, and other leaders of the international, North Atlantic literary life of the 1920s and 1930s. There was no unmediated "impact" of the great texts on the American critics who became devoted to them during the era of World War II. These critics were very much under the sway of a critical inheritance. Wilson's *Axel's Castle* had popularized in America the idea of a single and distinctly modern literature, but this critical landmark of 1931 mixed admiration for what Wilson called the "symbolist" writers with a conclusion that lost favor in the 1940s: These writers, Wilson had argued, could provide little guidance in the future. Eliot's own critical views were a more decisive influence on the development of the canon.[10]

Eliot's authority was the most imposing in regard to poetry. He dominated Cleanth Brooks's *Modern Poetry and the Tradition,* a book of 1939 that served as a rallying point for many critics of the 1940s. Brooks extolled the poems of Eliot and Yeats, and of Alan Tate and John Crowe Ransom, the American "agrarian poets" who were his friends. The work of these men implied a superior "conception of poetry" that could serve, according to Brooks, as a standard for upgrading the metaphysical poets of the seventeenth century and for downgrading the Romantics and Victorians of the nineteenth.[11] Since Eliot was a canonized poet himself, all the more could his activities as a critic serve to intensify in Eliot's epigones the feeling that authors and critics were united in a single cause, bound together in a very special intimacy from which were excluded even the most respected figures who fell outside the perimeter of the "modern" and its direct antecedents.[12]

Exactly who, besides Eliot, was understood at the outset by these American critics of the early 1940s to be within this perimeter, to most clearly manifest the unique spiritual powers of modern literature? Reverent lists like those quoted above from Blackmur and Zabel punctuate the essays of the era. Although neither D. H. Lawrence nor Virginia Woolf were listed in either of these two instances, their names were often invoked amid a selection of the authors already mentioned in this essay: Eliot, Yeats, Valery, Rilke, Pound, Joyce, Gide, Hemingway, Proust, Mann, Kafka, Conrad, James, Stein, Shaw, Pirandello, O'Neill, and Ibsen. There were other players in this little literary game, but there is no doubt that critics of a variety of methodological orientations and ideological predilections shared a basic sense of just what were the scriptures of modernism. It is tempting to see these lists as ballots for a "consensus all-modern team," electing Mann and Joyce at novel, Eliot and Yeats at poetry, and so on, as sportswriters elect tackles and fullbacks. This would render frivolous an enterprise that was earnest in the extreme; and it would also imply that the canon was a more concrete institution than it actually was.[13] To speak even of a "canon" and its "keepers" is to represent this episode in the history of literature and society in terms that some participants would find an insensitive caricature.

The canon was a very special agenda adopted by a loosely organized community of literary critics. The great texts were to be deciphered and discussed by this community on behalf of anyone with the capability of following the discussion and understanding the extraordinary importance for "our culture" of the items on this particular agenda. Hence the "burden for critics" contemplated by Blackmur: This was a body of difficult and forbidding literature that especially demanded the talents of *critics,* yet this literature was also of such crucial cultural significance that its study was not to be just another little exercise in the use of this or that critical technique. The modern canon was a set of ciphers, an agenda of mysteries, a collection of secular scriptures in which were embedded certain elusive but profound truths that could be discovered only by hard work.

Most of this hard work was done text by text, and author by author. Hence the basic medium for developing and reinforcing the mystique of the canon was the critical appreciation of individual artist-heroes. Yeats, for example, took on almost Christ-like stature in "The Modern Myth of the Modern Myth," an address at the 1947 meeting of the English Institute, one of the nation's most prestigious critical forums throughout the mid-century decades. Here, Yeats was represented by Donald A. Stauffer as having made a "lonely sacrifice of self . . . not forgetful of the people, but for their sake." Yeats's gift was a potentially enabling "myth" of individual freedom, formulated the most forcefully in regard to his own person. "Yeats's greatest mythical creation" may have been himself, Stauffer reflected, and "time alone will tell whether or not through his life," Yeats himself has become "a heartening hero, a myth 'for the common people, for all time to come.'" This hopeful prospect Stauffer contrasted symbolically to a more probable future: the "rough beast" slouching toward Bethlehem in Yeats's poem of 1921, "The Second Coming."[14]

These appreciations of the artist-heroes of modernism were "literary," of course, but they often entailed certain rudimentary ideas about power. If "poetry is a rival government," as William Carlos Williams once suggested, the critics of the mid-century decades were a willing and efficient civil service. They celebrated the power of art to enable, to revolutionize, and to integrate; while they tended to downgrade other potential sources of power. Science, especially, did they variously patronize, ignore, or subject to an invidiously constructed division of labor. So, too, did they diminish the powers of socio-economic classes and of the state in contrast to those of art. In the degree of their extravagant estimation of the social role of art, as in everything else, the critics differed somewhat from one to the other. Blackmur, as usual, did not disdain the voice of prophecy: He left no doubt that he and his fellows were making "a new claim for the arts, and perhaps the most ambitious yet in the long series since Aristotle." The claim, explained Blackmur in 1956, was more radical than Shelley's old notion of poets being the "unacknowledged legislators of the world"; that idea implied a harmonious relation between artists and society. The claim of the expressionist art of the 1920s, insisted Blackmur, was to "undermine, to readjust, to put into fresh order the frames or forms in which we make the adventure of conduct tangible to our minds," and the claim "therefore denies validity to pre-existent legislation on human relations."[15]

Of the critics caught up in the mystique of the canon, none was more widely known outside departments of English and comparative literature than Lionel Trilling. Yet Trilling had misgivings about the canon, and perhaps a bad conscience for serving so long in the ranks of its keepers. His ambivalent reconsideration of the educational benefits of the canon, published in 1961, is one of the most vivid and extensive representations we have of the experience of entrusting one's spiritual capital to the modern canon. Trilling professed to recant nothing, and insisted that the literature of modernism was the most "intensely spiritual" of all literatures, unsurpassed "in power and magnificence." Trilling implied that the modern canon was so very, very special that people might need protection from it, and it might need protection from them. The canon needed to be protected from the popularization and vulgarization that is a risk of trying to teach it in a college course, as though it were just another bunch of literary texts. But the reader, too, may need protection against the antisocial bias and the psychologically terrifying properties of these texts. Just how literally were we to take the sympathy for "the Abyss" that one can find in Mann and Conrad, in Nietzsche and Dostoevsky? When an undergraduate asked Trilling, in all seriousness, how one might "generalize" Mann's idea of "the educative value of illness, so that it would be applicable not to a particular individual, Hans Castorp, but to young people at large," was it Mann or the student who needed to be protected? The investment Trilling had made in the modern texts was simply prodigious, and for this reason the texts had to be kept at a certain distance, relevant to daily life in an intimate way, but not too intimate. "I do not venture to call" modern literature "actually religious," said Trilling with characteristic caution, "but it certainly has the special intensity of concern with the spiritual life which Hegel noted when he spoke of the great modern phenomenon of the secularization of spirituality." It was in speaking of the modern texts that Trilling invoked W. H. Auden's reverently passive notion of a reader being read by a book.[16]

Perhaps the most mysterious aspect of the modern texts was the quality, or qualities, that made them modern. Lack of clarity and consistency about the notion of the "modern" bothered few critics until the 1960s, when, as if the amorphousness of the concept had suddenly dawned on them, American scholars and their British counterparts produced a remarkable series of books and essays trying to identify the essence of modernism.[17] These efforts resulted in widely differing conclusions, and two of the most thorough students of the problem frankly threw up their hands: "the modern awaits definition," wrote Richard Ellman and Charles Feidelson, Jr., in 1965, when they organized their massive anthology, *The Modern Tradition,* around a series of autonomous, discrete themes.[18] This solution was fully consistent with the critical practice of the previous three decades. There had been a number of working touchstones for modernity, and one or another of them made their appearance quite casually when a critic discussed this or that text. These touchstones were most often called upon when a critic was eager to bring a given author's work more firmly into the canon, or to insist that a text from the ancient world or from the Romantic era was actually "modern" in its feeling. A representative example of this practice was Zabel's introduction to the *Viking Portable Conrad,* in which "apartness and alienation" serve as the abstract principles for the modernity that Zabel preferred to indicate by way of example.[19] It was a certain sense of the "function of metaphor" that united Donne and the moderns, according to Brooks.[20] A timeless synchronicity was singled out in 1945 by Joseph Frank, who announced in one of the period's most influential essays that the "peculiarly modern quality" of modern poems and novels was their "continual juxtaposition between aspects of the past and the present so that both are fused into one comprehensive view," transforming, in effect, the historical imagination "into myth."[21] These examples merely confirm that insofar as the modern texts were vehicles for a system of values, ideas, and insights, that system was a loosely organized, shifting mass, specific elements of which were affirmed or at least discussed on occasions created for different readers by different texts.[22]

So it has often been, no doubt, with many "isms" whose participants have been as self-conscious about identification with a movement as were the critics who took on the task of interpreting the artifacts of modernism. Part of the self-consciousness of these critics was a fierce determination to avoid reductionism, and a conviction that the distinct and prophetic qualities of the modern movement rendered naïve any effort to sum it all up, as one might sum up this or that conventional movement in the history of thought or the arts. The point of treating modern texts as an agenda of mysteries was of course that these texts manifest insights that were not accessible, in their profundity, through anyone's handy little summary; the texts defied facile analysis, and this was a source of their greatness. To list straightforwardly the "values of modernism" would be to diminish the power of the texts. For such simplicity one could refer students to the contemporary movement in philosophy known as "existentialism." This movement was sometimes said to be related to modernism; access to some themes in modern literature might be sought in the writings of Sartre and Camus.[23] A willingness to be gross about the nature of the modernism of literature, however, was rare prior to the 1960s. When that willingness became apparent, more than one observer took the fact as a sure sign that modernism, whatever it had been, was really over.[24]

One of the things it had been, apparently, was a vision of human beings and their world that was potentially at variance with the vision that had produced social democratic politics of the Anglo-American sort. The mystique of the great texts becomes more comprehensible when we see behind it a need to keep in check the potentially anti-democratic implications of modernism, a need to protect from modernism the actual political culture with which the American critics of the 1940s and 1950s were entangled. This problem transcended political differences among the critics. One did not have to be as radical as the old "Leninist" Philip Rahv or as conventionally liberal as Lionel Trilling to feel this tension. And the problem was not confined to the reactionary behavior of some of the artist-heroes; it extended also the suspicion found in many of the great texts that Enlightenment ideals were untenable.[25]

If "modernism" was not a "world-view" for the critics of the mid-century decades, it was certainly a *set of suspicions* about human beings and their world, a collection of senses *that could be explored the most safely if kept out of propositional form,* and outside the realm of prosaic argument. It was a function of the scriptures of modernism to create and maintain for the exploration of these suspicions *a privileged foundation:* a base free from the obligation to specify and to take a stand upon the political, moral, and metaphysical implications of these suspicions. The modern canon was thus a vital tool in the reconsideration of liberalism that figured prominently in the intellectual history of the 1940s and 1950s. It was enough to say, with an air of unflinching integrity, that the insights embodied in the modern texts called into question traditional liberalism, bourgeois morality, a naïve faith in the goodness of people, and the notion of a meaningful cosmos; one did not, while defending modern letters as profound, have to go on to consider the actual truth of these suspicions, and the demands that such truths might make on a liberal democrat trying to raise a family. To press such inquiries would be to become "moralistic," to view the relation of literature to society in the naïve, didactic perspective of the hated Victorian bourgeoisie. Now, literature was to be about society but not subject to it: *of* the world, but not *in* it.

This suspended quality in the "modernism" embodied in the canon was often expressed through the notion of "aesthetic." The texts were presumed to be capable of filling cultural space once occupied by philosophy, theology, and political theory *without losing their distinctive aesthetic quality,* and becoming, in themselves, subject to the rules of argument appropriate for philosophy, theology, and political theory. Modernism was a new way of "seeing," it was often said; the logic-chopping of philosophers was irrelevant to it. Blackmur explained that life "in our time" had become so complex that it seemed "capable only of aesthetic experience." It was not, then, a matter of peaceful or even hostile co-existence between the arts and prosaic discourse; the arts were now *it*. Since "almost the whole job of culture" had been "dumped into the hands of the writer," it is the *aesthetic* experience of Mann and Joyce and Gide and Eliot that we must grasp in order to give us "mastery" over the subjects these writers address, namely, the modern world itself. Bergson prompted Blackmur to say that the "true nature of what the institutions of society are meant to control" is given to us by the "serious arts," in "aesthetic experience."[26]

Hence the paradox: One could militantly and iconoclastically identify oneself with the insights into "society" found in Gide or Mann or Pound, yet one did so at such an aesthetic distance that one's ostensibly intimate identification with the great moderns carried few programmatic implications for social life. The hope remained, like Gatsby's green light: If only we work harder, apply yet more diligently and imaginatively our techniques of criticism, we might tap the creative potential of modern art, and achieve the spiritual renewal for which our society yearns.

How, then, are we to account for the spiritual authority exercised by the modern canon in American literary culture during the mid-century decades? To be sure, the great texts exercised more authority over some people than over others, and this authority must have been sustained in individuals by any number of distinctive personal needs and aspirations not to be addressed here. Yet the keeping of the canon was an enterprise sufficiently broad and public to prompt generalizations about it. I believe one can identify several circumstances in public life that impinged almost simultaneously on many of the men and women who became keepers of the canon, and that were at least conducive to the growth of its authority in their lives. These circumstances did not have an equally direct effect on everyone, but they did constitute a formidable set of pressures and incentives.

The potential of the great texts began to be widely recognized at a time most convenient for the profession of literary criticism in the United States. Just when a literature of exceptional austerity was in need of being interpreted, the burgeoning colleges and universities of the postwar era were taking on more and more professors of English and of other modern European languages.[27] Some members of this new, unprecedentedly large generation of Ph.D.'s made their way in academia by studying Beowulf or Dante, but it was the writing of so many books and articles about *modern* literature—and then about those critical works themselves—that led Randall Jarrell to attack "The Age of Criticism" on behalf of "real" writers.[28] Specialists in the techniques of literary interpretation were demanded; in the study of modern literature the new professors could perform services most akin to those being performed by professionals in other technically demanding disciplines. An agenda of mysteries was ideally suited to this generation of American critics. Blackmur's "A Burden for Critics" was a classically mandarin program, making extravagant claims on behalf of the esoteric and cloistered calling of Blackmur, his colleagues, and his students. It will not do, however, to attribute the authority of the canon to the business enterprise of a class of market-creating professionals. It is more reasonable to suppose that in the absence of this professional factor, the mystique of modernism would have been less intense, briefer in duration, limited to a smaller constituency, and subject to less notice from educated Americans generally.

Blackmur and his fellows had an easier time justifying their callings, and their choice of texts, as a result of the political events of the era of World War II. We have come to remember the 1940s and 1950s as a time of anti-utopian sentiment, according to which the preservation of the status quo and the defeat of monstrous evils like Nazism were valid enough political triumphs in a world whose socialist hopes seemed to have eventuated only in the iniquities of Stalinism. It was precisely in the context of Stalin's betrayal of socialist humanism that Kafka began to eclipse Marx in the interests of Philip Rahv, one of the principal editors of the *Partisan Review*.[29] The crises of Nazism and Stalinism widened and deepened suspicions that the world was indeed as intractable, ironic, and defiantly irrational a place as had been glimpsed in the pages of the artist-heroes whose reputations were then growing the most dramatically: Kafka, Conrad, and Dostoevsky.

This troublesome world was also addressed by Reinhold Niebuhr, Jacques Maritain, and other out-and-out theologians who won a very considerable following among educated Americans. But the Scriptures from which Niebuhr and Maritain read had already enjoyed a wealth of opportunities to teach whatever lessons they could. These Christian lessons, moreover, presupposed a continuity in the sources and character of the world's intractability, irony, and irrationality that not everyone was willing to concede. The new scriptures of modernism, even when they manifest a yearning for Christian solutions to modern dilemmas, did not demand any sacrifices to ancient gods. The modernists offered novelties and liberties that the theologians did not. Blackmur would play Augustine to Gide's St. Paul.

If both the dynamics of American academic life and the historic events we associate with the names of Hitler and Stalin were conducive to the growth of the canon's authority, yet a third relevant condition was the changing ethnic and social composition of the American intellectual elite. The modern canon was an ideal literary agenda for the new, ethnically diverse, secular intelligentsia formed primarily by children of East-European Jewish immigrants and descendants of native American, "WASP" families. Intellectuals from both of these backgrounds discovered each other while in the midst of revolts against each's own provincial inheritance, and shared the promise of a new, more cosmopolitan culture.[30] A vital part of this promise was a distinctly modern literature that spoke to universal human dilemmas, rather than to parochial concerns.

Nothing was more clear about the modern movement to most of its American commentators than its international character. Not only did the texts move rapidly from nation to nation; many authors of these texts had done their creative work away from home. Conrad had gone from Poland to England; Joyce from Ireland to Paris; and Ibsen from Norway to Germany. The native-born Americans who had contributed the most in the 1920s—Pound, Eliot, Gertrude Stein, and Ernest Hemingway—had been expatriates, true extremists in the case of anti-provincialism. Although Eliot himself and some of the "regionalists" sometimes praised provincialism, a more common theme in the celebration of the canon was its apparent capacity to transcend every province. Even if a given masterpiece had emerged from a homogeneous, traditional setting or had been inspired by an ancestral faith, its genius was said to be its universal character, its ability to speak to the modern condition. This genius could be compatible with the use of Christian or Jewish symbols, although it was essential to many members of the new intelligentsia that a modern literary culture be free from the domination of distinctly Christian or Jewish symbols. The keepers of the canon generally believed that the potential tribalism inherent in traditional religious symbols could be neutralized. Even the Christ-affirming T. S. Eliot was hailed as a "cosmopolitan" in 1945 by Delmore Schwartz, who was a social being of the type Eliot presumably had in mind a decade earlier when he had warned that free-thinking Jews were a threat to an ideal society.[31] One did not, according to Schwartz, have to accept Eliot's particular solutions to the problems of modernity in order to appreciate his diagnosis of them. "Modern life," explained Schwartz, is like a foreign country of which Eliot is a heroic explorer:

> Eliot is the international hero because he has made the journey to the foreign country and described the nature of the new life. . . . Since the future is bound to be international, if it is anything at all, we are all the bankrupt heirs of the ages, and the moments of the crisis expressed in Eliot's work are a prophecy of the crises of our own future in regard to love, religious belief, good, evil, the good life and the nature of the just society.[32]

The need for a literature to possess in common and to argue about was the most intense during the very late 1930s and early 1940s, when the modern agenda was in fact adopted with dispatch by a variety of American literary intellectuals. Not only were provincial memories then more intense and threatening than they were to become in later years; in that crucial era, too, intellectuals had cause to measure with dismay the low returns of their recent, secular investments of spiritual capital. Neither the agrarian program for the South nor the revolutionary program for the industrial proletariat had produced the results so recently and earnestly hoped for by their supporters. The bankruptcy of Stalin as revealed in the Moscow Trials precipitated an especially deep and sudden crisis on the part of intellectuals who had taken risks on account of their faith in him. Among American intellectuals of the era, there resided a great deal of spiritual capital ready for commitment. We need not be surprised that much of it found its way into texts. The scriptures of modernism had much to recommend them. If their doctrines were obscure, one could do what religious Jews and Christians had done often enough, when uncertain about doctrine: One could be committed simply to texts.

The reality of any critical community prior to about 1950 has sometimes been denied.[33] But throughout the 1940s the diverse enthusiasts for modern literature were very much aware of each other, wrote often for each other's journals, addressed each other's interpretations of the great texts, and sometimes interacted personally across ethnic, geographic, religious, and methodological lines.[34] The canon was kept in the *Partisan*

Review of Philip Rahv and William Phillips as well as in the *Sewanee Review* of Alan Tate and J. E. Palmer. It was also kept in the *Hudson Review,* a quarterly founded in New York in 1948 partly in reaction against what its editors found in the glib and all-too-clever style of the *Partisan.*[35] Although these little squabbles between quarterlies are the stuff of literary gossip, and too often of literary history, the fact remains that the *Hudson*'s commitment to the canon from the very beginning rivaled that of the *Partisan,* the most militantly and exclusively modernist of major American magazines in the mid-century decades. The *Hudson*'s inaugural issue left no doubt about its center of gravity. It opened with Blackmur on Dostoevsky, continued with Herbert Read on modern art, and with Mark Shorer—in what was to become a famous piece of criticism—on techniques in the fiction of Lawrence, Joyce, and Conrad. This founding issue of the *Hudson* also contained poems by the certifiably modern E. E. Cummings and Wallace Stevens, and carried a review of the work of the canonized Paul Valery. In its very next issue, the *Hudson* published Blackmur's vindication of the Augustinian criticism of the modern texts.

The authority of the modern canon also owes much to the continuity between the settings in which the texts were produced and the setting in which the American critics came to appreciate them. This is to say the whole range of considerations commonly drawn upon in explanations of cultural modernism as such may also apply to the positive reception of its literature. The distinction I drew at the outset between the pre-1930 texts and the uses made of those texts by mid-century readers need not lead us to overlook the fact that the readers of the 1940s and 1950s and the authors of the 1920s and before were subject to some of the same, broad historical conditions that enabled Blackmur to take seriously a comparison of his own time with Augustine's. The authors, we are told by some historians of modernism, reflect a certain stage in the history of the capitalist order, and were affected by the whole complex of transformations that sometimes go by the name of "modernization."[36] No doubt this is also true of the mid-twentieth-century American critics who are the subjects of this study, but to particularize the impact on them of these transformations is well beyond the reach of this essay. I have focused instead on conditions more specific to the American intellectual life in which the great texts exercised their most extensively acknowledged authority. Without these conditions, the role in the United States of modern literature would surely have been different than it was.

To take a skeptical view of the mystique of modernism during the mid-century decades is not to deny that a generic service of literature and the arts is to expand experience and perception beyond what they might be were they tethered always to the immediately apparent needs of liberal democrats raising families. That this service was performed admirably by the canonical works can, and in my opinion should, be affirmed even as the peculiar mystique so long surrounding these texts loses its hold. To understand that mystique as an episode in our intellectual history may even enable us, as readers, to confront on our own terms the poems, plays, and novels of which the critics of the mid-century decades were so often advocates.

6

DEMOCRACY AND THE

MELTING POT RECONSIDERED

Just how to distinguish "ethnicity" from "ethnocentrism" has been a matter of concern to a number of American social critics and politicians during the past generation. The basis for this concern, of course, is the worthy desire to defend one and to condemn the other: Ethnicity is warm and wonderful but ethnocentrism is a cold shoulder. In response to this concern, the old notion of "cultural pluralism" has enjoyed something of a revival. Cultural pluralism promises ethnicity for all who wish to affirm it, yet with the caveat that nobody's particular ethnicity is to be advanced at the expense of anyone else's. The recent attraction of American intellectuals to cultural pluralism and to ethnicity is dealt with skeptically in a book by the sociologist Stephen Steinberg that serves as a jumping-off point for the essay below.

Although this essay deals briefly with the history of ideas about ethnic relations in the United States, it is also intended to be a contribution to political argument. Hence it is of a genre somewhat different from that of the other essays in this book. I reprint it here because it speaks to the tension between cosmopolitanism and provincialism that is a major theme in the studies collected in Part One of In The American Province.

The ideal of an transethnic American nationality has often been a cover for an Anglo-Saxon ethnocentrism properly repudiated in our time. Yet this ideal, in itself, is now more viable than ever, I argue here. Appreciation for this ideal has been diminished, I believe, by a resurgence of uncritical ethnic particularism within the last generation.

Whatever the viability of the traditional, frankly idealistic conception of American nationality I try here to defend, there is a second point at issue. What shall and shall not count as one's "roots"? Inherent in ethnic particularism is a bias toward a narrow construction of one's historical antecedents. Genetic ancestors long forgotten are said to have an authentic, identity-endowing power not possessed by one's vividly felt cultural antecedents. A weaker version of the same bias singles out from these cultural antecedents an ethnic component, at the expense of regional, ideological, religious, vocational, and other components. It must be granted, to be sure, that in the case of any individual, ethnicity may or may not be the most vital and sustaining element of social identity, but I argue in this piece against the easy assumption that one's most authentic roots are to be found in the soil of one's "old world" clan.

"Two Cheers for the Melting Pot" was the title assigned this essay by the editors of the journal in which it was published, Democracy II *(1982), 89–97. I have restored the title of my own choice. The book under review is Stephen Steinberg,* The Ethnic Myth: Race, Ethnicity, and Class in America *(New York, 1981).*

Dᴉscussɪon of social identity in the United States is currently entangled in two incongruous metaphors. The master symbol for ethnic assimilation, the melting pot, is surrounded by plants of many varieties looking about for their "roots." The search for roots is made necessary, it would seem, by the fact that many of the plants were not autochthonous but were produced synthetically. Awkward as this relation of roots to chemistry may be, the popularity of the root-and-plant metaphor is fully in keeping with the two assertions about the melting pot most fashionable during the last twenty years. The point about the melting pot, insisted Nathan Glazer and Daniel Patrick Moynihan in 1963, is that it did not happen. The point about the melting pot, declared Horace Kallen back in 1915, is that it undermines democracy.[1] The rediscovery of Kallen's dictum and the appeal of Glazer and Moynihan's in the climate of the 1960s and 1970s is understandable: Just when many Americans were developing new and admirable sensitivity to the destructive effects of WASP ethnocentrism upon non-WASPS, it was reassuring to know that ethnic life "beyond the melting pot" was real, and was an important bulwark of a free society. The "Americanizers" had failed, thank God! Whatever ills

American society had, it was at least resiliently pluralistic in its culture. Whatever reforms or revolutions might be entailed by a critical renewal or revision of democracy, one could at least be sure that the task demanded enthusiastic support for ethnic particularism. To think otherwise was to betray a lingering affinity for the nativism of Henry Adams, or to descend to the political level of Archie Bunker.

The superficiality of the "new ethnicity" has not escaped everyone, but most critics of it have been willing to settle for the puncturing of a few of the more outrageous balloons floated by the likes of Michael Novak and Peter Schrag.[2] Stephen Steinberg's *The Ethnic Myth* is a more sweeping and aggressive critique of ethnic particularism and its chief ideological support, "cultural pluralism." It brings sharply into focus a number of truths that ought to help demystify the phenomenon of ethnicity and dispell the illusion that the reinforcement of ethnicity can do much to strengthen democracy. If there is a point to be made about the melting pot, it is, according to Steinberg, that the melting pot works, and in so doing serves democracy better than its critics have recognized. Steinberg also argues that an elementary understanding of American social structure and its historical development renders cultural pluralism a dream at best, and at worst an invitation to ignore the class basis of the problems of exactly those Americans who rail against the evils of assimilation.

Arguments over the transforming powers of the American melting pot turn on the significance of indicators that are in themselves subject to very little dispute. No one doubts, for example, that more and more grandchildren and great-grandchildren of the European immigrants of 1880–1924 have been marrying outside the ethnic group of their origin. It is with reference to this particular immigration that the issue of assimilation has been most energetically discussed, and Steinberg draws upon many of the studies showing a decline not only in intraethnic marriage but in the use of languages other than English, in residential concentration, and in the holding of distinctive attitudes toward politics, religion, sex, and vocation. There do remain ethnic enclaves, dominated by the least well-off of the descendants of immigrants and by the professionals whose livelihood depends upon serving an ethnic market. One can insist that these enclaves are saving remnants upon which a new cultural flowering can be based, but Steinberg warns that many of the forces that have diminished the once-large ethnic communities are stronger than ever. A continual and substantial flow of new immigrants from the parent country was a crucial support for these communities, but this support has not existed since Congress curtailed massive immigration in 1924. Economic opportunities continue to lie overwhelmingly outside the ethnic context; an ethnic culture can scarcely be expected to endure when the basic economic activities of most of its potential members are without an ethnic connection. The survival of such a culture would also depend on a degree of control over education that even the Catholic parochial schools do not provide. Moreover, the blatant prejudice against Poles, Italians, Jews, and others that once led members of such groups to depend chiefly upon one another has declined since the 1920s. What has most sustained the recent pride in "ethnic neighborhoods," it would seem, is not the fear that they shall cease to be ethnic, but that they shall cease to be white.

Steinberg has much less to say about the Asian and Latin American immigrations of the last fifteen years, but he believes the same rules apply. He sees no reason to doubt that in the long run, descendants of these Asian and Latin American immigrants will assimilate on terms comparable to those on which the Europeans and, more recently, the Japanese have done. The pace of the process is bound to differ, and will be primarily determined by the economic position of a given ethnic group at the time the process begins. Jews, Steinberg reminds us, were equipped by urban and commercial experience to take greater economic advantage of the American scene than were their peasant contemporaries among other immigrant peoples from Eastern Europe. A similar contrast can be drawn today between the often highly skilled Asian immigrants and their counterparts from Haiti and Guatemala. The case of American blacks is complicated, but here, too, Steinberg singles out economic opportunity as the crucial factor in their destiny in twentieth-century America: "If blacks had been allowed, at the turn of the century, to compete for the industrial jobs that provided opportunity to millions of immigrants, they would today occupy a position in the class system similar to that of Irish, Italians, Poles, and other immigrants who were entering the industrial labor market for the first time" (221).

Steinberg has no use for the popular notion that the *values* inherent in a given ethnic tradition determine the rate and extent of success in America. He delights in undermining the claim that distinctive attitudes toward women and the family controlled the different destinies of Irish and Italian women. The frequency with which Irish women entered domestic service and the infrequency with which Italian women did so depended, Steinberg points out, on economic and demograpic circumstances in Ireland and Italy, yielding in the Irish case many more young, single, female immigrants. These Irish women, Steinberg adds, "fled 'the service' just as quickly as they could establish families of their own or gain access to more desirable employment" (166). Steinberg makes analogous points about the relation between economic opportunity and the values associated with Jewish, black, and Catholic competitors in the great race for wealth and social standing in America. Steinberg consistently underestimates the staying power of systems of value, but this is less troubling than it would be were he not doing battle against the more widespread tendency to treat values as autonomous forces. Steinberg is correct to see the relevant systems of value as subject to modification, and as having been sustained, to begin with, by continuities in the "preentry" social and economic conditions experienced by each ethnic group. Although Steinberg's historical sketches are threadbare and unsophisticated, his summary of selected monographic works serves to get across the essential inequality of the American ethnic groups at their time of entry into the American social system.[3]

If this point is not altogether new, it needs the reinforcement provided by Steinberg's relentless pounding. The harmonious orchestra of cultures envisioned by Kallen and his successors might make some sense if all ethnic groups had entered American life roughly equal in wealth, education, and occupation. Each group might then be expected to go its own way, treating the American state as merely a useful legal canopy under which to stand while serving its own gods and perpetuating its own customs. Yet even those European groups whose original involvement in America was, to the degree allowed by the dynamics of world capitalism,[4] a matter of choice were unequal among themselves and were especially unequal in relation to the dominant "ethnic group," the native-born Americans of largely British ancestry. This inequality created pressures upon individuals to become part of the mainstream culture, where opportunities for a fuller life were obviously to be found. In the absence of genuine equality, therefore, the cultural pluralist program threatens to reinforce existing inequalities by discouraging the entry of individuals into the mainstream. Even when blessed with a supply of ethnic groups that have successfully struggled to reduce their own inequality, the cultural pluralist program is flawed. The members of these groups will have become less ethnic while becoming more equal. Without a panorama of distinctive and authentic ethnic cultures, the cultural pluralist program has nowhere to go.

Insofar as democracy entails the reduction of inequality, Steinberg has grounds for declaring that "democracy and pluralism are not as compatible as the ethnic pluralists would like to think" (260). He recognizes the democratic character of Kallen's aims, and grants that Kallen's ideas helped to protect immigrants from the "100 percent" Americans who would use the melting pot as a weapon of blatant WASP domination. Yet Steinberg sensibly goes on to acknowledge a conflict between the "democratic" principle that "guarantees individual freedoms and specifically proscribes various forms of discrimination," and the "pluralist" principle that "sanctions the right of ethnic groups to maintain their separate cultures and communities" (258). Democracy has been "enhanced," Steinberg observes, by legislation and court decisions that prevent neighborhoods, schools, and private clubs from discriminating "on the basis of race, religion, creed, color, national origin, or sex," but the same enactments and rulings "narrowly circumscribe the areas in which ethnic exclusivity is possible, and therefore make it difficult for ethnic groups to maintain institutions that are essential to their collective survival" (257–258). Ethnic groups generally try to have it both ways, Steinberg observes: "It is not uncommon" for them "to invoke democratic principles to combat the ethnic exclusivity of more privileged groups, but to turn around and cite pluralistic principles in defense of their own discriminatory practices" (258).

Glazer and Moynihan tried to reconcile the two principles by distinguishing between "positive" and "negative" discrimination: The latter is based on "naked prejudice," which the former is "for the purpose of defending something positive rather than simply excluding someone because of his race" (259). Steinberg properly dismisses this bit of casuistry: "Glazer and Moynihan forget that when Jews and Irish were excluded, upper-class Protestants also expressed a desire to preserve the ethnic character of their neighborhoods and clubs" (259). This reminder is made all the more forceful by Steinberg's informative chapter on Harvard University's successful effort in the 1920s to discriminate against Jewish applicants, and thereby to preserve much of Harvard's traditional character. The Harvard case differs from affirmative action, Steinberg insists, because Harvard's leaders sought "to give preferential treatment to an already privileged group," while "affirmative action programs are aimed at groups so underprivileged that they would otherwise be denied educational opportunity" (252). Thus Steinberg ends up with his own version of the positive-negative distinction. His version is at least based on an empirically visible difference, but readers in search of a theoretical justification of affirmative action as ultimately more "democratic" than the so-called merit system will need to look elsewhere. At least Steinberg is willing to live with, rather than to deny, the tension between democracy and the right of people to act in groups for the purposes of perpetuating particular traditions.

The limits of Steinberg's analysis are measured by his willingness, at the very end of *The Ethnic Myth,* to raise and to leave unanswered the question, Assimilate into what? This is the rhetorical question asked repeatedly by champions of ethnic particularism, and Steinberg walks into the trap with an innocence that he, of all people, should have overcome. "Our society has not created alternatives for the rich and closely knit communities that we identify with our immigrant grand-parents" (262), muses Steinburg, falling uncritically into the idiom of ethnicity's mystifiers, whose clinching argument for ethnic allegiance is always the cold and abstract quality of American life. To get real *Gemeinschaft,* we are invariably told, one must nuzzle up to one's old-world clan; there is no "peoplehood" to be had elsewhere in this supremely modern *Gesselschaft.* Steinberg mocks as the "ultimate ethnic myth" the "belief that the cultural symbols of the past can provide more than a comfortable illusion" (262), but having labored so long to identify this belief *as* an illusion and to establish the priority of class over ethnicity, Steinberg seems willing to avert his eyes while his readers drift on back to the world of their fathers. To those who ask, "What else is there?" Steinberg has nothing to say.

One thing he might have said is that identity with one's class is enough. To endorse the longing for something more dense and particular, one might argue, is to impede the development of class consciousness, to invite divisions subject to manipulation by more powerful classes, and to turn one's back on the historic universalism of the Left. This view would be consistent with *The Ethnic Myth,* but Steinberg is probably better off not trying to defend it. The legendary reluctance of Americans to identify themselves in terms of class scarcely needs to be belabored here; only someone prepared for a career of lonely prophecy should seek to convince

Americans that they must so identify themselves, and that they must, in the process, refrain from forming communities that appear to cross class lines. One has to be terribly sure of the direction of history, moreover, to demand that working-class people, in particular, should in the interests of the historic role of their class do without the sustenance that can be found in communities that cross class lines. Yet Steinberg could have indicated where Americans might look for a sense of peoplehood less likely than ethnicity to obscure the class basis of their discontents, and less subject, perhaps, to mystification.

American nationality is one obvious place to look. Yes, it too has been mystified, and has often enough served as a mask for exploitation, but its democratic potential has been overlooked in the necessary, if sometimes myopic, efforts of the 1960s and 1970s to renounce imperialism. The tradition of lambasting American realities on account of their failure to measure up to American ideals has been inhibited by the suspicion that making too much of "American" ideals has been part of the problem. Who, after all, has had more to say about American ideals than the men who led and defended the Vietnam War? Yet there are good reasons to try to overcome this inhibition, and to help make more available to Americans the sense of peoplehood that American nationality can provide.

One good reason is that the melting pot has now done so much to de-Anglo-Saxonize that nationality. Commentators on American society have often observed that a de facto Anglo-Saxon particularism once operated quietly under the aegis of the Enlightenment universalism basic to our political tradition and to the standard Statue-of-Liberty myth. National institutions, it was pointed out, have been dominated by "real Americans" of the stock who "built this country," which is to say, who endowed the United States with its language, constitution, and the controlling conventions of its public life. The domination by distinctly WASP elites has diminished during the last half-century. It is easier than ever for non-WASPs to feel that American traditions are truly theirs, available to be built upon or to be reformulated as one sees fit. Decisions concerning just what aspects of American culture deserve to be kept and developed need not be made on the basis of an analysis of the ethnic ancestry of each aspect. Jefferson and Melville were "British Americans," but critical engagement with them need not on that account be resisted by Americans of non-British ancestry or regarded as a duty by Mayflower descendants.

Another good reason for cultivating American nationality is the very degree of abstractness held against it by many of those who envy the more deeply rooted and homogeneous nationality characteristic of France, Germany, or Israel. To be an American, it has often been observed, is only to come into possession of a set of abstract rights. How rootless and superficial a nationality compared with that drawn upon by de Gaulle, Herzl, Bismarck, or Churchill! Yet the porous texture of American nationality has the virtue of mitigating the tribalist potential inherent in nationality itself. We live in an age when ancient religious and ethnic divisions are being reasserted, often fanatically, in many parts of the world: It is not a time for Americans to apologize for their relatively generous and flexible approach to national identity. An ideal sense of peoplehood surely entails a balance between concrete, historical elements and abstract, general ones; the first provides the dense and specific experience into which each new generation is submerged, while the second provides the tools for interpreting and criticizing that experience in terms of what can be discerned about the universe as a whole. American nationality, the product now of more than two centuries of struggle within a single, if evolving, set of abstractions, can be fairly said to embody a distinctive balance between these elements. America is not the only setting of democratic political culture, but simply to be an American is to enter a historic dialogue with democracy.

That this dialogue is an extension and refinement of many themes in Western history has sometimes been felt to render America too commodious and indefinite an entity for one to identify with in the way that one identifies with an ethnic group. "America," the old saw goes, "is a nation without a people." Yet this apparently problematic scope of American nationality can be another reason for actually preferring it. What looks vast and intimidating from within a local lodge of an ethnic fraternal order can be seen as smaller and more definite when viewed from a more cosmopolitan standpoint. Many of the people who helped form the ethnic groups of the United States had not thought of themselves, prior to immigration, as being *importantly* Italian or Hungarian; they had identified instead with smaller, local collectivities in the old world rendered obsolete by a new social setting in which being Italian or Hungarian came to seem very definite indeed. "Ethnic" identity is always historically contingent. Now that we possess unprecedented awareness of the diversity of the living world, and of the numerous civilizations that have come and gone, America ought not to seem so prodigious. If identification with it requires that one stretch one's soul a bit, it could be well worth the pain.

Does not such a process of enlargement make culture more coarse, sacrificing for a larger communion the finely wrought social webs that can sustain intimate rapport and stimulate the creative elaboration of particular cultural achievements? This results only if the sense of peoplehood is allowed to become an entire way of life. Simply "being American" is not an adequate life, any more than it is enough to simply "be" Norwegian or Jewish or Japanese. Senses of peoplehood are gross. Without this quality, they could not perform the vital but limited function of identifying a people as a people. This identity does sometimes spill across its ideal limits and drown in a conformist torrent the diversity of other, simultaneous identities—narrow or broad in scope, casual or intense in spirit—the precious capacity for which happily distinguishes human beings from other species. We are reminded of this danger by the history of committees on "un-American" activities. But these smaller identities threaten also to lose their ideal proportion, and to imprison people in what Steinberg describes as "parochial disregard for events outside the ethnic province" (262), an obliviousness to the world that can impoverish and endanger residents of any given province. It is a truism that any society experiences a tension between unifying and diversifying forces, but this experience is especially intense in the heterogeneous United States; it is in the course of mediating this constant and often creative tension that American nationality has evolved. So long as the United States remains the institutional framework within which are worked out the rules that most affect Americans of all faiths, regions, and ancestries, American nationality will remain a more realistic investment in social identity than will stocks of local issue.

If a sense of peoplehood is too coarse a thing from which to derive a detailed blueprint for culture, so also is it too coarse to provide any specific political program. Any sense of peoplehood does constitute a minimal foundation for politics, but even so explicitly political an entity as American nationality can be claimed with equal ease by Ronald Reagan and by democratic socialists. The direction that the American tradition ought to take will of course be contested. Yet in any specific contest, so blunt an instrument as a "sense of peoplehood" can perform only limited service; the temptation therefore exists to forsake altogether this level of abstraction, and to ignore the indications that many Americans are searching for a greater sense of peoplehood than has been available to them. Not everyone shares in this search, but signs of it surely include the recent quickening of religious interests as well as the preoccupation with "roots." Since the quality and quantity of energies put into public life depend in part on feelings of identity, anyone concerned about the state of American public life ought not to be silent when the question is asked, "Assimilate into what?

A sense of peoplehood may be a tiny fraction of a polity's life, but it can be terribly important, especially if it isn't there. A renewed commitment to American nationality as the locus of social identity is no substitute for the material and cultural benefits now conferred so largely on the basis of class, but this commitment can at least implicate people in a political language in which to seek more effectively the equitable distribution of these benefits. If the figure of the melting pot is to be replaced in the popular imagination by the figure of the reflective plant looking for its roots, Americans would do well to remember that the plant they have become is a formidable growth upon the extensive and cross-fertilized soil of Western culture. It will not do to try to find in little flowerpots the roots of American trees.

PART TWO

Studies in Historiography

7

T. S. KUHN'S THEORY OF SCIENCE

AND ITS IMPLICATIONS FOR HISTORY

Originally this essay was to have been entitled "Have You Seen the Ghost of Tom?" The point of invoking the old campfire song (Have you seen the ghost of Tom? / Long white bones with the skin all gone / P-o-o-o-o-r Tom, wouldn't it be chilly with no skin on?) was to poke fun at the historians and social scientists who were then rushing to redefine as "paradigm-shifts" an apparently infinite number of changes in thought and practice that had previously been described in other terms. It seemed to me, writing more as a defender of Kuhn than as a critic, that many of Kuhn's admirers had gotten the whole thing backwards. Kuhn was extending into the study of the history of science *some ideas that historians in other fields had long taken for granted. To be sure, Kuhn brought to the study of science many ideas that he did not pick up from old-fashioned historians of politics, philosophy, and the arts, but the old ideas were the ones most often attributed to Kuhn by those who wanted to "apply" him to fields outside the history of science. The first task of my essay is thus to identify just what insights historians have found in Kuhn's now-classic work of* 1962, The Structure of Scientific Revolutions, *and to try to state them in terms that will enable historians to (a) recognize the insights as largely their own, (b) make more comfortable use of them without getting entangled in false analogies to physics and astronomy, and (c) acknowledge frankly that it was Kuhn who had inspired them to come more fully to grips with their own methodological presuppositions. This is what the first one-third of the essay is about, and had I stopped there, my "ghost of Tom" title might have been tolerated.*

What led to the more conventional title actually carried by the piece was my determination to address also the more difficult and enduring issues around which the latter two-thirds of the essay revolve. I try to show that Kuhn is of some help— but not much—in clarifying the process by which scholarly communities warrant their truth-claims. Again, it is a matter of reminding ourselves that most of what Kuhn has to say is species-specific to science, not general to the life of the mind nor even to professional communities. Finally, I try to show that in the debates between Kuhn and philosophers over science as such, Kuhn serves as an important defender of the general mission of historical study. It is thus to Kuhn's arguments about science *that historians ought to attend; it is here, not in spin-offs concerning the scientific status of political science or concerning the paradigmatic status of the* ancien régime, *that we can learn something. Kuhn's historically inspired and historically defended claims about the nature of* scientific knowledge *form the soundest basis for rapport between Kuhn and historians.*

Kuhn's reputation is now somewhat different from what it was when I quarrelled with his critics in this essay a decade ago. Then, he was all too often dismissed by philosophers as a pretender, as a popular writer who really ought to have enrolled in the freshman course of a given philosophic critic. Now, Kuhn is counted routinely, if grudgingly, as one of the century's major theorists of science. The best point of access to the Kuhnian controversy is an anthology edited by Gary Gutting, Paradigms and Revolutions: Applications and Appraisals of Thomas Kuhn's Philosophy of Science *(Notre Dame, 1980).*

This essay was published in American Historical Review LXXVIII *(1973), 370–393.*

NOT SINCE THE PUBLICATION of R. G. Collingwood's *Idea of History* has a work of "theory" won from historians the amount of interest recently accorded Thomas S. Kuhn's *The Structure of Scientific Revolutions.*[1] If historians are conventionally aloof from philosophy of history, they are even less attentive to philosophy of science—yet contemporary footnotes prove that Kuhn's theory of *science* speaks to, and for, historians as few works of philosophy of *history* ever have. Even the revered Collingwood, for all his influence upon intellectual historians during the 1940s and 1950s, served to stop discussions as often as to advance them; a citation to Collingwood's profound but forbidding "Epilegomena"[2] enabled historians to perform an act of calm defiance: "we historians are on to something basic and complicated about human experience, which you can read about in Collingwood, and if you can't understand what he says, well, that's your problem." This defiant use of Collingwood may have been appropriate in some cases, and Collingwood will presumably continue to serve historians in this way without coming down off the shelf he now shares with a more mobile junior partner. Kuhn, unlike Collingwood, is being read carefully by many practicing historians.

Not since the time of Charles Beard has any guild historian attracted an audience among the academic intelligentsia as extensive as Kuhn's. Collingwood, too, was a historian, but he always remained the peculiar possession of historians and of a handful of philosophers; *The Structure of Scientific Revolutions* has become a major text for interdisciplinary discourse and has been acclaimed by the *cognoscenti* that reads Lévi-Strauss, Piaget, Erikson, Laing, Lukács, and Chomsky.[3] Kuhn's audience beyond history and philosophy comes to him for what he says, or implies, about the relation of permanence to change, knowledge to culture, and history to value. This interest in Kuhn constitutes, among other things, a quickening of interest in insights that have long been vouchsafed to historians, for Kuhn's vision of these relationships owes much to the professional subculture of history. Hence Kuhn's relation to historians is simultaneously that of outsider and insider; he is a philosopher of science from whom historians can learn and a historian who may help clarify the historian's outlook for the benefit of an era that has long since turned to sociologists, scientists, psychologists, and literary critics for definitions of whatever issues engage the intelligentsia as a whole.

The meaning Kuhn's work has for history can best be clarified by answering three questions. First, To what extent can Kuhn's description of the behavior of scientific communities function heuristically, as a methodological postulate, in the study of communities organized for purposes other than that of doing science? More specifically, How, if at all, can Kuhn's sense of historical development enrich political, cultural, and intellectual history and other fields outside the history of science? Second, What are the normative implications of Kuhn's philosophy of science—his sense of validity—for the attempt to improve the quality of the "knowledge" historians produce? Third, What stake, if any, do historians in general have in the controversy between Kuhn and many philosophers over the nature of science?

The Structure of Scientific Revolutions excites the imagination of working historians chiefly because much of what it says about scientific communities seems to apply so strikingly to other kinds of communities. David H. Fischer asserts that Kuhn is "relevant to all fields" of history, and any number of manifestoes have announced the applicability of Kuhn to general intellectual history and its subdisciplines.[4] In practice, Kuhn's terms have been employed explicitly by historians of art, religion, political organization, social thought, and American foreign policy, in addition to their more predictable use by historians of the social sciences and the natural sciences.[5] It is Kuhn's sense of historical development that attracts all this attention; specifically, historians are moved by Kuhn's sense of what a tradition is, what conditions sustain it, and what the relation is between tradition and innovation. Kuhn acknowledges that his view of historical development owes much to the conventional historiography of politics and the arts,[6] but *The Structure of Scientific Revolutions* has made such a distinctive contribution that two of our most methodologically sophisticated historians of political thought—J. G. A. Pocock and Sheldon Wolin—have gone all the way to the history of science to find, in Kuhn, the theory of change satisfactory to them.[7] Most uses of Kuhn by historians overlook or minimize the prior kinship with Kuhn that in fact makes rapport so possible; Kuhn's terms are often imported, in toto, from their context in the history of science, so that Kuhn enters the discourse of historians as entirely an outsider, as yet another emissary from sociology whose new-fangled ideas the historian feels obliged to summarize before "applying them to history." The result is that many "applications" of Kuhn take the somewhat incongruous forms of analogies between science and non-science; a Kuhnian "scientific revolution" is explicitly compared to the American decision to withdraw from Vietnam under the pressure of anti-war demonstrations at the Pentagon and at Chicago.[8]

The problem is that Kuhn's striking achievement in the history of science has made what we might call the species-specific aspects of his sense of historical development so available and compelling that we have difficulty getting through the species back to the genus of which Kuhn's theory is a part. Yet it is the generic in Kuhn that historians have been trying to employ, and this accounts for the fumbling apologies that so often accompany attempts to show that the history of society is, for all practical purposes, "just like" the history of tightly organized, technically equipped scientific communities. Insofar as *The Structure of Scientific Revolu-*

tions can enrich historiography beyond the sciences, insofar as the book's sense of historical development can function heuristically as a methodological postulate, it will do so less awkwardly if historians achieve a more comfortable relation with Kuhn, if they themselves seize more effective control over what they have found in Kuhn.[9] This requires a clear, general understanding of the sense of historical development that is embedded in *The Structure of Scientific Revolutions*.

Kuhn's notion of the "paradigm," his most celebrated and maligned term,[10] embodies the sense that activities are defined and controlled by tradition, and that tradition consists of a set of devices, or principles, that have proven their ability to order the experience of a given social constituency. An operative tradition provides a community with criteria to distinguish one activity from another, sets priorities among those activities, and enables the community to perform whatever common activities make it a community at all. Insofar as the community's common experience is contingent, that experience presents itself as a series of "problems" to be solved by the tradition, which validates itself by transforming the contingency of experience into something comprehensible and subject to maximum control. Tradition, then, is socially grounded, and its function is that of organization. Organization may be achieved through a number of modes and devices, ranging from formal institutions to informal habits and from codes of abstract principles to concrete examples of how problems of a given class have been solved in the past. Whether it is conduct or perceptions that require organization, whether the task is prescriptive or cognitive, the organizing devices have enough flexibility to sustain them through successive, contingent experiences; to the extent that a tradition can expand and adapt, like the English common law, it is that much more likely to retain its constituency.

But traditions do lose their constituencies sometimes, and it was of course the transition from one research tradition to another in scientific communities that Kuhn was especially concerned to explain. Kuhn's notions of "normal science," "anomaly," "crisis," and "paradigm-shift" (or "revolution") manifest an integrated set of senses concerning the relation of tradition to change. Change is possible within the terms of an operative tradition, as we have seen, insofar as the elements of the tradition are, like principles or precedents in the common law, able to expand their implications enough to deal with new experiences while not losing their identity. Such innovation within a tradition is energized by an essentially conservative instinct, to maintain the viability of tried-and-true ways of acting and thinking. However tenacious a tradition, its constituency may still find itself surrounded with problems that defy solution. Traditional organizing devices, even when stretched, may fail to control and comprehend the experiences that apparently fall within their province. This failure can occur in a variety of ways. The community may be suddenly subject to conditions radically different from those in effect when the reigning traditions were institutionalized; another culture may have set up housekeeping next door, thereby creating a constant source of novel stimuli too immediate and concrete to be ignored even by those who would prefer not to acknowledge the novelty's existence. Or the community's activities in one area may be affected by upheavels in another: Perhaps a political upheaval, replacing one governing elite with another, or replacing oligarchy with democracy, will produce new criteria for what counts as the satisfactory understanding and control of otherwise unchanged religious or economic life. The discovery of problems unsolved by the tradition may even result from a dynamism within the tradition itself: Endemic tenacity may extend and refine organizing devices to such a degree of precision that they can recognize as "unorganizable" something that cruder, less demanding devices might treat as routine.[11] Whatever the path to crisis, a community thus disorganized must come up with a way to put things in order, and here the pioneering instinct comes into play. Attempts to refurbish the old tradition are replaced by the conscious search for new and more functional devices of organization; tenacity and singleness of purpose are replaced by the intentional proliferation of alternatives. A community's entire store of cultural resources may be ransacked before a consensus begins to emerge that certain proposed devices are superior to others. The more complete the consensus, the greater the stability the community enjoys, and the more likely it is that the new organizing devices will become traditional. Certain communities may go through a full cycle of (1) secure tradition, (2) novelty and confusion, (3) disagreement over whether to resist innovation or encourage it, and if the latter, in what direction, (4) coalescence around a candidate that might become (5) another secure tradition. Other communities may never achieve the unanimity necessary for this "cycle" to come about; rather their traditions may be less secure, their confusion and conflict more permanent, and their "revolutions" less pronounced, if ever worthy of the name.

Once this sense of historical development is abstracted from *The Struc-*

ture of Scientific Revolutions it sounds like a set of truisms. This fact only serves to illustrate a point Kuhn has insisted upon: Concrete examples, like Kuhn's achievement in the history of science, have a staying power distinct from that of the general principles they embody. Had Kuhn written the foregoing two paragraphs instead of having written *The Structure of Scientific Revolutions,* it is doubtful that he would have inspired so many attempts to "apply Kuhn's ideas to history." Yet the foregoing may enable historians to recognize and control just what it is that Kuhn seems to say for them. Once defined generically, the sense of development found in Kuhn can be more easily distinguished from other ideas about historical development and evaluated comparatively. And one man's "truism" can be another's enlightenment: Theorists of social change, for example, now treat Kuhn as a significant and original contributor to that field.[12]

Among genera of theories of historical development, the one to which *The Structure of Scientific Revolutions* belongs acquires some of its distinctness from its indifference to the overall pattern and ultimate character of history. Connected to no total cosmic scheme, the theory stands somewhat apart from "speculative philosophy of history." There is no determinate life cycle, no implication that certain changes are "natural" for a cultural unit at certain times, no insistence that traditions will or will not attain a certain degree of stability, no reason, in principle, why a given tradition might not live forever. The theory neither holds that change is always gradual, cataclysmic, or dialectical nor insists that change is generated by elements exclusively within or outside of "social systems." The theory offers a thoroughly nonteleological view of change: no idea of progress is implied, nor one of decline; there is no sense that Athenian political organization was superior in the second century B.C. to what it had been in the fifth, no sense that New England's religious ideas were better, or worse, in 1730 than in 1630. No golden age stands behind or beyond, no *élan vital* energizes history, and no deities preside over it. Hence the generic sense of development that informs Kuhn's work is aloof from many of the concerns that drive the classical theorists surveyed recently by Bruce Mazlish and Robert A. Nisbet.[13]

Kuhn's general vision of change carries with it a minimum of anthropological and social theory. It does not specify as "natural" any particular relationships among the various psychosocial and economic drives that are served by organizing devices; it does not connect art and religion with economic needs, for example, nor does it suggest that all human activities have their being within a grand struggle between Eros and Thanatos. It depicts stability, equilibrium, and integration as goals, but these echoes of functionalist sociology are muted somewhat by the absence of anything like that school's emphasis on stasis: "the purposive end" of social systems, for the functionalists, is "the mere persistence and perpetuation of the system itself."[14] The Kuhnian vision emphasizes instead the terms on which a tradition justifies itself or loses its binding power: according to its ability to organize the community's contingent, historical experience. What is left open in the Kuhnian theory, considered generically, is the fundamental constitution of what is being stabilized and integrated. The aims of natural science help fill this gap for Kuhn in *The Structure of Scientific Revolutions,* but these are clearly "species-specific."

While the limited scope of Kuhn's general sense of development is the basis for much of its distinctness and utility, this cuts both ways. A historian concerned to explain a given temporal episode might find that Kuhn's vision frees the historian from grand developmental formulas and enables him to focus more directly on that episode, in its particularity; yet this same historian must look beyond Kuhn for a body of theory that will help him formulate and answer the questions left unasked by the Kuhnian framework. The latter simply would not predict, for example, that internal conflicts over the adequacy of competing religious faiths will be found to be functions of economic conditions. But neither would the Kuhnian vision prevent the discovery, through auxiliary means, that this was the case in a particular community at a particular time. Historians must be prepared to see things Kuhn does not lead them to look for, but Kuhn's sense of historical development may be able to neutralize the biases of a number of social and anthropological theories without excluding them from the matrix of inquiry. Kuhn's sense of development is different in scope and emphasis from Marxist, Freudian, and even functionalist theories, but its relation to them is not necessarily that of a rival: It can serve as a control, as a qualifier, whereby the traditional and fruitful eclecticism of the historian can continue to draw upon diverse insights about the nature of man and society without being victimized by attendant prescriptions concerning the nature of change. To the extent that historians employ generalizations in order to understand the particulars of history,[15] historians are best served by a sense of development like Kuhn's, which excludes the fewest of possible relationships from vision and retains the most.

The distinctness and potential utility of Kuhn's sense of development are functions not only of its limited scope but of its positive attributes. In the dynamics of change, for example, Kuhn's emphasis is on the role of tradition in helping to define a given contingent experience and in responding to it; traditions are not passive entities, helplessly battered about by circumstance, capable only of adapting to a concrete, externally defined given. Yet the ordinance that cultural forms have over experience is not to be understood as the triumph of spirit over matter, nor even of "ideas" over "events": The Kuhnian vision replaces this source of materialist-idealist disputation with a dialogue between traditions and contingent experience, in order that the historian can more freely investigate the functions of cultural forms as organizing devices. One can say of Kuhn what Gordon Wood has said about Bernard Bailyn in another context: He brings together idealism and behaviorism by showing that men are as much "victims" of their ideas as beneficiaries of them; traditions prevent men from seeing in their experience phenomena that an alternative tradition might lead them to confront. [16]

Furthermore, Kuhn anchors traditions firmly in social subgroup constituencies, and thereby he distinguishes his work from history that inquires less rigorously into exactly who is served by given institutions and ideas. Constituencies can be identified with relative ease in the developed sciences, but this species-specific aspect of Kuhn's work serves to encourage historians in general to ask more insistently, "Whose experience in connection with what activity is being organized by what cultural forms?" Hence Kuhn both promotes and socializes the "radical contextualism" of much of contemporary intellectual history, in keeping with which great pains are being taken to see that the choices attributed to historical figures like Hobbes and Locke were authentically available to them, not imposed on their milieu by history's subsequent elaboration of alternatives to positions they took. [17] More sociological than metaphysical or psychological in orientation, Kuhn's vision of historical development depends absolutely on "communities," whose internal and external relations in any particular case require careful definitions.

Essential to Kuhn's sense of what communities do are his emphases on conflict and problem solving. Subgroups in a community may propose devices for organizing whatever activities they must perform in concert with the community as a whole; when this happens the relation between the subgroups is one of competition. The proponents of each device attempt to persuade or overpower opposing groups, and in the process they may refine their devices to the point that they become more obviously functional: In this sense, competition can be productive. The alternative devices are candidates for the job of "problem solving," a notion so dominant in Kuhn's sense of development that all other activities are, in effect, translated into its terms. The plausibility of Kuhn in the present context depends largely on whether one believes this translation can be effected comfortably, behind the scenes, without turning "problem solving" into another heavy, mechanical formula, and without ignoring aspects of a community's life that we regard as essential to its history.[18] Certainly the assertive effort of scientists to expand knowledge through solving the "puzzles" of normal science is "species-specific" to *The Structure of Scientific Revolutions,* but this manifests the more generic sense that contingent experience functions in relation to a tradition as a series of "problems" that must be solved in order that the activities of the community, whatever they are, may be carried out in an organized, satisfactory fashion. The notion that all thought and action participate in "problem solving" is of course a familiar one, at least since the time of John Dewey.

Finally, a positive aspect of Kuhn's sense of development is its emphasis on elements of tradition that are prior to, or even apart from, principles, laws, and other conventionally "rational" organizing devices. Certain specific, concrete achievements within the remembered history of a community may function as models for thinking and acting without first being transformed into abstract principles. Kuhn thus reinforces compellingly the historian's practice of looking for prototypes of this sort, especially when trying to explain the behavior of a community that seems not to be following any principles at all. For example, English colonists in America enslaved Africans long before the principle of lifetime, heritable, racial slavery was acknowledged by English Americans. The behavior of the colonists was influenced by precedents from social situations they regarded as analogous.[19]

If *The Structure of Scientific Revolutions* can inspire attempts to depict in its terms the history of nation-states, no wonder this work has led historians to compare their own guild to Kuhn's scientific communities. While not "a science," the discipline of history is at least an academically organized branch of inquiry; it resembles Kuhn's scientific communities more obviously than do many of the cultural units that are said to partake of the same pattern of historical development. Increasingly, historians offer new interpretations, or suggestions for new research, as "paradigm-proposals," and historians have begun to regard basic changes in common outlook as "paradigm-shifts."[20] The introduction of this vocabulary has been especially easy since histories of the profession have long been grounded, quite firmly, in some of the generic insights that inform *The Structure of Scientific Revolutions*. Conceivably historiography could profit by yet more attention to the role of certain concrete achievements in establishing professional traditions and to the role of these traditions in controlling the response of historians to changes in their own intellectual and social environment; but the impression persists that we already have an abundance of exactly this sort of information about ourselves. The best of our professional histories was written by John Higham, Leonard Krieger, and Felix Gilbert soon after Kuhn's book appeared, but the authors of *History* seem not to have required Kuhn's help to direct their attention to questions of this sort.[21] Hence, while one could no doubt deliberate at length over the extent to which Kuhn's analysis of the historical development of scientific communities can, or should, be taken to apply to the professional community of historians, this question is finally not very interesting. A much more important and difficult question presents itself as soon as we acknowledge one crucial distinction between our relation to our own profession and our relation to conventional objects of historical study.

What matters most about the discipline of history is its ability to distinguish good history from bad history, accuracy from confusion, truth from fraud. However diverse and complicated the aims of doing history, we are at least dependent upon this activity for knowledge about certain things. While we care about the ways in which history is relative, we care even more about the ways in which it is true. Suddenly the fact that Kuhn wrote about science becomes important, as it decidedly is not when his work is read for its general sense of historical development. To what extent does Kuhn's philosophy of science—his sense of validity—provide the discipline of history with prescriptions for the improvement of its services? This question is grounded, then, in our engagement with the community rather than in our detachment from it; and its pursuit requires that we cease to read Kuhn as we have until this point, as a describer of the behavior of groups and the individuals within them. We need now to look within and beyond Kuhn's sense of historical development to find his sense of validity, or objectivity.

The relevance to history of Kuhn's sense of how the sciences achieve validity is more complicated than the tired question, Is history a science? Kuhn's admirers among historians include those least inclined to discard history's traditional autonomy for the more scientific standing presumably afforded by methodological integration with the social sciences;[22] historians differ from the sociologists and political scientists who take up Kuhn as yet another model of science against which their own activities can be measured. The difference follows from history's conviction that it antedates and transcends social science, that history partakes of art as well as science, that history is too much a "craft" to be subsumed under science. Historians have been less eager than social scientists to attribute to themselves the practice of "normal science" under controlling "paradigms," the mark of a truly "developed" science.[23] Yet historians, whether we regard them as craftsmen, protoscientists, or whatever, do operate with a sense that their discipline can be practiced with varying degrees of success. Hence historians can look to *The Structure of Scientific Revolutions* not to learn about the aims and methods of the sciences, but to understand how those aims and methods are fulfilled. The question is not the extent to which history and science share abstractly defined aims and methods, but whether Kuhn's account of how validity is achieved in the sciences can clarify and/or improve the status of validity in history. Historians continue to term good scholarship "objective," long after pretensions to "scientific history" have been forsaken. Can Kuhn's sense of validity help us, as historians, to clarify what we mean by "objective," and does Kuhn prescribe any means of achieving greater objectivity?

Certainly, without Kuhn's help, we could say that in the idiom of historians an "objective" account of some experience or event is valid on an intersubjective basis. This is to say that the truth of the account will be recognized by virtually all reasonable people, if they understand what is supposed to be the purpose of the account, if they follow the steps of its argument, and if they follow the pattern of its evidence. The account is about the event or experience, not about something else, and it is true, not false. Obviously there are questions begged in what counts as a "reasonable person" and what counts as "an experience or event," and these are among the issues about which philosophers argue. Positions on these issues divide one sense of validity from another.

One such division is between Kuhn and his critics among philosophers of science, some of whom insist that Kuhn has no sense of validity at all. Kuhn, it is charged, has so relativized even the developed sciences as to deny their claims to objectivity; Kuhn's philosophy of science allegedly turns the decisions of scientific communities into matters for "mob psychology."[24] This reaction is sparked by Kuhn's profoundly sociological orientation. His sense of validity is essentially the following: A truth-claim becomes valid when the most learned practitioners of a technically sophisticated field agree that the theory on which the claim is based explains the range of phenomena under common scrutiny more satisfactorily than does any other known theory. This view of what counts as true differs from any simple correspondence-theory, according to which truth is a function of correspondence with something "out there." It also differs from the "justificationist" philosophies of science, according to which science is distinguished by its use of certain standards of rationality that are not culture-bound. But for Kuhn the crucial questions are: Whose word do we take concerning what's "out there" (in other words, which theory explains the relevant phenomena the most satisfactorily?), and whose sense of "satisfactory" do we employ? In both cases Kuhn's answer is that we take the word of the professional community; but when he says this he is referring to tightly organized, self-contained groups of experts bound together by rigorously defined questions and highly technical methods. Only these professional communities in the "developed sciences" are given this extraordinary position "above the law," above all models of justification. Kuhn can ground objectivity itself in professional communities of this sort because they alone have produced an impressive supply of ideas about nature that work. Ideas "work" when they predict the behavior of natural phenomena so well that we are enabled to manipulate nature or stay out of its way. Within the store of ideas of this type, some "work" better than others, and the successive discovery of better and better ideas is the transition from one valid idea to another, not a transition from invalidity to validity. The fact that a truth-claim may be brushed aside by a later, more technically equipped generation does not detract from that original truth-claim's status as "valid science for its own time."[25]

What needs to be underlined here is that Kuhn's sense of objectivity, while it depends on agreement, is not entirely circular, as would be the case if the community's decision were taken in a vacuum. Rather the community has to take some account of the particulars that are observed under specified conditions. By thus acknowledging that there is something "out there" we do not reactivate the crude realism of the correspondence-theory; rather we recognize the obvious fact that any organized enterprise, however elaborate its working apparatus, must come to grips with its material conditions: Politicians in need of money can be expected to accumulate a certain amount of knowledge about the political values of the rich. Surely there are no insuperable philosophical difficulties in recognizing that physical phenomena have considerable influence over what physicists do, that millionaires affect much of the behavior of impecunious politicians, and that primary documents from the reign of Henry II exercise some control over what Angevin constitutional historians do. As for how we know that a given glob of reality is, in fact, "physical," "a millionaire," or "a document from the reign of Henry II," it ought to be sufficient to say that while these judgments are, technically speaking, interpretations, only the most hopeless solipsist would deny that some "globs of reality" admit more easily than others of the sets of definitions on which physics, capitalism, and constitutional history are founded.

Now, what about the relation of Kuhn's sense of validity to the discipline of history? Insofar as historians have produced a body of knowledge that "works" to the satisfaction of everyone who cares, it consists largely of the semiautonomous, name-and-date "facts" that take up the pages of standard biographies, and that are only incidental to the questions historians try the hardest to answer. The most strikingly successful "answers" to questions historians care about are proverbially and persistently unable to inspire the degree of support given to reigning doctrines in the natural sciences—even the unusually tight "research consensus" created by C. Vann Woodward's *Origins of the New South* cannot serve as evidence that history is one of those disciplines that are "beyond the law." Historians, including those within fairly narrow subfields, are continually involved in debate over exactly what questions should be asked—precisely the sort of discussion the developed sciences are freed from by their tightly constructed "paradigm." Historians, moreover, actively go about asking radically different kinds of questions, and they grant professional status to work controlled by a number of different ideologies and commitments. Grudging or not, this tolerance of diversity distinguishes history from Kuhn's developed sciences, which tolerate it only when they do not know what they are doing, when a "normal science" consensus breaks down. Furthermore, the very notion of a "professional" community applies only ambiguously to history and to some of the social sciences, for the constituency of these disciplines is hard to define. In history, especially, the evaluation of a scholarly work frequently involves the participation of readers who, while not "professional historians," are sufficiently cognizant of what historians do to make the latter seek the approval of this larger, more intellectually diverse constituency.

Fortunately Kuhn's sense of validity has a corollary for knowledge-producing communities that fall short of the tightly organized, clearly successful research consensus of the developed sciences. These "proto-sciences," as Kuhn calls disciplines like history and most of the social sciences, both generate and test—however imperfectly—"testable propositions."[26] The professional community of historians regularly applies inter-subjective standards to the scholarship of its members. The "profession," even if this term is stretched to cover the educated non-professionals whose approval is important to historians, does make judgments, does provide an atmosphere of organized criticism. This remains true despite the fact that the touchstone of "good history" is notoriously difficult for anyone to define: The entire notion of intersubjective validity in history must live alongside the suspicion, if not the conviction, that the knowledge-producing aim of history is secondary to, or in any case qualified by, the moral and esthetic aims that presumably distinguish it from all sciences, physical and social. Indeed some historians would deny that the term "knowledge" is useful for denoting the type of "meanings" that historians discover in (or assign to) things. It would be a mistake to look to Kuhn for the clarification of these persistent complexities in the aims of history, but his view of validity is potentially relevant to history so long as we stipulate that the "testability" of a proposition is not a function of the use of any single, specific model of justification. However we define the aims of history, it remains true that no work of scholarship in that field will be counted as "successful" unless it persuades its professional readers of the following: (1) That the questions it asks are comprehensible, and worth asking; (2) That the sources it has examined are indeed the ones most relevant to the inquiry; and (3) That its analysis of the sources has been rational. By "rational" we mean that the author's presuppositions about human nature, the behavior of groups, causation, and so forth are either shared by his readers or are perceived by his peers as respectable competitors to the views of the readers. The "knowledge" produced by historians is clearly distinguished from statements about the past that fail to persuade professional readers in these ways.

Hence we end up saying in a slightly different way something that has often been said about history: It is "imperfect knowledge." But when philosophers refer to history as "imperfect knowledge," they generally have the covering-law model of explanation in mind. In that view the knowledge produced by historians is imperfect because historians have not been able to explain particular events through the use of highly confirmed "laws," as the cracking of a radiator on a cold night can be explained by general laws concerning what happens to water at different temperatures and to metals under stress. On the Kuhnian analysis, however, the covering-law model of explanation is merely one of a number of possible values that may form part of a discipline's working assumptions, and the presence or absence of complete hypothetico-deductive explanation is not, in itself, enough to establish the validity or lack of validity of a truth-claim presented in its name. This is where we can see Kuhn's sociological orientation the most dramatically. Kuhn might be willing to grant that most of the developed sciences do, as a behavioral fact, strive for hypothetico-deductive explanations, but "imperfect knowledge" in the Kuhnian sense is imperfect on the grounds of the extent of agreement about its truth and among whom it is agreed. The "explanation" that a community, or part of a community, accepts may derive its coherence from properties that cannot be translated, without remainder, into "laws" of any kind: The cogency with which vast amounts of material are made to fit together by a particular, concrete achievement like Perry Miller's *The New England Mind,* or, again, Woodward's *New South,* may persuade professional readers of a work's rationality.

Whatever the structure of rationality in the developed sciences, or in the "imperfect knowledge" of disciplines like history, the structure's sociological base has aroused in several philosophers the fear that Kuhn's effect is to encourage a protoscience to impose, arbitrarily, a tight research consensus upon its practitioners in order that the discipline might more nearly approximate the mature sciences. Kuhn, it is said, encourages intellectual retrenchment, pedantic specialization, the avoidance of logical rigor, and, if not mob rule, at least the unjustified refusal to join issue with arguments presented by professional minorities.[27] On this view Kuhn's implications for history would be as follows. In order to make their work more completely objective, historians may determine what kinds of questions can be answered without controversy and then confine research to these questions. The sure-fire means of getting reliable knowledge is the elaborating of truisms and the collecting of information that, however dubious its significance, is at least true. Or, if more ambitious questions are to be allowed, objectivity can be won by expelling from the profession anyone unwilling to accept a given ideology. This would assure that research done by the remaining members of the group would not be subject to debilitating methodological criticism.

This reading of Kuhn's implications for history, and for any knowledge-producing discipline, is mistaken, I believe, and on grounds that demand clarification. Kuhn in fact presupposes a balance within professional communities between the drive to "perfect" their knowledge—even through retrenchment and the imitation of the developed sciences—and the drive to answer the very questions whose difficulty has prevented the prior achievement of a tight research consensus. Had Kuhn acknowledged this presupposition more openly, some of the confusion concerning his normative implications might have been avoided. Even when challenged to explain why his views do not encourage the hasty and arbitrary legislation of fundamentals and the repression of minorities Kuhn's response has been cryptic. The protosciences should be patient, Kuhn says, for maturity comes only to those who "wait and struggle" for it. But waiting and struggling presumably proceed on certain terms. What are they? And how shall "waiting and struggling" apply to crafts like history, which share only ambiguously in social science's quest for the "maturity" of the developed sciences?[28] Had Kuhn chosen to address these questions more directly, and had he outlined the normative implications of his philosophy of science for history, I believe he would have been bound to claim something like the following.

The professional community of history, or of any knowledge-producing enterprise, has available to it at all times the value-systems of other disciplines, including the developed sciences. Insofar as there is a loose consensus in the learned world as a whole about what it is to be "rational," history and similar communities are answerable to that consensus. As long as history claims to be a participant in learned discourse, history must maintain a substantial measure of rapport with what counts as "good sense" in this larger constituency. Within the learned world's vast store of vaguely compatible value-systems, historians will find a number of specific value-systems—including, for example, that embodied in the hypothetico-deductive model for explanation. Historians may take up these specific value-systems and see if they function well in the discipline of history, given the common aims that make it a community at all. Yet the "common aims of the community" are to some extent at issue when history, or any "protoscience," is trying to resolve a basic internal conflict or to choose among the various, specific value-systems available to the community. And Kuhn does not prescribe any *specific* standard for the resolution of such problems. Professional communities in the protosciences are not a "law unto themselves," to be sure, but they would seem to be under no more specific ordinance than the obligation to be reasonable. Kuhn's refusal to go further than this, his refusal to endorse specific value-prescriptions for the protosciences greatly alarms his critics, but it makes sense once we recognize its connection to the trust Kuhn has in the motives men bring to inquiry in general.

Kuhn's *Structure of Scientific Revolutions* as well as his recent efforts to clarify the argument of that book reveal a willingness to grant legitimacy to the basic questions around which inquiry does, as a behavioral fact, develop. Kuhn seems to assume that physical inquiry, historical inquiry, philosophical inquiry, zoological inquiry, political inquiry, or whatever, whether or not they have become developed sciences, or whether they ever will, do possess a kind of primal validity: The drives that bring these inquiries into being provide their practitioners with something to stand on in terms of the aims of the professional communities that may form around these inquiries. Kuhn, therefore, does not prescribe basic aims for the branches of inquiry; these aims are there and can be trusted. Indeed, Kuhn so took for granted the legitimacy of the aims of the developed sciences that at least one critic was moved to complain that Kuhn did not discuss "the aim of science." Kuhn's response to this has been that the developed sciences seek "to explain in detail a range of natural phenomena,"[29] an answer too vague, I am sure, to satisfy his critics. Kuhn is simply more willing than are many philosophers of science to entrust responsibility to people who are not philosophers of science. If this makes him an "irrationalist," I do not see how the charge can be refuted. The persons drawn to a given inquiry and acculturated into the organized community that has taken form around that inquiry are, Kuhn seems to imply, in a position to take the lead in evaluating the various approaches to their field that the surrounding learned world presents to the community. Kuhn assumes that these practitioners themselves are sufficiently loyal to their callings to look for answers that will neither abandon their basic questions nor repudiate what counts as "rationality" in the larger culture for whose benefit the inquiry is being conducted. Obviously, disciplines without a "normal science" consensus must live at all times in a state that approximates "crisis" in a developed science, and Kuhn assumes that the basic aims of such disciplines are compelling enough to enable their practitioners to endure the uncertainty and conflict that attend upon theory proliferation and energetic methodological criticism.

The scope of Kuhn's normative implications for history and other protosciences is thus extremely limited, encompassing chiefly the questions of who should decide what, to the relative satisfaction of whom? Some of the confusion about Kuhn's normative implications might have been eliminated, again, had Kuhn more boldly distinguished between prescriptions of this sort, which are intrinsic to his theory of science, and prescriptions that are in principle consistent with that theory although Kuhn himself does not make them. The latter could include prescriptions of almost any specific content, so long as they are generated, discussed, and adopted or rejected within the appropriate framework of relations among practitioners, their colleagues, and their larger constituencies in the learned world. The fact that Kuhn has chosen not to integrate specific value-prescriptions for sociology or theology into *The Structure of Scientific Revolutions* must not be taken to obscure his conditional approval of inter-disciplinary dialogue concerning the ways in which the basic aims of various disciplines ought to be interpreted and pursued.[30] Kuhn does, of course, separate himself from the schoolmarmish practice of the positivists, according to which the branches of knowledge are treated as pupils, some to receive gold stars for the mastery of certain methods, some to wear the dunce cap for speaking nonsense.

Perhaps Kuhn's position can be brought out more distinctly if we compare it to each of the polar attitudes that have defined the analytical philosophy of history during the past twenty-five years. As Rudolph Weingartner has pointed out, philosophers have been divided between those who wish to provide an account of what historians ought to be doing and those who wish to provide an account of what they actually do.[31] The most conspicuous of the former are the followers of Carl Hempel, the covering-law theorists whose philosophy of history provides historians with a specific model for explanation that, if it could be brought into more complete operation in history, would perfect the knowledge historians produce. Opposed to the "Hempelians" are a number of philosophers who take the methods of historians as self-justifying and who seek to provide an adequate philosophical account of what historians do. Historians almost always prefer the latter style of philosophy, for it can be taken to legitimize aloofness on the part of historians from methodological discussions in the social sciences and humanities generally. Historians interested in justifying this aloofness will not get much help from Kuhn, however, for he implies that history, insofar as it expects to survive as a recognized branch of inquiry, cannot afford to ignore frequently made methodological complaints about its procedures. Yet Kuhn does imply that historians have, in their own sense of their common aims, a legitimate place to stand when entering theoretical discourse with nonhistorians. For example, Kuhn would surely defend the reluctance of historians to put aside narratives, even though this reluctance creates ambiguities in "historical explanation" that diminish the standing of history in the eyes of some philosophers and scientists, who would prefer that explanation by covering laws proceed in a more forthright fashion.

If Kuhn would not regard the discipline of history as free from the need to justify itself, neither would he free subgroups of historians with special "perspectives" from the need to justify their point of view to other historians. We often speak of a historian's perspective as much more than a limitation on his objectivity; we see it rather as a positive opportunity to observe things that are obscure from other perspectives.[32] *The Structure of Scientific Revolutions* certainly supports this understanding of the function of a "point of view," but Kuhn's sociological sense of what makes an idea true exercises an important control on "perspectivism," and prevents it from turning into the more complete relativism of "every man his own historian." To the extent that what historians do has a claim to knowledge, this claim is based on the existence of a community, however amorphous, that evaluates the various "perspectives" of its members, as well as the relation between a given perspective and what is allegedly "discovered" within it. The community distinguishes among points of view that are comprehensive, parochial, and incoherent.

Community sanction is thus essential to knowledge, even when "imperfect," but this does not necessarily imply the repression of points of view the profession as a whole regards as "parochial." On the contrary, these ostensibly "parochial" perspectives have the same relation to the professional community of historians that the latter has to the other branches of knowledge. Just as historians can refuse to do away with "narratives" and still be considered, by most of the learned world, as producers of knowledge, so can the advocates of a "parochial" vantage point like Marxism remain doggedly "parochial" and still be contributors to history. But the Marxists, to take them only as an example, remain second-class citizens in the community of history in the same sense that history is a second-class citizen in a learned world where the developed sciences set the standard for knowledge. If Marxists refuse to abandon their parochialism in order to become better acculturated as historians, their situation is again comparable to the historians, in their entirety, in relation to the larger learned community: The parochial Marxists and the redoubtable narrative historians each have a set of commitments too essential to their callings to be relinquished, and in each case, also, the recalcitrance of the minority is tolerated by the larger group. The learned world tolerates narratives because it suspects that what works in physical inquiry might not, after all, work for every kind of inquiry, and the historical profession tolerates the Marxists because it knows that its collective judgment is too "imperfect" to justify the expulsion of a parochial minority with as much empirical and theoretical foundation as the Marxists. In both cases, then, the minority is taken seriously because it can make a case for itself in terms that can be at least understood by the majority.

Does this suggest that the appropriate balance between the demands of minorities and majorities is achieved automatically? Does it mean that Marxist interpretations of history have gotten no more and no less than their share of attention from the profession as a whole, decade by decade, during the twentieth century? Would Kuhn prevent us from saying that professional communities make mistakes? Since the meaning of these queries depends on whether they are taken to presuppose a transcendent standard for judgment, we are led directly into Kuhn's attempt to release philosophy of science from the need for such a standard.

That the history of a thing can tell you something about its nature has always been a controversial assertion with reference to science, an activity that even the nineteenth century was unable to historicize completely. Historians of science have been expected to write the history of an activity whose nature was known, or was in any case the business of someone else to define; not until recently have they been called upon to clarify the nature of science. Kuhn has been the most insistent advocate of this new role for history since 1962, when he introduced *The Structure of Scientific*

Revolutions with the claim that the historical study of science "could produce a decisive transformation" in views on the nature of science. These words gained some of their drama from their immediate context: Kuhn's volume was published as part of the *International Encyclopedia of Unified Science,* the summa of logical positivism, the movement that viewed the nature of science as the most strictly synonymous with its logic. Kuhn sought to historicize the most recalcitrant of subjects, science, and he threatened to drive the "Whig interpretation of history" out of its last well-defended enclave, the historiography of the sciences.[33] Kuhn would carry the insights of historiography into new territory.

Kuhn's assault on Whiggery in the history of science met with complaints very much like those raised by defenders of Whiggish history in other fields. We have often been told, for example, that the important thing about antebellum abolitionists is that they were right. Whatever the complex web of historical conditions that enabled the antislavery radicals to see the evil of slavery clearly and to act to try to end it, our rational and moral relation to these radicals can only be obscured by attempts to bring out these sustaining conditions in their full, historical, material complexity. Accounts of the psychosocial basis for the behavior of the abolitionists detract from its righteousness, the argument goes, just as a sociological orientation toward science obscures the two things about science that are truly important: its ideal logic of justification and its access to the objective natural order. The ideal structure of science and the morally right response of reformers are what we need to understand; we cannot be helped by studies that justify obfuscation and debunking in the name of "comprehensiveness and complexity." Certain ethical and logical ideals are so important to our survival, and so precariously held, that they need reinforcement, not the more complete "understanding" that risks the miring of these ideals in the swamps of human nature and history.

Oliver Wendell Holmes, Jr.'s attempt to historicize law produced a discussion similar to the one now surrounding Kuhn's work. Holmes's belief that the law was made by judges, that its life was "experience" instead of logic, that there was no "natural law" waiting to be discovered and declared, placed him in opposition to the brittle formalism of his generation's jurisprudence.[34] To be sure, the "legal realists" who claimed Holmes as their prophet went on to deny the influence of precedent and reason, of rules and logic, on the behavior of judges,[35] but the realists' relation to Holmes is analogous to the relation of Kuhn's followers in the "counterculture" to *The Structure of Scientific Revolutions.*[36] Far from "ir-rationalism," Kuhn's view of science is remarkably like the conventional view of law, now that the Holmesian insights have been detached from the excesses of the realists: Law (science) is part of culture, but culture brings great rational and moral resources to the improvement of law (science), and the lack of a transcendent standard does not endanger society's loyalty to law (science).

The controversy over Kuhn's work is even more strikingly reminiscent of the nineteenth-century *Angst* over the fate of the doctrine of design. In *The Structure of Scientific Revolutions* Kuhn predicted that the "main obstacle" to the historicization of science would be the same abstract convictions marshaled against Darwinian natural selection.[37] The subsequent decade has confirmed the prediction. Since certain organisms and their component parts were so supremely capable of doing their job, how could biologists explain their development without design? Since certain scientific theories work so well, how can any explanation of their development dispense with a theory-independent, objective, natural order? Today most of us believe that Darwin's opponents exaggerated evolution's threats to the integrity of civilization and to the identity of man; the defenders of design seem to have been motivated by a sense of permanence much too extreme and absolute. The present issue is whether Kuhn denies to science the stability of structure and environment required for its practice. Kuhn's critics charge, in effect, that Kuhn is naïve about how great and abiding is our need for cosmic anchors, for ideals of perfection unsullied by social, psychological, and historical functionality.

Kuhn's theory of science dispenses with the idea of a fixed, permanent natural order that can function both as a standard for truth in the case of particular theories and as a goal for the progress of science. Kuhn also rejects the a priori methodological unity of science, according to which specific, formalized rules of verification are assumed to attend upon the basic aims of science. Scientific progress for Kuhn is not progress toward completeness via the accumulation of correct observations; it is, rather, "evolution *from* primitive beginnings," from what scientists agree upon to explanations that increase and refine their "understanding of nature."[38] This "progress" of science is made possible by a conjunction of (1) continuity in basic aims,[39] with (2) the mysterious fact that parts of the natural world turn out to be "knowable,"[40] which is to say that the object of knowledge presents problems that can be solved to the satisfaction of enough people to enable a tight research consensus to come into being. This consensus, in turn, promotes the microscopic specialization that allows scientists either to expand the range of phenomena explained by their theories or to discover anomalies. The eventual explanation of anomalies may require the community to choose among alternative revisions of theory, and choices made by individual members of the community are controlled by a complex of preferences enumerated in no existing "logic of explanation." What the community decides will in any case settle the matter, will determine which theory revision will count as a progressive step in science. Such is the theory of science that Sir Karl Popper believes to be giving comfort to the enemies of "our civilization."[41]

We must aim at truth, said the late Joseph R. Levenson, "even if the truth cannot be known."[42] The fate of Kuhn's theory of science depends partially on the extent to which this tension is in fact bearable. In the context of contemporary thinking about the cultural relations of science, Kuhn's work raises the following question: Is it a necessary condition of the successful pursuit of science that scientists, and/or the societies to which scientists look for support, retain the conception of a "fixed permanent scientific truth"[43] as the goal of science? Kuhn himself has not confronted this question directly, but *The Structure of Scientific Revolutions* surely assumes that our ability to make judgments can survive the knowledge of how entangled those judgments are in our psychosocial matrix and that neither our reason nor our values are inappropriately threatened by a thoroughly historical perspective. To the extent that we see around us certain disciplines that abandon their callings for the academic equivalent of get-rich-quick schemes, Kuhn trusts that such hoaxes can be identified and criticized without a transcendent standard. In this view culture-bound standards are stable enough to define "mistakes," to sustain a critical attitude toward our intellectual environment, so long as we understand that the transition from transcendent objectivity to socially grounded objectivity need not be a substitution of terror and caprice for rationality. *The Structure of Scientific Revolutions* can be read as an invitation to forsake at last the fictional absolutes of natural theology.

Issues of such depth would not be raised by the historicization of science if this process were allowed to proceed within the terms of the now-classical distinction between the historical sociology of scientific knowledge and the philosophy of scientific justification.[44] In keeping with this distinction, conventional sociology of science does not attempt to integrate its sociological explanations of ideas about nature with an articulate interpretation of what makes such ideas valid or invalid.[45] Questions about the success with which science achieves its aims are supposedly beyond the scope of the discipline, as, indeed, they would be beyond the scope of any historical, psychological, or sociological study of science, if the above distinction were rigorously adhered to. Yet *The Structure of Scientific Revolutions* seeks explicitly to explain the success of science;[46] this work is clearly distinguished from historical approaches to science that ignore validity, or translate it into entirely neutral terms. Kuhn's attempt to account for the validity as well as the relativity of science endows his work with a significance for historians that will be missed by those who look only at his sense of development, and then at his sense of validity, without seeing how the two are actually related in *The Structure of Scientific Revolutions* itself. For the "science" that Kuhn would historicize remains throughout his work the real thing, the explicitly successful explanation of natural phenomena. Kuhn's "science" is an activity that we value greatly, an enterprise upon which "our civilization," as Sir Karl would say, and properly, is crucially dependent. Its historicization therefore brings into bold relief as nothing else now can the question of history's relation to value. Does a historical understanding of the "problem-solutions" we rely upon inhibit significantly our ability to defend, criticize, alter, and defend again those very "problem-solutions," those answers to life's questions that we believe in? Responses to this query have always affected the extent to which the insights of historians are solicited, ignored, or resisted. The discipline of history has a stake of its own in the controversy over the full historicization of science.[47]

8

HISTORIANS AND THE
DISCOURSE OF INTELLECTUALS

Essays on the practice of history tend to be very abstract, except when pointing to examples of things historians should not *do. Sustained attention to specific texts, it would seem, is the specialty of the reformer, and even more of the scold. Commentators with a more generous view of the craft are too often content to drop a few great names here and there. I try to reverse this emphasis in this sympathetic commentary on a major tradition within the practice of intellectual history. I try to identify that tradition more precisely than I believe it has been previously identified, and, by articulating what I take to be its methodological presuppositions, seek to promote its more effective practice.*

A number of readers have taken me to be trying to "define" intellectual history in general, and to thereby confine it to the study of the discourse of intellectuals. I thought I had warned sufficiently against this misreading, but I am glad now for the opportunity to make the disclaimer yet more explicit. Many, if not most of the scholarly works of the last fifty years that have been taken as "intellectual history" in the United States have been studies of the discourse of intellectuals. Although this essay aims to encourage such studies, and to explore some possibilities for their enrichment, I see no reason to insist on the exclusive application to them of the label "intellectual history," nor do I wish to doubt the wisdom of scholars who pursue historical inquiries about people less educated, less reflective, and less argumentative than the people we usually call "intellectuals."

Other readers have accused me of taking too generous a view of the tradition, and of attributing to intellectual historians in general a set of methodological insights that are more distinctive than I acknowledge, and that, if widely acted upon, would make intellectual history a considerably more rigorous enterprise than it has been. There is merit to this complaint. I trust that my discussion of my chosen examples is sound, but I have probably exaggerated the extent to which American historians of "ideas" have understood all along that they were studying "discourse." Perhaps the achievements of these historians, moreover, are less impressive than I have implied.

Finally, I wish I had cautioned explicitly against the connotations of passivity and civility that can be carried by the word "discourse." The ideas advanced in discourse are to be understood as ways of coping with whatever leads the speaker to take the action of speaking. That action is not always carried out according to the civilized conventions of the seminar or of the salon. Nor is access to discourse automatic: Social and political contexts obviously set limits on who gets to speak about what, and in whose hearing.

This essay was written for a conference honoring Merle Curti on his eightieth birthday. It was published in the proceedings of the conference, edited by John Higham and Paul Conkin, New Directions in American Intellectual History *(Baltimore, 1979), 42–63.*

MUCH OF THE SCHOLARLY WORK that goes by the name of "intellectual history" consists of efforts to study the discourse of communities of intellectuals. The obviousness of this fact is sometimes concealed by the easy way we have of speaking of our subject as "ideas" or "attitudes," and by our habit of describing these ideas and attitudes with such sweeping adjectives as "Western," "modern," "American," "European," "white," and "nineteenth-century." To be sure, there are works of history comprehensive enough to justify the use of these adjectives, and there are works whose subjects are indeed ideas and attitudes in their autonomy. By "autonomy" here I mean the absence, on the part of the historian, of conscious attention to any discourse in which an idea or an attitude might have functioned. Yet a great many of the books and articles produced by scholars known conventionally as intellectual historians are implicitly or explicitly addressed to the performance of minds in discourse. Moreover, many of these books and articles address the discourse of certain kinds of people whom, for want of a better term, we often call "intellectuals."

Why should these points deserve the explicit formulation and elaboration that this paper seeks to provide? That ideas are articulated in a communicative context of some kind is scarcely news to historians or to anyone else. How this basic insight is commonly possessed and employed by intellectual historians, however, is not quite so clearly and widely understood. The existing literature on aims and methods in the field, compatible as much of it is with what I want to say, focuses on other aspects of the endeavor. A critical explication of the role played by the notion of discourse in the work of intellectual historians may serve to increase the control practitioners have over their metier and thereby to improve its practice. This explication may also serve to help explain to historians in other fields, and to nonhistorians, just what it is that intellectual historians do.

By identifying "discourse" as a basic subject matter of inquiry I intend several implications. Discourse is a social as well as an intellectual activity; it entails interaction between minds, and it revolves around something possessed in common. Participants in any given discourse are bound to share certain values, beliefs, perceptions, and concepts—"ideas," as these potentially distinctive mental phenomena are called for short—but the most concrete and functional elements shared, surely, are *questions*. Even when one grants that the choice of questions on the part of contributors to a discourse is in itself an act of evaluation, and when one grants further that conflicting "answers" offered to these questions will be structured partly by the ethical, aesthetic, and cognitive agreements among the participants, it remains true that questions are at the active heart of the discourse. Questions are the points of contact between minds, where agreements are consolidated and where differences are acknowledged and dealt with; questions are the dynamisms whereby membership in a community of discourse is established, renewed, and sometimes terminated. To focus instead on a belief or value attributable to an individual or to a collectivity of individuals is at once to move back from those authentic, contingent relationships; when historical subjects are said to hold a belief or value, those subjects are endowed with merely abstract, static characteristics (for example, a belief in "progress" or in "republicanism") that may or may not be shared by a virtual infinity of other subjects who may or may not interact with each other. Yet when these same ideas are viewed in their capacity as answers to questions shared with other persons (for example, "What is the national destiny of America?" or

"What kinds of political conduct are virtuous?"), they become contributions to discourse.

They become so in different senses, depending upon the degree of explicitness with which a given question is being addressed. An idea about national destiny, for example, is easily understood to be a contribution to discourse if the context of its assertion is decidedly a discussion about national destiny. Yet a society that so takes for granted its national destiny as to obviate any discussion of it may also possess, in the unarticulated presuppositions of its members, an "answer" to what the historian may treat as a "question" about national destiny. Clear as the distinction may be between questions actually asked and those not asked— between what is talked about and what is not—the infinity of the unsaid includes within it a class of ideas that stand as answers to certain basic questions for particular groups of people and that silently serve, thereby, to limit, direct, and sustain what members of those groups actually say to each other. Presuppositions, then, lie in socially undifferentiated space no more than do explicit questions and answers; presuppositions have a distinctive role within specific systems of communication.

That the history of thought consists of a series of answers to questions was, of course, pointed out eloquently by R. G. Collingwood,[1] and it has been a prominent observation in recent theoretical literature. Yet the point of entry for this literature, as for Collingwood, is the particular historical artifact, usually the *text:* It is in order to discover the intentions behind particular texts, such as Hobbes's *Leviathan,* that historians are understood to scrutinize the realm of discourse in which such texts were designed to speak. The discovery of the meaning of texts is obviously essential, but a distinction exists between, first, the study of discourse as a means of interpreting particular texts and, second, that study as a project of its own. It is one thing to explicate Huxley's response to Bishop Wilberforce and it is quite another to write a history of the Darwinian controversy. My point is not that either of these two enterprises can go forward without the insights derived from the other; rather, we must simply acknowledge that the most rigorous of our recent theoretical literature describes and advocates the first of these and says little about the second.[2]

This fact about our own methodological conversations derives, I think, from the distinctive needs of the branch of intellectual history whose practitioners have written the most compelling and widely quoted methodological treatises in recent years: the history of political philosophy. By "distinctive needs" I refer first to the emphasis historians of political philosophy place on particular artifacts of intellect; indeed, if the history of political philosophy did not focus on texts like Hobbes's we would certainly need to create a discipline that did. A second distinctive need has been the imperative to overcome the residual Whiggery and moralism that there remain a more formidable obstacle to historical scholarship than they do in other fields. This second need has quite clearly been a motive force behind the theoretical literature to which I refer, just as— to cite a more well-known and momentous example of this syndrome— social scientists of the late-nineteenth century produced a substantial body of writing on the nature of "science" while trying to transform the various branches of moral philosophy into sciences. And, just as natural scientists were then—to carry the analogy a step farther—inclined to describe the nature of their own enterprise a bit more precisely and explicitly, so, too, is it now appropriate that intellectual historians articulate more clearly the general outlook that has been taken up and put to such creative and effective use by historians of political philosophy.[3] This articulation must include, above all, the reminder that discourse and the communities formed around it are "central subjects"[4] as authentic as are ideas and the texts in which ideas are embedded.

In the context of this conviction, a number of issues demand attention. Does the notion of discourse restrict itself to minds that were active at the same historical moment, and even to those aware of each other? Do communities of discourse necessarily correspond to national, linguistic, and occupational units? Must such communities consist of social equals? Can discourse be fairly construed to include paintings, statues, rituals, and other nonverbal modes of communication? Are discourse-defining questions presumed to be perennial? To what extent does the designation of communities of discourse as the primary unit of study restrict the attention of historians to ideas that appear to directly "answer" the discourse-defining question, and thereby exclude from inquiry aspects of the designated discourse generated by the engagement of its participants with other questions and other communities of discourse? Does the notion of discourse imply any general theory about the impetus for, and sustaining conditions of, intellectual change, including changes in questions as well as answers? To what extent would the more conscious reliance upon the notion of discourse entail acceptance of the "archaeological" outlook on discourse advanced recently by Michel Foucault?

Let me try to speak to several of these issues by translating into their terms the prominent features of several well-known works of intellectual history, none of which, I trust, is so idiosyncratic as to render it an inappropriate example of what many intellectual historians do. I have in mind three works written about different centuries by students of different national cultures: William J. Bouwsma's *Venice and the Defense of Republican Liberty,* Charles Coulston Gillispie's *Genesis and Geology,* and Perry Miller's *The New England Mind.*[5] None of the authors of these books has made a pointed methodological assertion about "communities of discourse," but I believe this notion fits their work comfortably.

Bouwsma's title refers to the Venetian writers who sought to defend the interests of their republic through the theoretical refinement and articulation of Venice's political tradition in the immediate context of the imperatives of the Counter-Reformation. These writers participated, with spokesmen for Rome and for Florence, in a Catholic discourse about the proper structure of authority in a Christian society. Specifically, the questions at issue were the extent of papal powers vis-à-vis those of secular states, and the foundations of those powers in the nature of things and in the history of the Mediterranean world. If these questions were created for the disputants by their common membership in the geographic, political, economic, and religious continuities of northern Italian life, the grounds for differing answers were laid by the contrasting circumstances of the commercial city, Venice, and the capital, Rome, responsible for the maintenance of the universal Catholic order. The "republican liberty" that had flourished in the trader's world was placed in a new light by the appearance, in the Reformation, of a particularism more radical than that of the Italian republics; hence the questions were sharpened, and the contrasting interests of the opposing Italian parties became more threatening to each of those parties. Bouwsma concludes with Paolo Sarpi, the last—before his republic's decline—Venetian polemicist to create out of the terms of the argument with Rome a compelling theoretical statement of Renaissance republicanism. Sarpi's writings eventually became vehicles for the recollection, on the part of Europe as a whole, of the example of freedom set by the Venetian republic. Since the memory of Venice was indissolubly bound up with a more "modern," particularistic, secular world view, that memory, in turn, was an agent in the political imagination of Europe for several centuries.

The discourse of these northern Italian Catholics of the late-sixteenth century thus emerges from Bouwsma's account as a distinctive historical moment, significant for the functions the discourse itself performed in the larger history of Europe. Bouwsma's ultimate interest throughout is actually in attitudes and values of a general order, not in the exact questions around which the discourse revolved. The methodological point I want to make at the risk of belaboring it, however, is that Bouwsma's means of getting at the salient values and attitudes (for example, "particularism," "historicism,") is to study exactly those now-arcane questions and answers that were on the surface, that carried debate forward, and that drew out of one group of participants a distinctive exemplar of Republicanism.

Gillispie's book is about British geologists from the turn of the nineteenth century to the eve of the Darwinian controversy. These geologists argued over the merits of various theories designed to account for the origins of the earth (for example, catastrophism and uniformitarianism), but their arguments turn out to be demonstrably conditioned by commitments each had developed in his capacity as a Protestant, and, less demonstrably, by commitments developed as a citizen of Britain. There were three discourses, then, that overlapped: While the primary one had to do with technical questions in geology, the contributors to this discourse simultaneously sought—with varying degrees of conscious intentions—to answer questions in natural theology and social philosophy that were being addressed at the same moment by natural theologians and social philosophers. Gillispie is aware that geology was not confined to Britain (although British naturalists were then preponderant in geological research and writing), but he chooses to single out for study the British participants in geological discourse precisely because this enables him to more vividly show the presence of Protestant natural theology and British social philosophy within geology.[6]

Students of American intellectual history need no guide to the most commanding and justly famous work in our own scholarly tradition, Perry Miller's *The New England Mind.* I can allude briefly to its relevance to the concerns of this paper. The first volume of *The New England Mind* gives some attention to the intellectual and religious origins of Puritan ideas, but treats these ideas, for the most part, as a structure, and attributes the structure to a community of interacting minds. Miller's aim was to describe the contents of the minds of the first generation of New England's intellectual leaders; at one point he explicitly characterized these contents as "the premises of all Puritan discourse."[7] And what is the second volume if not the narrative of that discourse during the following two generations? The questions addressed by Miller's subjects run a gamut from explicit theological issues, such as the extent to which one can be "prepared" for salvation, to such implicit issues as the relative goodness of human nature. Throughout, Miller is concerned with how the formulation and attempted resolutions of these questions is conditioned by not only the "premises" outlined in volume one, but also by a variety of contingent experiences, including, among others, the growth of commerce, the transformation by events in England of issues in church polity and in the relations between church and state, the general emergence in Europe of the "new learning," and the development over time of attachments to America as a place. Specialists may complain that Miller's judgments require correction—as they may complain that Bouwsma subsumes the Venetians and their foes too strictly under "medieval" and "modern" world views, or that Gillispie distinguishes too sharply between "scientists" and other educated Englishmen—but complaints of this order need not distract us from recognizing the kind of history Miller has executed. Volume two of *The New England Mind* is held together less by "ideas" than by the seventy-year conversation to which those ideas were contributed; to read this book chapter by chapter is to immerse oneself in a succession of disputes, of discussions, of arguments—here, if anywhere in our professional literature, is the life of the mind depicted as a *life* rather than as a set of discrete units of thought or artifacts of intellect possessed of either common or unique attributes.

It will scarcely have gone unnoticed that the examples I am using address, in each case, a discourse carried on predominantly in verbal form among disputants who were essentially peers, who were cognizant of each other's views, and who shared both a language and what we could loosely call, even in the instance of Bouwsma's northern Italians, a national culture. Moreover, the temporal scope of these works covers two or three generations. The notion of a community of discourse need not be given so restricted a denotation, but I begin with works of this sort because so many studies of intellectual history do, in fact, operate within this perimeter. This pattern in the selection of topics is a result not only of sloth, but of the historian's proverbially tenacious loyalty to the particularity and density of experience more easily grasped within these parameters than beyond them.

This loyalty to what Gilbert Ryle and Clifford Geertz have now led historians to think of as "thickness"[8] has made the work of Arthur O. Lovejoy anomalous, and therefore instructive here as a contrast to the books I have cited. Lovejoy's brilliant *Great Chain of Being* exemplifies "thin" description. Here is a study of a single "idea"—or, more precisely, a mutually reinforcing cluster of three beliefs about the nature of things— over many centuries and within many languages and national cultures. What makes the book "thin" is Lovejoy's purposive disregard of the distinctive contexts in which the idea of the great chain ostensibly appeared and was put to service. Lovejoy does observe that the great chain was an answer to a question that kept getting asked throughout Western history,[9] so one could insist that Lovejoy performs for a single "premise" of all Western discussion of "being" the same sort of analysis Miller's volume one achieves for many premises of Puritanism. This insistence might save—formally—the notion of a community of discourse, but in fact Lovejoy does not study the evolving constitution of the question supposedly involved, only the continuity of the answer. Now, the very idea that a single question can exist in so many times and places I do not find so thoroughly outrageous as do some of Lovejoy's critics, but most of us can surely agree that no question, however general, can escape being constituted by some particulars of the language, the national culture, and the genre of expression in which a given formulation of the question may have existed. Lovejoy would not dissent from this, but the insight has little impact on his work because he frankly eschews the desire to understand ideas as they variously function, a desire that of course lies behind most discourse-conscious scholarship. Lovejoy explicitly directs his ideal historian to "cut into" philosophical argument, for example, in order to isolate the "unit ideas" the historian will then similarly isolate by cutting into art, science, literature, and so forth.[10]

Reference to Lovejoy's aloofness from the discursive thickness of the ideas he studies need not imply that such aloofness is endemic to histories with multigenerational and multilinguistic subjects. In epistemology, for example, or in physics, it is not invariably a mistake to regard members of different societies living in different centuries as participants in a single discussion. To so regard certain aspects of the history of epistemology and physics does not necessarily imply a timeless status for the questions to which these disciplines are addressed, nor even that epistemologists and physicists lack salient involvement in other, more temporally and geographically bound, contexts of discourse. What is implied, rather, is only that questions in epistemology and physics can sometimes be *demonstrated* to be so constant, even as such questions are addressed by persons greatly separated in time and place, that there exists as an appropriate subject a community of discourse having boundaries very different from those within which Bouwsma's Italians or Miller's Massachusetts clergy conversed. For example, one could say that there has been, among a substantial number of British, American, German, and French philosophers since the time of Kant, a considerable agreement on what the problems of epistemology are; it is not necessarily wrong to regard Kant, Josiah Royce, and some of today's philosophers as participants in a continuous discussion.

A number of issues remain; in order to eliminate any inference that the scholarly tradition I am seeking to explicate is moribund or esoteric, I will explore these issues through texts "closer to home": American history imprints of 1975, 1976, and 1977. A convenient example is a book of 1977, Theodore Dwight Bozeman's *Protestants in an Age of Science.*[11] This book, which is much narrower in scope than any to which I have alluded until now, is about Baconian ideas as held by the conservative faction of antebellum American Presbyterian theologians. Now, one can call it a history of "ideas" if one wishes, but in so doing one might not convey the fact that Bozeman's Princetonians are discussed in explicit relation not only to other Presbyterians, but also to their Unitarian and Evangelical enemies. The discourse in which Bozeman's crowd participated also embraced most of the intellectually ambitious Protestant clergy in America and Scotland, but Bozeman's "narrow" book is no less grounded in that discourse than would be a volume that sought to interpret all of it. Strictly speaking, Bozeman's book is not a description of Baconian ideas as they can be found in the writings of these professors; it is rather an explanation of the appeal of these ideas and an analysis of their function in the apologetic endeavor thrust upon Old School Presbyterians by the religious behavior and thought of those of their contemporaries and immediate predecessors about whom these Princetonians greatly cared, and of whom they took careful notice. The book is also an attempt to discover the role that Princeton Baconianism, in turn, played in the larger discourse to which it was a contribution: How, for example, it affected the context in which the Darwinian controversy could take shape among American Protestants during the next generation. Hence *Protestants in an Age of Science* is built on a grid strikingly similar to that on which Bouwsma's undeniably more imposing and important work was constructed.

Bozeman's book, like the others I have cited thus far, focuses on arguments made by people whose chief business it was to argue, and to do so as rationally as they could. It is in relation to studies of this kind that the word "discourse" makes the clearest intuitive sense.[12] Yet the notion can also be an anchor for studies of a very different kind, as is shown by the example of Ronald G. Walters's *The Antislavery Appeal.* The immediate abolitionists who are Walters's subjects bear to the world of antebellum American reform a relation not unlike that borne by Old School Presbyterians to American Protestant theology; both have a position on a set of related questions that are being argued over with other parties. Debates among antebellum American reformers, however, entailed more direct and extensive efforts to change the social behavior of masses of people than did debates among theologians, and the community of reformers did not put nearly so high a value on logical consistency as did the community of theologians. Now, one could still write a book on the arguments of the immediatists, and of the ideas embedded in those arguments, but Walters has instead addressed the immediatist movement on the level of the "structure of perception"[13] that integrated its world and informed the full range of its activities, from the most earnest efforts at rational argument, through the most frank of emotional appeals, to the most direct of political action. Walters explores this structure of perception by documenting certain patterns in the way slaves, slaveholders, and related social conditions were depicted by immediatists in a variety of modes of expression, including diaries, fiction, letters, drawings, speeches, and treatises. Hence *The Antislavery Appeal,* while a study of neither the arguments contributed by the immediatists nor even of the style of thought embodied in those arguments, defines its topic according to a specific referent point in reformist discourse—the immediatist position—and illuminates that topic by showing how a distinctive set of perceptions conduced more directly than others to the assertion, in discourse, of a particular position. One could insist that a book more about "seeing" than about "thinking" is marginal to intellectual history as a discipline, but that would not render the volume's foundation in the notion of discourse any less striking.

By now I trust it is clear that the notion of discourse can apply to communities with varying degrees of commitment to the ideal of rationality, can sustain studies of parts as well as of wholes, and, further, that the notion entails neither an obliviousness toward the ways in which distinctive communities of discourse overlap nor an insensitivity to the fact that a single artifact of intellect may serve as an answer to more than one question. It ought to be clear, moreover, that the notion does not imply any attribution of sufficient causal efficacy to any generically defined component or sustaining condition of a discourse, including values, beliefs, perceptions, social structure, economic function, political position, and psychological state. All these things may or may not be agents in a given discourse, and it is the responsibility of a given historian to persuade us of the validity of whatever causal claims or implications he or she introduces with regard to a given aspect of a given discourse. The point about "discourse" is not a point about causal explanation at all, but about the nature of the reality to which causal claims and implications often apply. In any event, a truism that seems always in need of repetition is that providing causal explanations is only one of the things historians do; it would be impossible to translate without remainder any of the books I have mentioned into the strict terms of a causal explanation.

I trust it is also clear by now that the notion of discourse applies the least ambiguously to studies of men and women of words. The histories I cite are, for the most part, devoted to preachers, scientists, philosophers, theologians, political polemicists, and to a lesser extent, writers of fiction, rather than to painters, sculptors, architects, and performers of religious rituals. The extent to which an etching and an essay can be said to "share a question" is an interesting issue, and one that can no more be resolved by complacent affirmations of the integrity and autonomy of contrasting modes of expression than by the prior conviction that each age has a spirit that manifests itself in all cultural activities.[14] It is rather a matter for empirical study on a case-by-case basis; we have a number of books that convincingly treat certain nonverbal artifacts as contributions to the same discourse to which certain verbal artifacts have been contributed. A number of classics could illustrate this point, but I will instead mention a recent book by John F. Kasson simply because the volume's treatment of the arts is so representative of American scholarship during the past generation, and because the book also exemplifies the study of discourse across the lines of class and power.

Kasson's *Civilizing the Machine*[15] is about those literate Americans between the Revolution and the end of the nineteenth century who remained loyal to "republicanism" as a political culture and who sought to assess the implications of the growth of technology. These Americans participated in a discourse in which questions were less sharply formulated than in that of Bouwsma's Catholics or Bozeman's Princeton theologians, but it was one in which the assertion of technology's benign and "republican" character was undoubtedly a position held in opposition, for example, to such other positions on technology's moral and political meaning as the more skeptical ones taken by working-class leaders, some of whom saw in technology the potential replacement of republicanism with slavery. Kasson does not insist that technology's claims to benignity and republican virtue were *argued,* strictly speaking, by paintings like John Ferguson Weir's *Gun Foundry,* etchings like J. O. Davidson's *Southern Cotton Press by Night,* or the railroad scenes by Currier and Ives; but only the most querulous of Kasson's readers will doubt that the positions he attributes to these artists were indeed advanced and publicly reinforced by them, regardless of what other functions, discursive or otherwise, their art may have performed. To be sure, some of Kasson's subjects did not hear each other's answers to their shared questions as clearly as do the subjects of most studies of political or philosophical discourse. Distinctions between degrees of directness in communication must be maintained, but our access to these distinctions need not be lost when we simply recognize how thoroughly Kasson's book is grounded in the awareness that the attitudes he studies were not invented independently by a succession of mysteriously similar individuals; rather, Kasson's book is informed by the insight that these attitudes were generated, learned, possessed, asserted, criticized, and defended in a historically and socially specific context of public discussion. In that context, certain questions endured and certain answers seem more compelling than others to people who had particular economic relationships with machines. Currier and Ives helped to extend the domain of "Republican technology" within the public culture of the United States, and Mark Twain's *Connecticut Yankee* extended the domain of certain doubts about technology's consistency with republicanism; to regard the industrial landscapes of Currier and Ives and this novel of

Twain's as contributions to a discourse does not, I believe, strain the notion of discourse altogether beyond its descriptive utility.

The extent to which the writer of an essay and the maker of an etching "share a question" is of course only a sharper form of an issue that can legitimately be raised about contrasting verbal modes, or even about particular works within one of these modes, such as the essay. The issue, as it is most often put, is one of *intentions:* Did a given person, through whatever he or she wrote or otherwise created, intend to speak to a given question, and thereby intend to express the particular ideas that we as historians are inclined to attribute to him or her? Near the beginning of this paper I referred to the distinction between the instrumental use of a discourse in order to better understand a given text and the study of discourse itself. The latter enterprise might be said to use texts as instruments in order to better understand discourse. Since the two types of study reinforce each other so vitally, it would be a mistake to get scholastic about their distinctness; yet their differences on "intention" need to be clarified because it is on this single but important matter that methodological essays for one cannot speak effectively on behalf of the other.[16] The difference can be put both negatively and positively.

To state the difference in the negative, when a text (or other artifact of intellect) is used as a means of understanding a discourse, the historian need be concerned neither with the *complete* recovery of all the intentions behind a work, including intentions to speak to a variety of questions which themselves are the foundation for discourses other than the one the historian is addressing, nor with the rigorous determination of the author's hierarchy of priorities; when, by contrast, the point of the inquiry is to establish the intentions behind a text, all the discursive contexts in which the text appears to participate become tools for the interpreting of the text. Joseph Wood Krutch's *The Modern Temper,*[17] for example, is a text that speaks to a number of questions of interest to students of twentieth-century intellectual history. Now, the text may have a particular, definite structure of intentions the recovery of which is a legitimate enterprise, but the explication of this entire structure is not incumbent on a student of the efforts of Krutch and his contemporaries to define the meaning of love, say, or upon historians differentially addressing discourse about the social role of art, about the moral implications of laboratory science, or about the extent to which civilization was making "progress."

What *would* be incumbent on the historian of any one of these discourses—to turn now to the positive way of stating the difference—is above all reference to how Krutch's text functioned in the designated community of discourse, and to whatever freight from Krutch's various "other" involvements was brought into the life of the designated conversation. The same obligations, of course, attend upon the contributions of other participants than Krutch in the designated discourse. Thus the meaning of a text for the historian of discourse consists not exclusively in the intentions of its author, but also in the text's functions, including the answering for readers of questions that the author had not been especially concerned to answer.[18] Just as one enterprise employs the apparent functions of a text as a clue to its intentions, so does the other employ its apparent intentions as a clue to the text's function in discourse.

So conceived, the study of discourse can include inquiries of a number of kinds, as the examples of Bozeman, Walters, and Kasson indicate.[19] Although this breadth in the tradition is exactly what I want to emphasize, it would be a mistake to lose sight of the contrast between this tradition and other sorts of intellectual history. Obviously Lovejoy and his immediate followers have pursued a calling very different from the one I am describing. So, too, have the many historians of philosophy, of the social and natural sciences, and of political thought who have sought to show how thinkers in the past responded, in effect, to questions cast in the terms peculiar to *today's* discourse. These "Whiggish" historians, after all, were the object during the 1960s of much-discussed critiques by Thomas S. Kuhn, George W. Stocking, Jr., and Quentin Skinner, all of whom asked, for one or more of these branches of the history of thought, the development of a historiography congruent with the broad but resolutely "historical" scholarly tradition I have been describing.[20] Less obvious is what to make of the most methodologically articulate and distinctive cluster of scholars within the ranks of American intellectual historians, the "myth and symbol school."

It is possible to project onto some of the better works of this school—especially Henry Nash Smith's *Virgin Land*[21] and John William Ward's *Andrew Jackson: Symbol for an Age*[22]—a vast community of Americans of various stations addressing in several contexts a set of related questions about the meaning of their society. But even these two carefully designed books are more vague about the social constituency of the images they attribute to the collective mind of the United States and are less tightly focused on the particular uses to which such images were put than is Kasson's book, which otherwise resembles the books by Smith and Ward. Perhaps the works of the "myth and symbol school" could be more successfully defended against critics had the notion of community of discourse been more operative in the execution of these works and more explicit in the methodological pronouncements of its authors.[23]

Christopher Lasch's *The New Radicalism in America, 1889–1963*[24] is far indeed from the "myth and symbol school" and from "the American mind," but this provocative, extensively discussed volume can also serve as a counterpoint to the tradition of scholarship I am concerned to explicate. Lasch's successive chapter-biographies of selected twentieth-century intellectuals aim to chart the growth of a collectivity of *individuals* who manifest the general social characteristics (for example, detachment, reliance upon the mind in work and play) that Lasch believes can distinguish "an intellectual" from other individuals. As with the works of Ward and Smith, it is not impossible to project onto Lasch's book a community of discourse. Yet what the reader then might take as Lasch's account of a given thinker's contribution to the ongoing life of that community Lasch himself has consciously and consistently depicted as just one more occasion for the emergence of a single and generic "social type."[25]

This recognition about the nature of Lasch's book can bring us now back to my opening observation that most intellectual historians study the discourse of certain kinds of people whom, for lack of a better term, we call "intellectuals." The introduction of this notorious term into methodological discussions is usually an invitation to swap red herrings with all interested parties, but before trying to eliminate those red herrings let me underline two related disclaimers that until now have remained only implicit: (1) There is no reason in principle the notion of a community of discourse could not inform the study of *any* population that has left a record of having addressed "shared questions," regardless of the nature of the questions and of the educational level and mental capabilities of those who shared the questions; and (2) there is no reason in principle the term "intellectual history" has to be confined to the study of the discourse of "intellectuals."

What then, are we to do with the appellation "intellectual"? Or, to put the issue more sharply, what is it that gives the "discourse *of intellectuals*" a measure of identity sufficient to mark it off as a major variety of intellectual history? Certainly, the standard distinction between "elites" and "ordinary people" has much to do with it. Even if members of the powerless and uneducated classes of Renaissance Venice or Cambridge of the 1890s expressed opinions on the nature of liberty or on the structure of the universe, they shared questions only superficially with Paolo Sarpi and Josiah Royce. The same must be said of a large percentage of the "elite" population. Much of the intellectual activity that goes on within social and political elites belongs to what we now call popular culture or popular ideology. Moreover, someone who belongs to an "elite" for the purposes of some discussions may be "ordinary" for others. In our historiographical tradition, then, the "discourse of intellectuals" is identified chiefly by the extent to which participants draw upon and bring into precise focus the theoretical knowledge, literary and religious traditions, and other cultural resources that historians know to have been accessible to the most well-informed members of a given society at a given historical moment.

The demarcation to which I allude is not to be translated into the terms of the distinction between "articulate" and "inarticulate," for this distinction is often taken to imply either that persons who speak effectively and extensively do so not only on their own behalf, but also on behalf of silent neighbors with varying social characteristics, or that persons who do little to perpetuate or advance the scientific, literary, political, and theological debates of their time are "inarticulate" about all other matters, too. The distinction I wish to make is a more strictly behavioral one, which I hope can be clarified by reference to how differently a group of children may relate to "lego," the popular toy.

When children are given several boxes of lego, some will single out one or two structures to build and play with, while other children, given the same amount of time, will manage to use most of the lego in all of the boxes, and in so doing create definite and well-connected structures. The children who only use a few pieces are not necessarily "inarticulate." They may have simply chosen, for whatever reason, to exploit in an articulate fashion fewer of the resources at hand than have the children who end up using most of the pieces. To make the example stronger, one can confine the contrast to children with essentially the same apparent purpose, to create, say, a vehicle for the transportation of a single imaginary person; this purpose for one child can be achieved by a half-dozen pieces, or even a single piece, while another may require 100.

Why does one child use only a few pieces? Has this child not seen all the pieces in one box, or not noticed the other boxes? Does he or she simply put little value on the building of things, including imaginary vehicles? Does he or she simply not like lego, and prefer other modes of expression? Has another child hidden the other boxes of lego while we adults were not looking? Why do some people apparently interested in supporting a given claim about the authorship of the Bible settle for using one or two of many ideas at hand without taking seriously the potential utility of the other ideas? Do they not understand the relevance of these other ideas? Is their experience too limited to enable them to employ these other ideas? Do they simply not care very much about the issue, and devote their intellectual energies to other interests of which the historian may or may not be aware? Do they think the issue is important but so easily answered as to require no fuss? What role in these differences is played by education, intelligence, class position, cultural thievery, economic function, personal temperament, and so on? Pursuing these issues is an interesting and valuable activity, but the resolution of these issues is not a precondition for making the basic distinction to which I refer. It ought to be sufficient to observe that interaction among people who are using most of the pieces in all of the boxes, and who are able to order them in a variety of ways, is different from interaction among people who use no more than a handful of pieces and who arrange them in few ways.

This observation recognizes that questions of a general kind can indeed be shared by persons with varying resources for the formulation and pursuit of such questions, that communications across educational levels can be authentic, and that "ordinary people" as well as intellectuals think, even formally and systematically, with or without the same analytic tools used by contemporary intellectuals. Yet the observation *also* recognizes that relatively distinctive discourses can develop among people who precisely formulate questions that may be shared with people who remain oblivious to these more specific and often more precise formulations. Participants in these distinctive communities of discourse may come to see as constitutive of these very questions a range of highly particular elements—elements that must be ignored if the historian looks only upon the denominators common to both this specific discourse and the larger, more general one. Certainly, histories can be, have been, and should be written about intellectual experiences common to intellectuals and other sentient beings, but these histories, as well as those confined either to those experiences in which a given class of intellectuals apparently did not share or to those that seem to have been peculiar to intellectuals, can best locate their own subjects and define the relations between those subjects and the subjects of other histories by more deliberate attention to the discursive setting of thought.

This is to suggest that many of the traditional missions of historians, including the asking of exactly what ideas were formulated and possessed by whom, and put to what use, can be reinforced and equipped with more rigor if the notion of discourse is made somewhat more prominent in the methodological consciousness of scholars, and if it is conjoined with the operational definition of intellectuals outlined above. The discourse of intellectuals, then, has in any given case boundaries that are ostensibly empirical, that mark shifting differences in intellectual behavior, and that, by virtue of their very distinctness, encourage historians to inquire more diligently into the relations between these bounded entities and other communities of discourse than, perhaps, historians inquire if they fail to view as distinctive the thought of a society's apparent intellectual leaders. Inquiries into how and why a set of preoccupations moves from one interacting group to another, for example, are more likely to be stimulated when distinctive discourses are recognized.[26]

This sensitivity to the distinctness of communities of discourse may promise an enriched scholarship, but nothing could more resoundingly betray that promise than a literal-minded determination to fix boundaries more exactly and firmly than good sense will allow. Devoutly as one may wish for general rules of method with which rigor may be consummated and the "precise" boundaries of communities discovered, such rules (for example, the imperative to identify shared questions) are more effectively grasped and applied when learned from concrete examples of historical scholarship than when stated in the abstract. Examples such as those that form the elements out of which this essay is built can convey both rules and the sorts of limits imposed on their application by the concrete sources with which a historian works. The boundaries of many communities of discourse are no more or less definite than the boundaries of the historiographical tradition this essay seeks to explicate; just as one could go on, at yet greater length than I have above, trying to clarify the perimeter of this tradition, so could a historian of a given community of discourse risk losing sight of that community's essence by relentlessly seeking to verify in each of its apparent members the existence of a fully uniform pattern of intellectual behavior.

If the promise of a more rigorous exploration of relations between ideas and their various social constituencies is one benefit of a heightened recognition of the discursive context of thought, another benefit is the placing in perspective of an "idealist" vocabulary that, when used uncritically, misrepresents the tradition as actually practiced. The notion of discourse avoids the deleterious effects of the idea-event dichotomy while preserving the recognition of the intellectuality of the subject matter of intellectual history: An idea contributed to a discourse is no less an "event" (and no less trivial or momentous, in itself) than a bullet fired in a war or the invention of a machine. The notion of discourse sidesteps the Cartesianism that afflicts the language of many prefaces, if not of the texts that follow; it recasts the "internal-external" problem in terms that transcend the conceptual prison of "intellectual" versus "social" phenomena; and it recognizes in our subject matter an authenticity that the rhetoric of a dessicated rationalism has too often concealed from both practitioners and critics of intellectual history.

The notion of discourse, as I have tried to indicate throughout, implies the historicity, temporality, dynamism, and contingency in human thinking that have long been seen as the special province of historians and that are helpfully brought into bold relief by this notion at the present moment, when historians are so admirably eager to absorb as much insight as possible from such ahistorical disciplines as anthropology, linguistics, philosophy, and sociology. A hint of how endemically "historical" is this notion can be gleaned from the *Oxford English Dictionary's* entry for discourse, in which static meanings are well submerged beneath those entailing development.[27] A more dramatic and instructive index is the work of Michel Foucault. There, an effort to retain the notion of discourse within a program designed to obliterate the historical way of looking at human knowledge has located Foucault's argument in an undercurrent that constantly threatens to pull him down into historical depths the very reality of which it is his great mission to deny.[28] Nothing nettles him so much as to be mistaken for a writer of intellectual histories, and nothing in his theoretical writing is more obscure and unpersuasive than his efforts to explain why this characterization of his *Order of Things,* for example, is a mistake.[29] Although this is not the place to attempt an adequate exposition of Foucault's prescriptions,[30] attention to some of their features can serve to distinguish this paper's implications from Foucault's and to underline more of the methodological attractions of the notion of discourse.

Foucault charges "archaeology" with the tasks of discovering the "rules" that govern particular "discursive practices," and transcribing the changes from one set of rules to another. What goes on in discourse at any given time, then, is analyzed by Foucault in pointedly synchronic rather than diachronic terms, and what transitions there are—the substitution of one synchronic, rule-bound discourse for another—archaeology does not seek to explain, only to record. Foucault professes no interest in the political and social matrix of discourse, and is so determined to focus on what he regards as the unmediated, empirical surface of discourse—the dispersion of enunciative events—that he altogether eschews reference to "questions." These imply a measure of agency and coherence on the part of participants in discourse that is not implied by the mere existence of objective rules according to which utterances, including those a speaker may subjectively regard as questions, are constructed. Foucault's vision of discourse is in effect dehumanized, in comparison, at least, with the outlook basic to the historiographical tradition I have reviewed. How, then, can anyone seeking to critically extend that tradition learn anything from Foucault, and experience while reading his work an increase in enthusiasm for the notion of discourse?

In his effort to drain effective volition from artifacts of intellect, particularly texts and oeuvre, Foucault attributes to discourse itself a vivid positivity, a truly primal existence in contrast to the almost phantasmic being allowed to books, careers, genres, traditions, and other presences commonly felt to be concretely visible in discourse. To profit from this suspension of such conventional "unities" as books—to treat them, that is, as a mere space in which a population of events are dispersed—one need not accept Foucault's demand that only on the basis of discovered rules for discursive practice can the reality of these unities be reestablished, nor need one accept Foucault's radically antihermeneutic claim that the "population of dispersed events" that makes up discourse is available in its primal state if we but exercise the appropriate effort to apprehend it. This suspension has its attractions: It can subject to more rigorous interrogation the texts, oeuvres, genres, and traditions that appear to be *given;* of them one can ask, with conscious naïveté, "What are they?" What are the networks of which a book is a "node"? Out of what "complex field of discourse" is it constructed? "What specific phenomena" does it "reveal in the field of discourse?"[31] By refusing, for a moment, to answer these questions only in terms of the obvious antecedents of texts (for example, the intention of an author or the influence of an exemplar), the historian can gain critical distance from the presuppositions he or she brings to the study of discourse, and may be more likely to discover connections and gaps between artifacts of intellect that have been overlooked. It is Foucault's rasping, audacious, almost exasperated testimony to the substantiality of the particulars of discourse that most commends his work, and is also the most easily detached from his Olympian faith that these particulars are controlled by discoverable rules immune to human agency.

The heuristic suspension of conventional categories, like other benefits of heightened awareness of discourse, can apply in a general way to almost everything intellectual historians write about. In practice, however, the notion of discourse has a more constant and intimate utility for studies of historical figures who share well-defined questions and who are conscious of their common engagement with such questions—studies of the sort represented by Bouwsma, Gillispie, Miller, and some of the recent American history imprints discussed or cited early in this essay.

Even for such studies, the benefits of the notion of discourse are not to be misconstrued as ready solutions to the methodological dilemmas that practitioners regard as standard. How does one decide, for example, exactly where and how the perspectives of the major theoretical traditions in the human sciences ought to inform the selection, design, and execution of a project in the historical analysis of thought? The role of the notion of discourse is not to answer such questions, but clarify the setting in which they need to be asked.[32]

9

PERRY MILLER AND

PHILOSOPHICAL HISTORY

What we most need to know about Perry Miller, many historians insist, is the extent to which he was correct. No doubt this is the most important question, but it is not one that this essay is able to answer. Fortunately, there are now hundreds if not thousands of monographic articles and books that pursue this question in connection with this or that segment of Miller's work. A historian who has stimulated such extensive discussion, and implanted his or her claims and concepts throughout a field is, however, an appropriate subject for a study of the sort I do attempt here: an inquiry into the intellectual preoccupations and commitments that shape the scholar's work. I treat Miller's work as an artifact in itself and ask, as the literary critics might put the question, "What is going on in the text?"

The answer to this question has not always been obvious. Miller was a most unusual historian, and I think it safe to say that he has caused more genuine puzzlement on the part of graduate students in American history than any other historian whose works are normally required reading prior to one's preliminary examinations. I invoke here the perspective of a graduate student because the essay is written from exactly this perspective. I wrote it in a historiography seminar at Berkeley, while trying to make sense of Miller for myself. I was pleased to find that some other readers of Miller, including some well beyond graduate school, found the piece helpful. Hence it found its way into print.

I would not reprint the essay were I not still convinced of the soundness of the interpretation, as far as it goes, but I want to acknowledge that other analyses of Miller have recently gone further. My essay is now most useful, I believe, if read in conjunction with these more recent studies: James Hoopes, "Art as History: Perry Miller's New England Mind," American Quarterly *XXXIV (1982), 3–25, and Francis T. Butts, "The Myth of Perry Miller,"* American Historical Review *LXXXVII (1982), 665–694.*

This essay was published in History and Theory *VII (1968), 189–202.*

THE ACHIEVEMENT OF Perry Miller (1905–1963) will be understood "only when historians become philosophers and philosophers become historians," Edmund S. Morgan suggests in what is only the strongest of many assertions about the complexity and metaphysical nature of Miller's work.[1] Despite a growing awareness of Miller's historiographical stature, little effort has yet been made to analyze in depth his view of American history. Miller was so "engaged" that the text of his published works reveals much about his mind, providing a sound basis for such an analysis. For this purpose, the most useful segment of his voluminous study of "the meaning of America" is the strikingly personal *Jonathan Edwards* (1949), but the interests and tensions which define it appear throughout his work, including his grandest contribution to historical literature, *The New England Mind* (two volumes, 1939, 1953).[2]

The most fruitful approach to Miller is to understand two conflicts within his own view of the world, two tensions which fascinated him so endlessly that they seem to have controlled his formulation of dozens of problems, large and small. The first is a variant on three traditional dichotomies in Western thought, Subjective-Objective, Spirit-Matter, and Free Will-Determinism; the three are articulated most clearly in Miller's vocabulary as a tension between "the Conscious" and "the Mechanical." In this usage, "the Mechanical" refers to an absolutely material cosmos devoid of a moral dimension, of beauty, of purpose. Man, being part of "process," exercises no control over his fate; he is a creature to whom things happen, however much he may treasure the illusions of selfhood and choice. "The Conscious" *is* beauty, ethics, purpose, freedom, indeed the whole realm of value. Thus, strictly speaking, the inherent moral nihilism of "the Mechanical," if accepted as a description of reality, cancels out "the Conscious": How can its properties exist in a universe governed by the sequence of physical law and subject only to the amoral observation of science? But if one lives by "the Conscious," there arises the danger of a subjectivity so confining that it destroys contact with the finite world. As Miller put it, "the modern problem" is centered upon the "incompatibility . . . of the objective and the subjective, of the mechanical and the conscious."[3]

The second tension exists within the "Conscious" half of the first tension. It, too, is an amalgam of traditional dichotomies: Reason and emotion, order and chaos, science and religion, confidence and fear, to name only the most central, but it is not equivalent to any one of them. Parts of each are subsumed under the words—extraordinarily expressive in the context of Miller's work as a whole—"Understanding" and "Mystery." Miller's most explicit statement of this tension is bound up with his claim that Edwards faced it. Edwards's task was to mediate "between the pure understanding which was reason and Chauncy, and the mystery, which was terror and the spider." Granting that Edwards failed in his task, Miller asks "who has yet succeeded?" and insists that "every sentient being struggles still with the same antinomy, now grown unbearably severe."[4] As consciousness strives to establish value, two polar insights arise: Man's rational powers can discover enough order in the world to make it comprehensible; reality as a whole is so overwhelmingly incomprehensible that man's paltry discoveries seem pretentious. If consciousness sacrifices either of these insights to embrace fully the other, it fails to perform its function. It loses the deep and comprehensive awareness of reality required in any attempt to transcend the self-sufficient material mechanism in which consciousness is embedded. The nature of both these tensions will become clearer in the course of this discussion.

The most instructive introduction to Miller's involvement in the first tension is his use of it in analyzing some of those figures who most intrigued him, especially Jonathan Edwards and Henry David Thoreau. Miller's entire interpretation of Edwards is built around the tension, expressed through Newtonian physics and a variant on Lockeian psychology. The blistering passion Miller exhibits in tracing Edwards's conception of the problem is in itself a clue to the degree of his own involvement, but Miller does not leave us to guess his own mind. Clearly and repeatedly Miller goes beyond the limits of a mere analysis of Edwards to remind his readers of the similarity between Edwards's problems and those of thoughtful men today. Edwards simply confronted them in a more primitive form: "today, the terms forced upon us, albeit more complex, are essentially those that confronted him: a behavioristic psychology and a universe of a-moral forces."[5] Edwards's understanding of the implications of these conditions for the problem of value was so profound that his contemporaries could not grasp it: "only from the perspective of today" can his thinking "be fully appreciated."[6] Edwards's sermons, Miller assures us, "are experimental wrestlings with the two gigantic issues of modern philosophy: of the link between the objective and the subjective; and of semantics itself. . . ."[7]

> Far from being street-corner evangelism, Edwards' sermons are immense and concentrated efforts to get across, in the simplest language, the meaning of the religious life, of the life of consciousness, after physics has reduced nature to a series of irreversible equations, after analysis of the mind has reduced intelligence to sensory conditioning. . . . How can a perception have moral or passionate value if the sequence of causes is implacably fixed without regard to values?[8]

Miller felt less personal identity with Thoreau, but his novel interpretation of the "perverse pilgrimage"[9] of the Concord sage in the light of the same tension feeds the suspicion that Miller's fascination with it was more than a passing interest. Thoreau emerges not only as the highly narcissistic seeker of selfhood with whom students of American letters are familiar, but as an affirmer of "consciousness" (a word which extravagantly dominates Miller's discussion) and a fugitive from "circumstance." His avoidance of women and his delicate circumvention of friendship, and especially his attempt to overcome death, constitute for Miller a singular assertion of "consciousness." Miller finds a phrase from Thoreau that expresses, surely, the same nihilism that the inevitable sequence of law signified for Edwards: "What is man but a mass of thawing clay?"[10] Miller's Thoreau believed that "no self-appreciating consciousness" would concede that "circumstances shape man's purpose."[11] Reflecting on Thoreau, Miller muses: "When man strives to become conscious of himself, standing alone in the universe, without divine support and distrusting any promise of immortality, history remarks that he is promptly overcome with a sense of finitude . . . by the realization that . . . he is only a reed which happens to think."[12]

No scholar got as much out of the contradictions implicit in Puritanism's part-Platonic, part-Peripatetic view of nature and man as did Perry Miller. The Puritans could not wholly adopt the internally based conscience and intuition of Platonism without risking socially destructive individualism, a theologically inadmissible self-sufficiency on the part of

mankind, and the implication that their ideas did not correspond absolutely with objective reality; yet if knowledge came only through the
senses, as in Aristotelian doctrine, "there loomed ahead the threat of
nominalism, of a fearful world controlled by continuous arbitrary
power."[13] "The Conscious" and "the Mechanical" are even more obviously
at work in Miller's analysis of the covenant theology. Only in the Edwards
volume does Miller's language state the tension more clearly than in this
passage from *The New England Mind:*

> Through the maze of dialectic with which the covenant theologians rephrased
> conventional tenets runs one consistent purpose: they were endeavoring to mark off
> an area of human behavior from the general realm of nature, and within it to
> substitute for the rule of necessity a rule of freedom. They were striving to push as
> far into the background as possible the order of things that exists by inevitable
> equilibrium, that is fulfilled by unconscious and airless motions, that is determined
> by inertia and inexorable law, and in its place to set up an order founded upon
> voluntary choice, upon the deliberate assumption of obligation, upon unconstrained
> pacts, upon the sovereign determinations of free wills. They were struggling to
> extricate man from the relentless primordial mechanism, from the chains of instinct
> and fear, to set him upon his own feet, to endow him with a knowledge of utility
> and purpose, with the faculties to implement his knowledge, so that he might
> rationally choose and not be driven from pillar to post by fate or circumstance.[14]

"The Responsibility of Mind in a Civilization of Machines" carries
Miller's interest in the mechanical-conscious antinomy out of the cloistered haunts of intellectual historians into the fustian world of *The American Scholar.* In this essay Miller finds the qualities of consciousness en-
dangered by the most overt manifestations of the specter of mechanical
determinism: the machines which play so central a role in the lives of
twentieth-century men. Confronted with the prospect of "a mechanical
intelligence infinitely more advanced than the computer, a true robot,"
faced with the possibility that "consciousness itself" will be obliterated by
The Bomb, whose eventual explosion human power seems unable to
prevent, Miller's contemporary American has regressed "into the womb of
irresponsibility" and verges upon abdication of the function of mind:
whatever will be will be. "What, then can we say?" asks Miller. "We may
say that without recourse to romantic isolationism we are able to resist,
and will resist, the paralyzing effects upon the intellect of the looming
nihilism of what was formerly the scientific promise of mechanical bliss."
Calling on humanity to accept the benefits of technology but to apply

mind strenuously to the world's problems, Miller concludes that "the responsibility for the human mind to preserve its own integrity amid the terrifying operations of the machine is both an exasperation and an ecstasy."[15]

This basic tension between "the Conscious" and "the Mechanical" illuminates Miller's work in a way more important than is even hinted in any of these examples. It is expressed in his entire conception of cultural process, including his affirmation of the place of mind in history and the ambivalence with which he contemplated the demands the environment made on it. Any history other than intellectual history was for him virtually meaningless; meaningless in the sense that it is written with something other than the consciousness of the community as its primary referent. To deal with the mind was to deal with at least the potentiality for value; to study such topics as "trade routes, currency, property, town government and military tactics"[16] was to reduce oneself to observation of the merely mechanical, of that part of the process of culture the farthest removed from the locus of value.

And the process of culture, for Miller, was primarily the interaction of mind and environment, which correspond to "the Conscious" and "the Mechanical." Miller's preoccupation with the mind-environment relationship is everywhere apparent. *The New England Mind: From Colony to Province* is not a study of merely the intellectual life of New England—Miller scorned such an enterprise as "not worth the effort"—but is offered as "a case history of the accommodation to the American landscape of an imported and highly articulated system of ideas."[17] The distinction is crucial: Many historians, primarily concerned with the thought of an age or society, must confront the mind-environment problem in order to do their job adequately; Miller finds the problem so compelling that he uses it to justify the book's conception and scope.

Miller was by no means uniformly exultant over the contributions of mind nor invariably distressed by the influence of environment. His ambivalence is an index of the depth of his involvement in the tension. Miller sometimes found the environment "pressing" and "terrifying," and as such it seems to represent the vaguely feared power of the material world to control all, while mind represents the efforts of consciousness to have some influence upon its own destiny.[18] On other occasions, however, mind seems to represent a certain sterile rigidity which requires the impact of a more dynamic "matter" to reactivate it. As an example of the first, consider the language of Miller's dissent from Turnerian environmentalism: While Frederick Jackson Turner advanced the "conception of the ruling and compulsive power of the frontier," a theme of Miller's *Errand into the Wilderness* is "the struggle of Protestant culture in America against its weakening hold on the Puritan insight into this law of the mind, namely, that form controls matter. . . ."[19] The impact of the wilderness on mind is ultimately defined by forms—an intervening body of inherited ideas and cultural characteristics. Turner was "the foremost victim" of the fallacy that eventually came to rule American thinking, the fallacy that things rather than forms define reality.[20]

Something quite different is going on when Miller, with obvious fascination, discourses on the reaction of mid-nineteenth-century America to industrial steam:

> Words ring countless descants upon the majestic theme—not to any particular mechanism activated by this marvelous "motive agent," but merely to steam itself— the pure white jet that fecundates America. The imagery frequently becomes, probably unconsciously, sexual, and so betrays how in this mechanistic orgasm modern America was conceived.[21]

The impact of the wilderness on the inherited culture was not so explicitly a "mechanistic orgasm," but Miller is anything but aloof from the material environment in proclaiming that "the Great Awakening was the point at which the wilderness took over the task of defining the objective of the Puritan errand."[22] After having lovingly described the covenant in the first volume of *The New England Mind,* Miller can applaud its eventual demise: "It broke down because it tried, in disregard of experience, in disregard of the frontier and a thriving commerce, to stereotype the image of America, to confine it to the Procrustean bed of a priori conception."[23] The treatment given Increase and Cotton Mather as compared to that given Solomon Stoddard and John Wise in *The New England Mind: From Colony to Province* demonstrates what little regard Miller had for men who tried to isolate themselves from experience. While Miller had a genuinely ambivalent view of matter in general and of environmentally induced change in particular, his ideas were not really contradictory. By asserting the primacy of form Miller was enabled to accept the reality of matter; matter was, of course, inevitable and indispensable, but its threat to "the Conscious" is greatly diminished if consciousness has some control over the channels through which it is apprehended. This allows Miller sometimes actually to applaud as nature breaks through form, as the wilderness smashes ideas which have outlived their usefulness: The new forms are still, above all, *forms*.

Miller tried to make all of this clear by comparing cultural process to the formation of an individual human personality: "the achievement of a personality is not so much the presence of this or that environmental element as the way in which a given personality responds."[24] Physical conditions are important, but "these are not what make the personality we deal with, the nation we must understand. What constitutes the present being is a series of past decisions; in that sense, no act is spontaneous, no decision is imposed."[25] The explanation for America is not to be found "in the conditions of America's existence," Miller adds, but in the existence itself. "A man *is* his decisions, and the great uniqueness of this nation is simply that here the record of conscious decision is more precise, more open and explicit than in most countries."[26] A culture, then, is the product of its entire experience, much of which is a history of environmental stimuli. But as each interaction of mind and environment issues in a new configuration of ideas and emotions, the culture makes an important contribution: Every response of mind to environment owes as much to the disposition of mind prior to the confrontation as to the nature of the impinging environment. And it is this disposition of mind, this ever-changing product of cumulative experience that Miller chiefly seeks to understand and explain; insofar as what men "do" is history, their actions are significant as manifestations of this dually determined state of mind. When Miller says, in his most provocative utterance on the nature of cultural process, that "the mind of man is the basic factor in human history,"[27] he means not that ideas rather than some social or economic factor "cause" historical events, but that human history is what the mind is, and does, and what happens to it.

With attention so tightly focused on it, it is not surprising that mind should yield a tension within itself. In order to maintain the level of awareness required to sustain itself amid the cosmic machine, consciousness can ignore neither the insights of "the Understanding" nor those of "the Mystery." Miller's heroes kept both in their minds at once, never abdicated intelligence but never accepted it as adequate. Miller's villains are the extreme rationalists who, through science, reduce consciousness to a passive observation of matter and motion, and the enthusiasts, who, through terror and blind faith, reduce it to a sea of quivering, undirected emotion:

> The rationalist and the enthusiast alike are in the machine, and sooner or later, when their schemes prove incapable of coping with the multiplying accidents and the torments of existence, when their intoxication wears off and they are left with nothing but the dead, dull frame of exhaustion, then the real terror comes, not the terror of hell and flames, but the emptiness of the soul that has seen nothing worth seeing, has understood nothing worth understanding.[28]

Miller found it convenient to organize his most successful volume, *The New England Mind: The Seventeenth Century,* around a tension between "piety" and "intellect." Puritan piety was a peculiarly intense variant of the Augustinian religious tradition. At its heart was a "sense of overwhelming anguish" which flows from "man's desire to transcend his imperfect self, to open channels for the influx of an energy which pervades the world, but with which he himself is adequately supplied."[29] Piety was most directly expressed in the concept of God as "hidden, unknowable, and unpredictable. He is the ultimate secret, the awful mystery."[30]

> Puritans, as long as they remained Puritanical, could never banish from their minds the consciousness of something mysterious and terrible in life, of something that leaped when least expected, that upset all the regularities of technologia and circumvented the laws of logic, that cut across the rules of justice, of something behind appearances that could not be tamed and brought to heel.[31]

Puritan intellect, in the most inclusive terms, was the fourfold heritage of the Reformation, Renaissance humanism, scholasticism, and the intellectual preoccupations of the seventeenth century, but what defined it most crucially was the drive for an intelligible universe. At the center was the extraordinarily confident logic of Petrus Ramus, which was fundamentally "an assertion that the cultivated mind, unexalted by divine influence, is competent to gather accurate knowledge of things, and to assign particular truths to the proper place in the universal system. . . ."[32] Fascinated by the attempts of the Puritans to reconcile this strain with piety, Miller repeatedly summed up segments of the book with passages like this:

> Within the framework of their thinking, the colonial parsons were responding to the same impulses that were prompting Bacon, Descartes, and Locke. They were seeking to understand, to draw up explicable laws, to form clear and distinct ideas,

to maintain order and logic in the universe. . . . They still had too vivid a sense of the arbitrary Jehovah, of the *Deus Absconditus,* of the God of the whirlwind, ruling the world by irresistible might and wrenching the course of events to suit His pleasure, for them to indulge as yet in such assertions as the more advanced philosophers would hazard. However, even while paying the proper respect to the terror and the fury of God, they could contrive to take many steps in these directions. . . .[33]

Beginning with the Antinomians (who stressed piety at the expense of intellect) and the Arminians (who did the opposite), Miller liked to define representatives and inheritors of the Puritan tradition with reference to this basic tension.[34] But "the Understanding" and "the Mystery" do more for Miller than provide a habit of classification, a mere series of observations that Channing or Emerson or Bushnell represent a deviation from the Puritan synthesis in this way or that. The tension between them is at the heart of his judgments about American history and contemporary culture. Distressed that America had chosen to follow the optimistic, rationalistic line of Benjamin Franklin and William Dean Howells, that it has been generally uncomfortable with paradox and impatient with mystery, Miller assiduously sought out the minority that shared the insights he valued; he effected a kind of scholarly epiphany whenever he found an American who had faced a paradox. Lamenting that the life of the mind in his own time was dominated by John Dewey, Miller exalted Morris R. Cohen for balancing a commitment to intellect with a reminder to "a generation infatuated with practical and social applications that there exist 'physical or cosmic issues' obstinately unamenable to the instrumental theory of value."[35] He applauded Reinhold Niebuhr's attacks on secular liberalism and took every opportunity himself to laugh at those who "expect to cure evil by such natural implementations as education and sanitation."[36] Although he often quoted Niebuhr and Paul Tillich, Miller was basically displeased with twentieth-century theology; he strenuously condemned it for lassitude. If scientists found inspiration for such dazzling exploits, theologians had no excuse for doing so little of merit with the highly promising tradition of Pascal: the monuments of physics "challenge the religious intellect to show whether it has anything like the industry and creativity of the scientific. . . ."[37]

Miller was so eager to identify the "meaning of America" with experiences somehow connected with this darker strain that he arrived at some startling interpretations, some of which later gained wide acceptance, while others are still regarded as merely eccentric. Miller offered his *Jonathan Edwards* as an open demand that the author of the Enfield sermon be more firmly enthroned beside Hawthorne, Melville, and Twain in the American canon of lonely prophets of darkness.[38] His projected three-volume synthesis of the American mind in the early national period was conceived with revivalism as the initial, most basic element in American culture. Miller went to unreasonable extremes in denouncing Tocqueville while exalting the insights of the German-born churchman Philip Schaff (who perceived a deeply religious undercurrent in American life).[39] Miller defied almost every shade of scholarly opinion on the colonization of Virginia with his insistence that commercial and political motivations had only a supporting role: "Religion, in short, was the really energizing propulsion in this settlement, as in others."[40] In one of his most controversial essays, Miller argued that except for a handful of urbane rationalists, the controlling conception that made the Revolutionary War meaningful was the national covenant: Oppression at the hands of Britain was an affliction sent by God, within the terms of the covenant ultimately derived from Abraham, to punish Americans for sinful ways; the means of removing the affliction were first self-abnegation and repentance and then, God being satisfied, military measures whereby American soldiers would become the instruments God would use to remove the affliction. In this view, the rank and file fought primarily because of their fear of "the vengeance God denounced against the wicked"[41]; even in the great age of the American Enlightenment, Miller chose to emphasize not the rational understanding, but the terror.

Miller's conception of the "meaning of America" undoubtedly had many dimensions, but the dominant one involved the relative balance of "the Understanding" and "the Mystery" within a consciousness peculiarly pressed by its material surroundings. Hence the meaning of America is to be found in the terms of an especially compelling confrontation with a tremendous problem: the relationship of the human spirit with "reality." In the beginning the vast environment was relatively free from the influence of man; here there could be an interaction between the purest forms of "nature" and "culture." Not that culture, in this view, is any more apart from natural process than nature (remember: Miller was a naturalist), but insofar as there is any part of reality in which man's participation can be identified, it was here to be found in an uncommonly stark encounter with that part which does not involve human participation. Culture was an identifiable commodity; its content could be neatly exposited and its interplay with circumstances be traced with some confidence. With the growth of civilization in America the clarity of the encounter was lost: The material environment in which culture developed was no longer naked, and culture bore definite marks of American experience. But even before the interaction of mind and environment under the terms of this original formulation ceased to be interesting, before America became like Europe, circumstance and culture combined forces to bring into being another formulation of the problem, this time frighteningly reversed. No longer did the environment seem passive and culture relatively free; rather the mechanization of American life made man's role seem passive and the machine's active. The process of reality in which men are enmeshed had caught up with Americans, who had so long enjoyed the illusion, so fascinating to study, of independence and control. The human spirit now confronted matter not in the relatively simple, clearly identifiable form of wilderness, but in the bewildering configuration of literal mechanisms partially the product of man's own participation. This new formulation was almost as distinctive as was the errand into the wilderness: America was not only in the forefront of mechanization, but the America that faced the machines had within its culture the psychological marks of a radically different kind of experience, an experience in which the assertive selfhood expressed in colonization was allowed by circumstances to develop relatively free of the constraints of a complex European environment.[42] It was an optimistic and confident culture which, unlike the Europe which listened to Marx and Coleridge, innocently affirmed technology and industrialization until it was shockingly enmeshed. As it tried in the twentieth century to assimilate Europe's experience, it searched its own more closely for elements of tradition that would help it develop the deep and comprehensive awareness of reality that must define the spirit in which mind attempts to cope with environment. The greatest hero in the story turned out to be Jonathan Edwards, the genius who saw through the illusions of Arminian America and knew that there would come an apocalyptic time when process would overtake it. The sin of America was its luxuriant acceptance of itself in defiance of mystery and terror. But culture and circumstance being what they were and man being what he is, there was no more escaping sin than escaping process.

The two tensions come together in this rough conception of the meaning of America, but their presence in Miller's thought transcends the particularity of this formulation and all that feeds it: The entire corpus was produced by a mode of intellectual activity which in itself expresses Miller's world view. That mode of intellectual activity is essentially art, but it is an art acutely epistemological and profoundly historical in conception.

Miller was primarily an artist not because he wrote with resonance and verbal richness, but because his organization, architecture, and intricacy of conception reveal an intensely purposive and creative activity; Miller's work is antithetical to that which purports to "let the facts speak for themselves." A close reading of Miller makes all too obvious the truth of a proposition for which J. H. Hexter and David Levin, to cite only its most recent champions, have tried with difficulty to gain wider acceptance: A historian's language is not detachable from the "substance" of his work.[43] Unquestionably, Miller's best work reveals a depth of aesthetic sensibility, achieves a level of artistic merit rare in his generation of historians. To term him an example of "the historian as artist and as scientist" is to vulgarize the mind of a scholar whose work translated that cliché into something substantial and sophisticated.

Miller's art was historical not simply because his interest in a specific historical problem—the development of American culture—influenced his choice of a field, but because "the human predicament is given in time." Therefore, "the field of investigation is not only the perpetual laws of physics and the mind, not only the logical structure" of what interests us, but their extension "through temporal changes." Miller found Edwards "intellectually the most modern man of his age" for discovering that "the heart of the human problem is history."[44] As one for whom "facing finitude" was a cardinal virtue and whose view of reality was markedly temporal, Miller found the study of history especially congenial. C. D. Broad and Gilbert Ryle spoke to some of the same questions, but Miller's less literal—and certainly less useful, if precision is the only criterion— exploration of them is riveted to a study of cultural experience through time.

Miller's art was "epistemological" because informed by definite ideas about the relationship between perception and "historical knowledge." In declaring that "history is what the mind must perceive in a fashion dictated by the mind itself rather than by data and documents"[45] Miller rejected the simple realism that affirms the "objective" truth of what historians "discover." What he proposed instead was not the capricious relativism of "Everyman His Own Historian," in which virtually all interpretations have an equal claim to validity and the forms are arbitrary. He wanted a harder relativism in which the forms are vitally important, in which the knowledge that a historian is the victim of his past perceptions, of his entire personality and world view, impels the scholar to a more rigorous construction of forms to help him perceive historical reality. Miller's description of this sort of relativism parallels his account of mind and environment in cultural process; just as a culture responds to an environment in ways largely determined by the culture—*not* simply by the nature of the environment—so the historian draws from the sources a cognition which owes as much to the entire experience of the perceiving historian as to the document before him. What man sees as "the truth of history" is what his "disposition" determines.[46] In this Miller was not only giving uneasy lip-service to behaviorist psychology, but participating in a recent phase of the development chronicled most effectively in Stephen Toulmin's and June Goodfield's *The Discovery of Time* (1965) and culminating in Thomas S. Kuhn's *The Structure of Scientific Revolutions* (1962): The reluctant but growing recognition that our ideas about even the physical world are profoundly subjective, that our perceptions occur within "paradigms" which can be enlarged only with great difficulty. Miller, who stressed the priority of form over content in defining a liberal art and who, in scholarly disagreements, implicitly charged that others were simply unable to construct forms which would afford the most comprehensive apprehension of reality,[47] would surely be willing to apply to history Toulmin's and Goodfield's summary of how things stand in science:

> For scientific thought has advanced, not by men's stripping veils from Nature and reporting on what they see, but through a continuing effort to construct more consistent, precise and adequate conceptions of an invisible reality. As the Count in *Prospero's Cell* (Lawrence Durrell) insists, this does not mean regarding "the hard and fast structure of the sciences" as providing "nothing more than a set of comparative myths, some with and some without charm": rather it is to recognize that "there is a morphology of forms in which our conceptual apparatus works." The scientific ideas of a given age are much more than a bald portrait of Nature: they reflect men's untiring desire to match their forms of thought against the testimony of things.[48]

Although this "mode of intellectual activity" was Miller's way of dealing with the tensions which beset his world view, it is utterly incorrect to say that in so doing he transcended or "resolved" those tensions. On the contrary, their defiantly unresolved character is their essence, is almost, if I may speculate freely, what made them so engaging to a mind believing, in the words of F. Scott Fitzgerald, that "the test of a first-rate intelligence is the ability to hold two opposed ideas in the mind, at the same time, and still retain the ability to function."[49] If someone had convinced Miller that the tensions he confronted *could* be resolved, or were somehow "non-problems," one suspects that he would have found others even less amenable to resolution: Antinomy in itself seemed to excite his passion. Whether this characteristic was simply derived from an assumption that reality is, from what we can see, ultimately paradoxical, or arose from some emotional need to "look directly into the blinding sun,"[50] I shall not venture to guess.

10

THE VOICE OF INTELLECTUAL HISTORY

IN THE CONVERSATION OF MANKIND:

A NOTE ON RICHARD RORTY

This essay, more than any other in the volume, was written with a distinctive professional group in mind: those historians who identify themselves as specialists in intellectual history. It was published in the Newsletter of the Intellectual History Group, No. 4 (Spring 1982), 23–28. *This accounts for the note's focus on Richard Rorty's vindication of the calling of intellectual history. But the note is also designed to address a larger significance Rorty's work has for historians, even those not especially worried about the position of intellectual history within the historical profession. This larger significance is in Rorty's determination as a philosopher to confront the historicity of ideas, including philosophical and scientific ideas. Historians do not, as a rule, try to make a philosophy out of the insights that serve as presuppositions for their practice, but Rorty comes close to doing exactly this on our behalf. Rorty is a "historian's philosopher"—like Kuhn—in that he articulates and defends in circles beyond the historical profession a basic historicism with which historians are generally quite content.*

    But historians are generally content, also, to coexist more or less peacefully with the familiar, history-eschewing philosophers whom Rorty attacks. It could be argued that historians can be such relentless relativizers and demystifiers because they are implicitly aware that history is not the whole intellectual ball game, that other people—philosophers!—are engaged in the not altogether absurd task of developing standards for deciding what's "good" and "true." In this view, the complaint of historians to the effect that philosophers are "ahistorical" expresses not a demand for the rebuilding of philosophy after the blueprint of intellectual history, but only the more modest wish that philosophers would take fuller account of the historically conditioned character of any and all notions of the good and the true.

Rorty, however, takes the matter more seriously, and in his radicalism presents a challenge not only to philosophers but to anyone accustomed to relying on philosophers for advice. It is for this reason that nonphilosophers—including historians—have an interest in the controversy surrounding Rorty.

I want to mention here several aspects of this controversy as it has unfolded since the note below was written. Many of Rorty's critics have shown themselves eager to absorb much of his historicism, while he has shown himself uncomfortable at the prospect of being absorbed, of having his radicalism neutralized in the interest of a somewhat more historicist, but still rather traditional, discipline of philosophy. For a fascinating effort to domesticate Rorty, or, to be more precise, to keep ready for him a room in the house of philosophy from which he claims to have run away, see the essay-review by Robert Schwartz, Journal of Philosophy LXXX (1983), 51–67, *esp. 62–66. Although Schwartz goes far toward the reform of philosophy along lines that will please historians, he chokes at the crucial moment, wondering whether there will remain any point to "theories of mind, language and knowledge" that have "no transcendental or essentialist status" (65–66). Rorty has brought out a new collection of essays,* Consequences of Pragmatism (Minneapolis, 1982), *in which he insists that a real choice eventually must be made between what he denotes as "scientific" and "literary" self-images, the first being represented by such diverse but traditionally philosophical thinkers as Kripke, Kuhn, and Rawls, and the second represented by an equally diverse trio, Heidegger, Foucault, and Derrida. In a perspicacious essay that addresses both* Consequences of Pragmatism *and* Philosophy and the Mirror ōf Nature, *Bernard Williams makes more effectively than I do below the complaint that Rorty slights both the distinctness and the cultural potential of science: Williams, "Auto-da-Fe,"* New York Review of Books (April 28, 1983), 33–36. *My concern about the political coordinates of Rorty's philosophy has been reinforced by William Connolly, "Mirror of America,"* Raritan III (1983), 124–135. *Finally, it should be observed that in* Consequences of Pragmatism, *Rorty goes further toward acknowledging (see esp. xlii) the element of genuine contention, of struggle, that is masked in* Philosophy and the Mirror of Nature *by his extensive reliance on the notion of "conversation" to describe the process by which culture is constituted and revised.*

ANY GOOD IDEA can be devalued by insensitive imitation or application, so let me insist at once on the innocence of my apparent parody of an idea central to Richard Rorty's *Philosophy and the Mirror of Nature*.[1] The notion of "the conversation of mankind" was developed by Michael Oakeshott with particular reference to poetry,[2] and serves Rorty as a way to indicate the historical contingency and the deliberately discursive character of those parts of "culture" we know as the arts and sciences. It is philosophy's voice in this conversation that Rorty wants to redirect, and it is philosophy's apparent obliviousness to the historicity of culture that Rorty wishes to correct, but his book is not without interest for intellectual historians. If Rorty's reform of his own discipline were to be actually carried out, the voice of philosophy would begin to sound rather like the voice of intellectual history. This change might make for some appealing harmony, and most historians will be delighted at the prospect. Even if Rorty fails to get more than a bit of nervous throat-clearing out of his philosophical colleagues,[3] his book splendidly vindicates the social worth of services that intellectual historians have long sought to provide.

It is in terms of alternative services that Rorty's argument is most profitably considered. The voice of philosophy has been preoccupied, especially since the seventeenth century, with the providing of *epistemological* services. It has tried to clarify the conditions that make knowledge possible, and that explain, in particular, the success of modern science. Rorty calls upon philosophers to face up to how meager are the results of this project. Surely, it is time philosophers found something more productive to talk about. Moreover, they needn't look very far. The learned world very much needs *hermeneutic* services, and philosophers are very well qualified to help provide them.

What does Rorty mean by "hermeneutic" and by "epistemological"? What makes him believe that the conversation of mankind can get on well enough without a prominent place for epistemology on its agenda? Let me try to answer these questions briefly before commenting more directly on the implications of Rorty's work for people who already think of themselves as intellectual historians.

To be "hermeneutic" is, for Rorty, to seek to understand and critically engage diverse practices without reducing them to the terms of a single, universal language or system. Rorty's hermeneutics is more an attitude than a method, and is ideally manifest in "the informed dilettante, the polypragmatic, Socratic intermediary" who can compromise or transcend the disagreements between disciplines and discourses (317). "Hermeneutics sees the relations between various discourses as those of strands in a possible conversation, a conversation which presupposes no disciplinary matrix which unites the speakers, but where the hope of agreement is never lost so long as the conversation lasts" (318). When Rorty looks for positive examples of hermeneutics, he refers to cultural anthropology and intellectual history, two polemically anti-Whiggish disciplines that have traditionally encouraged a generous measure of empathetic identification with a great range of thinking subjects. When Rorty looks for examples of what hermeneutics is not, he focuses on epistemology. Indeed, Rorty's sense of what hermeneutics *is* depends for its cogency on the way he depicts its functional opposite, epistemology. If epistemology presupposes, for example, that discourse proceeds "within a pre-existing set of constraints," a structure of reason "which the philosopher discovers and within which we have a moral duty to remain," hermeneutics consists largely of the repudiation of this presumption. Hermeneutics is a "willingness to view inquiry as muddling through, rather than conforming to canons of rationality—coping with people and things rather than corresponding to reality by discovering essences."[4]

To be "epistemological" is, as some of the foregoing already implies, to carry on the quest for "some permanent neutral framework of all possible inquiry" (211), and to thereby perform the office of the "cultural overseer" who "knows what everybody else is really doing whether *they* know it or not, because he knows about the ultimate context (the Forms, the Mind, Language) within which they are doing it" (318). Central to the epistemological tradition has been the notion of the mind as a mirror; the theory of knowledge has been the enterprise of commenting upon this mirror, and awarding such labels as "cognitive" and "real" to the representations said to be found in the mirror. Rorty sees the history of epistemology as a series of efforts to endow one or another social practice of justification with an exalted status—unique access to the real—that is rendered suspect by a properly historical and sociological understanding of discourse.

Rorty takes particular pains to warn against the misunderstanding that he is proposing hermeneutics as a "successor subject" to epistemology, or that he merely wants to divide up the cultural turf differently, with more room for hermeneutics and less for epistemology. Hermeneutics, Rorty declares, "is an expression of the hope that the cultural space left by the demise of epistemology will not be filled" (315). The various arts and sciences, as they contribute their voices to conversation, simply do not need the kind of schoolmasterly supervision that philosophers, as keepers of the great mirror, have tried to provide. Philosophers ought to accept the discursive character of knowledge, open themselves to the course of conversation, and do everything they can to keep the conversation going. Insofar as we want to understand the entire process by which the conversation proceeds, "cultural anthropology (in a large sense which includes intellectual history) is all we need" (381). We do not need a discipline that believes it can "transcend" the whole conversation and specify just what contributions to that conversation do "mirror" the nature of things.

Any suggestion that we can get along without such a discipline is routinely equated with "relativism," and with an inability to provide defensible standards for condemning Nazis and praising good mothers. How, after all, are we to know which contributions to the conversation of mankind are the most worth listening to unless we have a standard by which to judge them? And of what use is any standard not anchored in something outside the realm of "mere" discourse? And what better way is there to be sure we have such a standard than to assign a bunch of smart people to study the "foundations" of knowledge?

Much of *Philosophy and the Mirror of Nature* is devoted to neutralizing these concerns. Rorty goes about this task with a rigor and sophistication that I cannot here pretend to convey. He is refreshingly forthright at every turn, including the points at which these issues come up in an exceptionally fruitful symposium with Hubert Dreyfus and Charles Taylor in the September 1980 issue of the *Review of Metaphysics*.[5] Rorty is willing to live with the "piecemeal and partial" style of critical evaluation available to someone who has dispensed with "eternal standards" (179). Reference to such putative standards was useful during the scientific revolution and the process of secularization, but the "moral and scientific" heritage of Galileo and of the Enlightenment no longer needs the "mirror of nature" to defend it (333). Threats to this heritage now come not from repressive social practices of justification, but "from the scarcity of food and from the secret police" (389).

More detailed attention to Rorty's arguments about "relativism" would be appropriate for almost any readership except one made up of historians, who are among the last people to fear that the entire enterprise of justification will be undermined by the more widespread recognition of its historicity. This fear on the part of some philosophers is a matter of genuine puzzlement to many historians. A note for the *Newsletter of the Intellectual History Group,* therefore, can simply report that Rorty takes up the good old cause where Thomas S. Kuhn left off. Indeed, Rorty provides one of the most thoughtful and fair-minded discussions of the Kuhnian controversy now in print (see esp. 322–342). Historians interested in the argument between Kuhn and his critics will find Rorty's book of special importance. While essentially sympathetic to Kuhn, Rorty takes Kuhn to task for conceding too much to his orthodox philosophical critics. On the other hand, Rorty's sense of justification as a "social practice" is strikingly free from the preoccupation with social and economic interests that has informed "externalist" social history of science as carried out under the leadership of the Edinburgh School.[6]

If Rorty's consideration of familiar Kuhnian themes is one attraction *Philosophy and the Mirror of Nature* may have for historians, a second claim on our attention is the book's implicit warning against the over-professionalization of intellectual history. Rorty's sense of how important is the calling of hermeneutics to the entire learned world cuts against a recent trend among those of us who think of ourselves as "intellectual historians": the trend toward the consolidation of a subdiscipline of scholars trained as historians, teaching in departments of history, and speaking more and more consciously to one another. The *Newsletter of the Intellectual History Group* is clearly a manifestation of this trend, the advantages of which are obvious enough. Yet this consolidation, however neatly it provides intellectual historians with a niche next to the niches filled by colonial historians, family historians, diplomatic historians, and so on, threatens to isolate intellectual historians in a way more damaging to their mission, perhaps, than comparable isolation might inhibit the successful doing of colonial, family, or diplomatic history. This is not to offer intellectual history as the supervisor of all discourse, as a successor to epistemology, but only to remind us that the discipline of intellectual history established itself professionally by providing to nonhistorians as well as to historians a number of rather ambitious hermeneutic services, and that these services were often performed with distinction by scholars who had not even done Ph.D's in history.[7] The special character of intellectual history's constituency has recently been addressed by Dominick LaCapra in a paragraph I quote here because it expresses concerns to which

Rorty's book is highly relevant: "The intellectual historian should," says LaCapra,

> recognize his or her audience as a tensely divided one made up of both experts and a generally educated public. The intellectual historian is required to come as close as he or she possibly can to an "expert" knowledge of the problems being investigated. But a goal of intellectual history should be the expansion of the "class" of the generally educated and the generation of a better interchange between them and the "experts." This means helping to put the generally educated in a position to raise more informed and critical questions. It also means attempting to prevent expertise from becoming self-enclosed within its own dialect or jargon. In these senses, intellectual history faces complex problems of "translation," and its own concerns bring it into contact with larger social and cultural questions. One such question is how to resist the establishment of common culture on a relatively uncritical level and to further the creation of a more demanding common culture that, within limits, is genuinely open to contestation.[8]

Intellectual historians can also find in Rorty's book a bracing reminder that positivistic social science has not taken over the world. During the past couple of decades intellectual historians have been eager to remain on the best of terms with a historical profession increasingly enthralled with American sociology, political science, and economics; as a result, once-vital lines to the classically humanistic disciplines have fallen almost silent. The professional community that sponsored, energetically discussed, and ambiguously rejected *Time on the Cross* still constitutes much of the setting in which intellectual historians work; how different are the methodological fashions in the atmosphere surrounding Rorty's work! There, people can be found willing to seriously debate the proposition that "the old-time Diltheyans" are indeed "falling forward on their faces as all opposition ceases to the reign of universal hermeneutics."[9] One doesn't have to assent to that charming (to some of us, at least) proposition in order to explore more aggressively the intellectual provinces in which it thrives.

Sympathetic as I am to Rorty, I want to express two reservations about the drift of his work. The first of these concerns science; the second concerns politics.

In his laudable eagerness to demystify scientific practice, and to insure that the conversation of mankind takes place between equals, Rorty ends up slighting science. A passage in his response to some sharp questioning by Charles Taylor reveals this mistake especially vividly. Hasn't science "illuminated the natural universe?" Of course, says Rorty,

> just as the nineteenth century novel illuminated the human universe. But there is no answer to the question, "How did the scientists manage to do it?" any more than there is an answer to the question, "How did the novelists manage to do it?" In particular, I don't think it helps to offer as an answer to the latter question, "Because they found some subject-independent terms."[10]

The comparison of science's success to that of the novel is a fine heuristic device for anti-epistemological purposes, but the novel, however generously we may assess it, remains a smaller cultural contribution than science. What would we make of any historian of the "conversation of the West" (394) since, say, 1500, who claimed that Henry James had done as much to change the terms of that conversation as Newton or Darwin did? Rorty's ungenerous attitude toward science is disturbing because it seems to contradict what is elsewhere a stoical determination on his part to take the history of conversation for what it has been, and to struggle only to change its *future*.

I wish Rorty had said more about what he might take to be the political coordinates of the basic philosophical outlook set forth in *Philosophy and the Mirror of Nature*. There is no doubt that Rorty shares with the classically liberal tradition of Mill and Dewey a primary commitment to free inquiry and free expression, yet one wonders just how interdependent are (1) Rorty's basic philosophical outlook and (2) the defense of (or gradualist reform of) the established democratic societies of the West. If criticism of one's culture can be only "partial and piecemeal" in the absence of "eternal standards," one would presumably want to condemn Argentinian repression, for example, on some basis other than the philosophy of the American Declaration of Independence. The latter philosophy, Rorty would presumably say, was useful for the purposes of an eighteenth-century revolution, but we can now vindicate human rights on grounds other than visions of the essential nature of things. The tradition of political thinking with which Rorty appears to be identified has sometimes been criticized for trusting too much in "pluralism." One wonders how Rorty would respond to that criticism. To put the matter more generally: If one believes what Rorty says in *Philosophy and the Mirror of Nature,* how ought one to do political philosophy?

Although I have stressed the continuity between what intellectual historians do and what Rorty wants philosophers to do, it would be a mistake to expect the two voices to become one. Intellectual historians are bound to go beyond the role of the translator and "informed dilettante"; they will retain a determination to formulate and defend specific claims about particular aspects of the history of thought. Even if philosophers give up on the task of telling people how to "get things right," intellectual historians are likely to continue to try to get "right" their own inquiries without falling into the epistemological arrogance against which Rorty so wisely warns philosophers. That is to say intellectual history will remain a more empirical enterprise than will philosophy, even of the sort Rorty wishes to encourage. Just how vital this empirical enterprise is to the successful performance of hermeneutic services is indicated by *Philosophy and the Mirror of Nature* itself, which seeks to "get right" the history of Western philosophy in order that we might transcend it. Thus the book speaks alternately and comfortably in both voices: that of the scholar and that of the dilettante, the latter "informed," in Rorty's important modifier, by the former.

It would be a mistake also for intellectual historians to regard *Philosophy and the Mirror of Nature* as a license for complacency. This book does manifest real respect for intellectual history, even to the point of trusting that intellectual history can help the voice of philosophy figure out what to say. Yet Rorty offers no assessment of intellectual history as actually practiced. It is for the rest of us to reflect on how close recent work comes to filling the ambitious, demanding, and culturally strategic role Rorty assumes intellectual history can play in the conversation of mankind.

11

AMERICAN INTELLECTUAL HISTORY:

ISSUES FOR THE 1980s

This piece was commissioned for a collection of state-of-the-art essays addressed to the various subdisciplines of American history. In it I have tried to identify and justify two agendas for American intellectual history. One of these agendas is America-centered, and consists of problems peculiar to American history, while the second proceeds from the recognition that America is a province of a larger, North Atlantic civilization that encompasses the national cultures of European countries as well as that of the United States. The point of reasserting the truisms embodied in these two "agendas" is to overcome a historiographically debilitating reticence about things "American." I hope it is not an error to observe that historians, reacting against the celebration of American uniqueness carried out in what we patronize as " '50s scholarship," have become a bit shy when it comes to generalizing about American culture and about the role of that culture in world history. Here, I have tried to indicate how we might move toward making such generalizations again, without getting tripped-up by the uncritical nationalism that we are now so quick to discern in the pages of the American intellectual historians of a generation ago.

I have also tried, in this essay, to caution my colleagues against the temptations of "linguistic imperialism." More than one reader has informed me with a smile that the temptations I warned against have yet to be even felt by most American historians. Be that as it may, I want here to call attention to two very helpful treatments of the "linguistic turn" that have appeared since this essay of mine was written: Martin Jay, "Should Intellectual History Take a Linguistic

Turn? Reflections on the Habermas-Gadamer Debate," in Dominick LaCapra and Steven L. Kaplan, eds. Modern European Intellectual History: Reappraisals & New Perspectives *(Ithaca, 1982), 86–110, esp. 106–110; and Keith Michael Baker, "On the Problem of the Ideological Origins of the French Revolution," in LaCapra and Kaplan, as cited above, 197–219, esp. 197–203.*

This essay was published in Stanley I. Kutler and Stanley N. Katz, eds., The Promise of American History: Progress and Prospects *(Baltimore, 1982), 306–317.*

THE STUDY OF American intellectual history now confronts a series of opportunities and dilemmas that are too often obscured by the tendency of historiographical discussion to dwell on such ephemeral issues as this field's relative status in the profession, the morale of its practitioners, and the exact location of its boundaries with other fields. Basic to all three of these distractions is a lamentable preoccupation with professional rather than intellectual challenges. Challenges of these two kinds are of course connected, but even challenges defined primarily by the dynamics of the profession are most appropriately met by directly addressing intellectual challenges, instead of the other way around. American intellectual history should be approached not as a distinctive population of practitioners whose interests are at stake but as an intellectual expanse occupied periodically by scholars operating out of many networks and possessed of a variety of skills—an expanse that is the property of no one, even of scholars who spend enough of their time in it to become known as "intellectual historians." We would do well to see this expanse as a *commons* instead of an estate. The opportunities and dilemmas found there are best recognized in the context of what has been taking place on this commons in recent years.

The study of American intellectual history is surely one of the most diverse, eclectic, and loosely organized of the subdisciplines of American history that retain a single name, and that form the basis for undergraduate courses and for major headings in indexes of dissertations and of scholarly monographs. This has always been so, but what counts as "American intellectual history" is now a more open question than ever before. Teaching and scholarship were once sustained in part by the notion that there exists a distinctive American intellectual tradition:

Courses could be organized around this tradition, and monographs could be written on episodes in its growth and transformation. Whatever else this tradition might encompass, it was known to include the thought of the Puritans, Edwards, Franklin, the Founding Fathers, the Transcendentalists, and the Pragmatists. With the waning of belief in the reality of a distinctive national tradition, at least one with this old cast of characters, the field of American intellectual history lost its hold on what was once thought to be a challenging and durable set of specific problems. The result can be seen in both teaching and scholarship.

A given syllabus may be organized around popular culture or the history of "intellectuals," around uniquely American preoccupations and cultural products or American participation in intellectual movements common to the extended culture of modern Europe, around "social thought" or literary culture, around political ideologies or religious-philosophical world views, to list only the most obvious of the choices on which the teaching of this field is currently based. Although one can be reasonably certain that a course in diplomatic history will address Woodrow Wilson's decision to enter World War I, or that a course in economic history will take up the Panic of 1819, similar predictions are risky for intellectual history, especially with reference to the period since the Civil War. The people and problems studied by Morton White in 1949 and Henry May in 1959 are no longer assumed to be basic. The textbooks of Ralph Henry Gabriel, Merle Curti, and Stow Persons have exercised little influence during the past two decades. A once-standard anthology edited by Perry Miller has been out of print for years.[1] Nowadays, Bruce Barton and Benjamin Spock are as likely to be assigned as are Thorstein Veblen and Reinhold Niebuhr, and often for good reasons.

Scholarly works manifest this same diversity. While the field's grasp on a set of specific problems embedded in a single national tradition has loosened, "intellectual history" has turned up in many places. "We no longer need intellectual history" as a specialty, one leading historian has proposed with reference to European as well as American studies, "because we have all become intellectual historians."[2] There are studies of aspects of feminism, antislavery, and education, for example, that deal primarily and self-consciously with ideas, and are easily received as contributions to intellectual history. One can argue that American intellectual history is not really a "field" at all, but merely the extension into the field of American history of a particular way of doing history.

Yet references to American intellectual history as a field have persisted even while more and more historians have become comfortable with the study of ideas. These references now refer more decisively than ever to a methodologically defined entity. Among historians of the United States, at least, intellectual history has come during the last ten or fifteen years to be more, not less, distinct from its sibling subdisciplines. Commentaries on American intellectual history have always addressed its "aims and methods," but not since the days when Perry Miller and Henry Nash Smith were considered innovative has this field been so consistently understood to be a *kind* of history rather than a set of problems to which a given mode of analysis has a natural relation.

This understanding has sharpened primarily with reference to three basic commitments long associated with intellectual history, but cast into more bold relief during the last ten or fifteen years while subject to some skepticism from the profession at large. To specify these commitments is not to define the "essential nature" of intellectual history, if there is such a thing. As K. M. Minogue has recently observed, "intellectual history . . . is, of almost all academic activities, one of the most resistant to reduction to form."[3] The three commitments to which I have alluded simply indicate the interests and sensitivities for which the study of American intellectual history has recently been a vehicle.

One commitment is to *thinking* itself, a human activity that demands historical study no less than migrating, fighting, building, multiplying, praying, farming, and a host of other activities that make up the events historians study. This proposition might seem so banal as to be beyond dissent, but there remain some historians who regard mental activity as important only when it can be shown to be a cause or a consequence of "real" events "outside the mind." Although Bernard Bailyn is too sophisticated for a formulation as bald as that, his 1981 presidential address to the American Historical Association betrays this bias: Bailyn contrasts the "interior" worlds of "attitudes, beliefs, fears, and aspirations" to "the exterior world of palpable historical events," and insists that "in the end the question historians must answer is the relation" of the former to the latter.[4] Historians who depict acts of mind as "events," too, may have only a semantic quarrel with Bailyn, but a more substantial issue in priorities divides Bailyn from those who would focus on these events, rather than treat them as considerations relevant to the order of "palpable" events.

The commitment to the historical significance of thinking has been strongly affirmed, however, by another recent president of the American Historical Association, William J. Bouwsma. What we need, asserts Bouwsma, is more "studies in the construction of meaning." Such studies are not the possession only of scholars who have called themselves intellectual historians, but such scholars have made their "greatest impact on historiography" when addressing "the history of meanings." Although Bouwsma toys with the possibility that this "history of meanings" could take the place of an "intellectual history" he believes has been too cerebral in its sense of how meanings are created, he vindicates interests and sensitivities with which the study of intellectual history has been persistently identified. Central to his prescriptions is "the concept of man as an animal who must create or discern meaning in everything he does"; historical scholarship would do well to focus less on "what happens to people," he insists, and more on "what human beings have made out of that experience."[5] This was exactly the advice of Perry Miller, who did more than any other single scholar to indicate to Americanists the possibilities of intellectual history as a distinctive enterprise.[6]

The sense-making efforts that most engaged Miller's attention were made by what we have come to call "intellectual elites." This belief in the historical significance of thinking done by people who were reasonably good at it, who specialized in it, or were at least expected by groups within their society to take the lead in doing it, is the second of the commitments for which the study of American intellectual history has been a vehicle. Indeed, the scholars who label their own work as "intellectual history" are more often than not devoted to the study of the discourse of these out-and-out "thinkers." Studies of this kind have sometimes been oblivious to what may have been going on in the minds of "ordinary" people, or have assumed uncritically that much of the population shared, at least in rudimentary form, the ideas articulated by society's leading intellectuals. Recent scholarship has been less casual regarding the relation of elites to the populations surrounding them. Still, some historians are convinced that whatever we need to know about the American past, we are not going to learn it by studying the likes of Jonathan Edwards, Josiah Royce, and F. Scott Fitzgerald. One might imagine that individuals who actually made *arguments* about the issues of their day, or who expressed through art a distinctive sensitivity to the dimensions of these issues, would be appropriate candidates for historical study, yet it is exactly here that skepticism about the orientation of American intellectual history has become the most strident and moralistic. Laurence Veysey has implied that scholars involved in the study of intellectual elites may have reason to suffer "guilt" for their pursuit of "the most arcane thought processes of exceptional individuals."[7]

If virtue attends upon the study of ideas held in common by large populations, the third in this list of commitments ought to carry with it the guarantee of a clean conscience. This third item is the operating assumption that social action necessarily takes place within a framework of meanings that serve to enable and to restrict what people do. The behavior of statesmen and strikers, pioneers and whaling men, bureaucrats and poets is to be understood at least partly in terms of ideas common to publics of which they were members. The meanings men and women associate with their actions "form the very structure" of their "social world," Gordon Wood reminded readers of *New Directions in American Intellectual History,* although he granted that the insight is hardly "new." Since ideas define and help to create social life, adds Wood, "it makes no sense to treat ideas mechanically as detached 'causes' or 'effects' of social events and behavior."[8] This concern with the enabling and delimiting functions of structures of meaning has been advanced with particular reference to political languages by Quentin Skinner and J. G. A. Pocock, two methodologists of intellectual history quoted extensively during the last decade by Americanists.[9] This third commitment, like the others, is subject to some skepticism. It violates a distinction that some historians continue to find indispensable: "Social realities" are one thing, and the presumably epiphenomenal worlds of thought are another.[10]

If these three intellectual commitments now endow the professional study of American intellectual history with what shape it has, it does not follow that everyone involved in that study has invested equally in each of the three, nor that given practitioners are more interested in these commitments than they are in the particular topics on which they work. It would be a mistake, also, to infer from the field's lack of programmatic focus that the quality of monographic work done on the commons is inferior to that being done in other fields. One could argue that since so many scholars who come to the commons do so well, there is little point in assessing the state of the arts practiced there, and even less in prescribing agendas for future work. Yet as the term "commons" implies, there are issues of common interest to scholars who work there. To bring these issues into focus and to make suggestions about their resolution might remind us that the commons should not be parceled out into small, private lots. Yet this privatization of the commons is now a real danger: Some scholars have become so complacent and autonomous in their work that what was once the most synthetic of American history's subdisciplines threatens to become the least.

One cluster of issues has to do with "America." If there really is such a thing, it would be a shame to miss it. Yet the notion of America has become a matter of some controversy. Many generalizations made about it in the past are now felt to apply only to distinctive groups within American society. The revolt against holism in American studies is only one source of the controversy. There is also the spreading recognition that so very, very much of the intellectual life of the United States—especially of its learned elites—is defined by questions and traditions that transcend any national culture. Historiographical brows have sometimes furrowed concerning the "relation of American to European thought," an uninspired phrase that stops short of acknowledging that the intellectual history of the United States is in many crucial respects a province of the intellectual history of Europe, and is, as such, comparable to the intellectual histories of Great Britain, Germany, France, and other distinctive nations within what Richard Rorty calls "the conversation of the west."[11] The question of "America," then, has antithetical local and cosmopolitan dimensions: Particularism within and universalism without have drawn upon the intellectual energies of Americans, and recognition of this fact has made the concept of "America" less central, analytically, than it once was.

The "locals" do not pose quite so striking a challenge to this concept as do the "cosmopolitans." Americanists generally do not doubt that groups of Americans defined regionally, ethnically, and religiously belong in American history. The efforts of southerners, Presbyterians, and blacks to think out and act upon the implications of their group identity in relation to American nationality provide the basis for standard scholarly fare among historians of the United States. The "cosmopolitans" are more likely to get out of American history altogether, and to become figures only in the specialized, international histories of biology, sociology, or philosophy. Perhaps this is as it should be, but if it will not do to assume that everything written in America expresses some mystical American spirit, neither will it do to assume that Americans participating in international discourse do so on terms that can be fully understood without assessing their simultaneous involvement in their national community.[12]

The problem of the "cosmopolitans" has sometimes been dealt with through a distinction between "American thought" and "thought in America." This distinction has most often been invoked with reference to philosophy, theology, and the natural sciences, where the nationality of ideas has been harder to specify and often irrelevant to understanding the ideas and their function in the lives of those who hold them.[13] It is one thing, according to this distinction, to talk about ideas and discursive practices that are peculiarly American, and another to talk about ideas and discursive practices that engage people who happen to be Americans; it is one thing to address an American intellectual tradition and another to address intellectual traditions present in America. This distinction cuts differently from period to period as well as from tradition to tradition. After American intellectuals came into comfortable leadership of the international circles of scholarship and science in the twentieth century, especially after World War One, they brought to their participation in those circles less of the cultural nationalist baggage carried by nineteenth-century predecessors preoccupied with their status as Americans in an essentially European world. The intellectual life of the colonial period, too, differs from the America-conscious epoch that stretches from Thomas Jefferson's Declaration of Independence to the late novels of Henry James, but colonialists have long been distinguished by the sophistication with which they treat the thinking of their European-American subjects.

Historians have had good reason to treat this distinction very gingerly. Many of the creative activities of American intellectuals have consisted of efforts to participate in the "conversation of the west" while at the same time acting upon or seeking to clarify the imperatives of American nationality.[14] Yet the distinction between "American thought" and "thought in America," if not taken too literally, offers an appropriately flexible orientation toward nonnationalistic American participation in international discourse. It invites, at the same time, a renewed, critical discussion of the problem of a unique, American intellectual tradition. This dual promise is best expressed in terms of two agendas that might well be posted on the commons, near enough to one another that scholars would be encouraged to keep both in mind.

One agenda would aim straight at the problem of "America," directing attention to whatever myths, languages, and arguments can be shown to serve at least some Americans *as Americans*. It would take as its most obvious datum the activities of public moralists: those who have taken it upon themselves to speak to, or on behalf of, what they have understood to be *the* American community. Prominent among these "public moralists" have been political controversialists, including politicians and office holders like James Madison and Abraham Lincoln as well as polemicists and commentators like Thomas Paine and Walter Lippmann. The role of public moralist has also been filled, of course, by clergymen, capitalists, novelists, jurists, social scientists, artists, labor leaders, and literary critics, but they, too, have made clear, in the process of performing this role, that their pronouncements on a host of cosmic and social issues were intended to enlighten a distinctly American public. This first agenda, then, would seek to develop a richer and more comprehensive account than we now have of the intellectual structure of American public life at given times, including the political languages within which people have formulated issues in that public life and have argued about its nature and destiny. We might well call it our Tocquevillian agenda.

As the adjective "Tocquevillian" implies, we already have an enormous professional literature addressed, more or less, to this first agenda. No doubt scholars now treat the singularity of American culture less casually than those who gave so bad a name to studies of the "American mind," but it is a purpose of the Tocquevillian agenda to harvest critically some of the results of this older scholarship, and to reformulate and pursue its concern with a distinctive, American intellectual tradition. This purpose might be defeated if use of the term "American" were restricted, in a fit of fastidiousness, to aspects of American life that involved every inhabitant. Just because some Americans resisted, or were excluded from, or never gained access to the kind of "selfhood" analyzed by Sacvan Bercovitch does not mean that Bercovitch is mistaken to call that selfhood "American."[15] Some Americans were "more American" than others in a specific and noninvidious sense: They were more extensively involved in, and dependent upon, a public culture created by men and women who were highly conscious of being Americans. We still have much to discover about how this culture was created, and about whose interests were advanced and hurt in the process of its creation.

If the first agenda would build upon the insight that there does exist an American national culture, the intellectual structure and demographic

extent of which are matters for continuing inquiry, the second agenda
would build upon the insight that America is, for some purposes, part of
Europe. This second agenda would consist of major problems in the
intellectual history of the Europe-centered West, and would presuppose
that these problems transcend as well as draw upon the national histories
of each of the major Western nations. These problems need not be expressed only in terms of "isms," but "modernism" is an especially useful
example because it denotes a specifically Western phenomenon that is
obviously a vital presence in the United States, yet is scarcely seen as a
problem in American intellectual history. To be sure, we have studies of
"modernist" endeavors on the part of some Americans in the arts and in
literature, but these studies tend to be designed, executed, and read with
reference only to the history of particular arts, and of modernism as such.
By contrast, the problem of modernism is prominent on the agendas of
students of the intellectual history of other Western nations.

The intellectual reality of America's involvement in Western thought
has been obscured by a professional convention that contrasts the field of
American intellectual history to the intellectual history of Europe, rather
than to that of Great Britain, of France, or of Germany. This convention
magnifies, universalizes, and renders more remote from America the intellectual history of the West that America actually shares with the various
national cultures of Europe, whose students seem consistently able to
maintain a more comfortable relationship with that larger history. Improvement will not come through patriotic and extravagant claims for
America's impact on the intellectual history of the West; what is needed is
simply a more widespread recognition that Americans sometimes *make
and are made by* that history. An agenda designed to advance this recognition is not so easy to represent with any scholar's name, for none whose
work can be seen in its terms have the stature of Tocqueville. In the
absence of an exemplary student, we might well think of this second
agenda as "Jamesian" in honor of both Henry and William James, two of
this agenda's most exemplary *subjects*.

As the adjective "Jamesian" implies, aspects of American intellectual
life relevant to this second agenda have not been altogether ignored. Yet
most of the attention, as invocation of the James brothers might also
suggest, has gone to American thinkers who won a large popular following within America while helping to make the intellectual history of the
West. This is as it should be, but the second agenda can also encourage

attention to thinkers and groups of thinkers less popular than the James brothers, less striking in their mark on modern history, and less decisively American in nationality. One might consider three movements of the middle decades of the twentieth century: logical positivism, the new criticism, and structural-functionalism. Each of these belongs to the history of a specialized discipline, but this fact need not result in their removal altogether from American history; each of them flourished, after all, more extensively in the United States than anywhere else. Any portrait of the intellectual life of educated Americans in, say, the year 1950, would be quite inadequate without attention to these three movements, just as studies of any of the three would be curiously restricted in scope if they ignored the national culture which turned out to be its most sustaining habitat.

Neither the Jamesian nor the Tocquevillian agenda, nor both together could bring the entirety of American intellectual life at any given historical moment into their scope, and one can trust that the diversity of the field of American intellectual history can survive any and all efforts at agenda-making. The point of this particular exercise is simply to call attention to important tasks that are not likely to be carried out at all unless done in the name of American intellectual history, and that could easily be pushed to the margins of the commons because of uncertainties attending now on the notion of "America."

If these uncertainties constitute one set of issues deserving our attention, a second set of such issues revolves around the notion of "language." "My language is the sum total of myself," observed one of the American thinkers most influential in the entire learned world of the West, Charles S. Peirce, in 1868. This aphorism has recently become a favorite epigraph for scholars in many disciplines seeking to come to grips with a transformation in philosophy of language described by Ian Hacking as "the switch from the primacy of private thought to that of public discourse." In the "Cartesian epoch," explains Hacking, "language had been a wonderful system of signs for conveying thoughts from one mind to another, but language was always secondary to ideas in the mind." Finally, in modern times, there "came at last the strange reversal; language became a necessarily public institution within which human selves are formed and by which people constitute the world they live in."[16] Historians have often taken for granted that "ideas" and "meanings" are the common coin of discourse carried out in the public realm of language.[17]

Yet the term "ideas" has long-standing connotations of interiority; ideas are felt to be things "inside people's heads." The term "ideas" is not likely to fall out of use, but the term "language" is proving increasingly useful. Not only does it indicate more accurately the strata of human experience and striving in which the study of intellectual history is generally carried out; it promotes greater rigor in the design and execution of scholarly projects. When historians refer to the conviction that frameworks of meaning serve to enable and restrict social action, they increasingly do so in linguistic terms.

The current popularization of the insight that human society is ultimately constituted by language thus presents professional as well as intellectual opportunities. Why not translate as much political and social history as possible into the terms of language (and hence "intellectual history"), thereby transforming the commons into the seat of an empire of language extending as far as possible throughout the profession? Sensitivity to the imperial possibilities presented by twentieth-century views of language has been shown more by Europeanists than by Americanists. Although Michel Foucault prefers to call himself an "archaeologist" rather than "intellectual historian," many historians have had no trouble finding themselves in his program, nor noticing that program's omniverous absorption of the human past into a language-centered study. A recent manifesto by another Europeanist is worth quoting because it catches the intellectual opportunities presented by a more linguistically conscious history, and thereby clarifies the foundations for the potential imperial role of such history. Did the "masses" make the French Revolution, asks Keith Michael Baker?

> On the contrary, the power of their actions depended upon a set of symbolic representations and cultural meanings that constituted the significance of their behavior and gave it explosive force. [The masses] cannot be invoked as a political *deus ex machina* without considering further the structure of discourse defining the political arena in which they intervened.

Baker goes on to speculate about the possibility of "a multiplicity of overlapping and competing languages from which princes and parlementaries, reforming ministers and grain rioters, philosophers and jansenists, scientists and quacks (and many others) could each draw a voice," and to suggest that "the search for the ideological origins of the French Revolution will require us to understand how, within this multiplicity of discourses, a new political language was generated that cast many different kinds of behavior into a new symbolic order."[18]

Baker thus distances himself from the history-is-made-by-sweaty-armpits school, but his alternative need not become a new reductionism, according to which the gutsy masses are translated without remainder into the genteel terms of what Foucault would call a "discursive practice." The point is not to doubt Baker's ability to resist the temptation to linguistic imperialism, but to indicate how real it could become to scholars who grasp the intellectual potential of the study of the history of languages.

Perhaps we shall soon witness a linguistic imperialism comparable to other imperialisms of the recent academic past: the sociological imperialism that once proclaimed "social forces" to be more "real" than ideas, the logical imperialism that once declared meaningless all utterances not subject to the tests for truth and falsity ostensibly employed by physicists, and the quantitative imperialism that once envisioned reservations for aborigines who had not taken up multiple regression analysis. Among the potential volunteers for these new International Brigades, with battalions no doubt named for Saussure and Peirce, are scholars who think of themselves as "intellectual historians." These scholars have vivid memories of raids on the commons made by cadres from these older empires. An exasperated Pocock, for example, speaks for many when he growls about the "practice of referring to the extra-intellectual or extra-linguistic as 'reality,' and to the intellectual or linguistic equipment, at least by implication, as non-reality"; Pocock finds this practice "so rooted and widespread" that only students of ideas and language are faced with "constant reductionist pressure to abolish" their inquiry "and restate its findings in other men's terms."[19] How easy to understand the temptation to turn the tables when the opportunity is now presented by the changing fashions of the learned world! Yet as the captains and kings of the declining empires depart in keeping with the prophecy of Kipling, the would-be soldiers and administrators of the new empire of language would do well to inspect their own motives closely, and to be sure that intellectual promise rather than professional opportunism determines what is done to the commons and surrounding lands that might, conceivably, be annexed.

Whatever the destiny of the new empire of language now gaining ground in departments of philosophy, anthropology, and comparative literature, the study of American intellectual history will best prosper if it remains a commons, resistant in true "Republican" fashion to the ambitions of private developers and imperialists.

NOTES

1. WILLIAM JAMES AND THE CULTURE OF INQUIRY

1. *The Works of William James* (Cambridge, Mass., 1975–) are under the general editorship of Frederick H. Burckhardt; Fredson Bowers is textual editor and Ignas K. Skrupskelis is associate editor. The volumes of the *Works* now in print, and the abbreviations used in the present essay, are as follows: *Pragmatism* (1975, introduction by H. S. Thayer) P; *The Meaning of Truth* (1975, introduction by H. S. Thayer) MT; *Essays in Radical Empiricism* (1976, introduction by John J. McDermott) ERE; *A Pluralistic Universe* (1977, introduction by Richard J. Bernstein) PU; *Essays in Philosophy* (1978, introduction by John J. McDermott) EP; *Some Problems in Philosophy* (1979, introduction by Peter H. Hare) SPP; *The Will to Believe* (1979, introduction by Edward H. Madden) WB. The Harvard Press has also published a one-volume paperback edition of P and MT, with an introduction by A. J. Ayer. This essay will also make reference to, and abbreviate as indicated, some work of James yet to appear in the Harvard-ACLS edition: *The Principles of Psychology* (2 vols., New York, 1890) PP; *The Varieties of Religious Experience: A Study in Human Nature* (New York, 1902; Modern Library Edition, 1936) V; *Collected Essays and Reviews* (New York, 1920) CER. James's words quoted in this paragraph are in WB, 7.

2. WB, xiii, See also Thayer, in P, xiv.

3. Logically distinctive as agnosticism, positivism, and materialism may be, the three were taken by James and by many of his contemporaries to constitute a syndrome. Of the three terms, "positivism" is the most vague; its essence for James was the demand he mocked in SPP, 17: "Give us measurable facts only, phenomena, without the mind's additions, without entities or principles that pretend to explain." James sometimes referred to the entire sensibility in question as "agnostic positivism," e.g., WB, 50. See also P, 15.

4. WB, esp. 21–26, 49–52, 77–80.

5. V, 509. For James's conception of this work as a contribution to scientific inquiry, see esp. V, 424, 500–508.

6. PP, Vol. 2, 618, 633–640, 665–669.

7. [William James,] Review of [P. G. Tait,] *The Unseen Universe*, in *Nation* XX (1875), 367; EP, 4; CER, 137–146; PU, 15–18, 148; SPP, 111–113.

8. P, 13–15, 144.

9. P, xxvii.

10. P, 14.

11. P, 140–144; see also V, 475–476, 494.

12. P, xxxiv.

13. P, 17, 140.

14. P, 34–36. See also MT, 42–43.

15. P, 100, 107, 139. See also P, 82–83, 122; and WB, 19, 87–88.

16. P, 111–112.

17. P, 118–119. See also EP, 20–21.

18. P, 119. See also WB, 26, 96, 103; MT, 51–52; and EP, 169.

19. The most influential work in this now very diverse movement in contemporary scholarship has been, of course, Thomas S. Kuhn, *The Structure of Scientific Revolutions* (Chicago, 1962). It is no coincidence that of the historical studies recently contributed to this movement, many of the most aggressive are addressed to the same Victorian context that aroused James; see, e.g., Barry Barnes and Steven Shapin, eds., *Natural Order: Historical Studies of Scientific Culture* (Beverly Hills, Calif., 1979).

20. MT, 40. See also WB, 49–50, 236.

21. P, 34.

22. P, xxix; MT, xxvi. Thayer's comments on James's way of talking about truth are discerning and helpful, especially in MT, xxvii–xxxvii, where Thayer demonstrates that James took for granted—but regarded as trivial—a point that his critics charged him with ignoring: that true statements partake of "objective reference." See also James's discussion of "objective reference," ERE, 33–37.

23. P, 34.

24. P, 97.

25. Richard Rorty, "Pragmatism, Relativism, and Irrationalism," *Proceedings and Addresses of the American Philosophical Association* LIII (1980), 722.

26. MT, 123.

27. ERE, 209.

28. WB, 5.

29. James identified himself with "pragmatism" in his address of 1898 to the University of California's Philosophical Union; it is reprinted as an appendix to P, 257–270.

30. MT, 23. See also CER, 318.

31. The shadow Royce's idealism cast over James's *Principles of Psychology* is convincingly detailed in Bruce Kuklick, *The Rise of American Philosophy: Cambridge, Massachusetts, 1860–1930* (New Haven, Conn., 1977), 181–186; see also MT, 23; and CER, 276–284.

32. ERE, 31–32. See also PU, 147.

33. MT, 6–7.

34. ERE, xxxvii.

35. ERE, 42. See also ERE, 34; and MT, 42–43.

36. PU, 18.

37. PU, e.g., 93, 100, 149.

38. PU, 106.

39. V, 446–447, 478–479, 504.

40. PU, 143–144. The magnitude of James's shift toward panpsychism should not be exaggerated; for an indication of how easily panpsychism was absorbed into James's long-term views, compare the passage quoted here with his account of God's place in a "pluralistic, restless universe" in an address of 1884: WB, 136–140.

41. PU, 118, 143, 148. See also WB, 53; and SPP, 73.

42. PU, 113.

43. WB, 18.

44. WB, 105.

45. For a recent study reaffirming this judgment, see Larry C. Miller, "William James and Ethnic Thought," *American Quarterly* XXXI (1979), esp. 535.

46. Two influential, and intellectually rigorous discussions in this vein are Morton White, "William James: Pragmatism and the Whole Man," in White's *Science and Sentiment in America: Philosophical Thought from Jonathan Edwards to John Dewey* (New York, 1972), 170–216, and Elizabeth Flower and Murray G. Murphey, "William James, The Tough-Minded: An Appraisal," in Flower and Murphey's *A History of Philosophy in America* (New York, 1977), 2:635–692.

47. Richard Rorty, *Philosophy and the Mirror of Nature* (Princeton, 1980), 394.

48. I have stressed the importance of this sensitivity for intellectual history generally in my "Historians and the Discourse of Intellectuals," in John Higham and Paul Conkin, eds., *New Directions in American Intellectual History* (Baltimore, 1979), 42–63, and in chapter 8 of this book.

49. WB, 55.

2. THE PROBLEM OF PRAGMATISM IN AMERICAN HISTORY

1. Henry Steele Commager, *The American Mind: An Interpretation of American Thought and Character since the 1880's* (New Haven, 1950), 97, 443. See also James Truslow Adams, *The American: The Making of a New Man* (New York, 1943), 382, and Henry Bamford Parkes, *The American Experience: An Interpretation of the History and Civilization of the American People* (New York, 1947), 266–270.

2. Gail Kennedy, ed., *Pragmatism and American Culture* (Boston, 1950), viii. See also Adrienne Koch's essays of the 1950s, collected in her *Power, Morals, and the Founding Fathers: Essays in the Interpretation of the American Enlightenment* (Ithaca, 1961), 1–3, 138–151.

3. Two famous examples are Lewis Mumford, *The Golden Day: A Study in American Literature and Culture* (New York, 1926), and George Santayana, *Character and Opinion in the United States* (New York, 1920). See also the chapter "Pragmatism as Americanism," in William Caldwell, *Pragmatism and Idealism* (London, 1913), 168–195.

4. Bernard Bailyn et al., *The Great Republic* (Boston, 1977).

5. The three leading pragmatists are the subjects not only of a steady stream of books and articles (especially in the *Transactions of the Charles S. Peirce Society*), but of ambitious editorial projects. The most important of these will provide a chronological edition of the papers of Charles S. Peirce, only a small segment of which were published either in Peirce's lifetime or in the eight-volume *Collected Papers* produced by the Harvard University Press, 1931–58, under a succession of editors. The first of a planned fifteen volumes of this new edition of Peirce was published in 1982 and the second in 1984 by Indiana University Press under the editorship of Max H. Fisch. Dewey's works are being reproduced in a uniform edition by the press of Southern Illinois University at Carbondale, under the direction of Jo Ann Boydston. Frederick Burkhardt is the general editor of the Harvard University Press's new standard edition of William James.

6. For an interesting discussion of this historiographical situation, see the symposium, Thomas Haskell et al., "Intellectual History and Intellectual Specialization," *Newsletter of the Intellectual History Group* 1 (Spring 1979), 3–13.

7. Professional philosophers, in turn, have been the authors of most of the recent books purporting to treat pragmatism as a whole. See H. S. Thayer, *Meaning and Action: A Critical History of Pragmatism* (Indianapolis, 1968); Charles Morris, *The Pragmatic Movement in American Philosophy* (New York, 1970); and John E. Smith, *Purpose and Thought: The Meaning of Pragmatism* (New Haven, 1978). Cf. Israel Scheffler, *Four Pragmatists: A Critical Introduction to Peirce, James, Mead, and Dewey* (London, 1974).

8. Particularly influential in drawing and pursuing this distinction have been Murray G. Murphey, "Kant's Children: The Cambridge Pragmatists," *Transactions of the Charles S. Peirce Society* IV (Winter 1968), 3–33, and Bruce Kuklick, *The Rise of American Philosophy: Cambridge, Massachusetts, 1860–1930* (New Haven, Conn., 1977). The impulse to exaggerate the continuities between Peirce, James, and Dewey is also resisted by Paul K. Conkin. See Conkin, *Puritans and Pragmatists: Eight Eminent American Thinkers* (New York, 1968), 193–402, in which the ideas of each thinker are outlined in their particularity. How different Dewey's path to pragmatism was from James's is splendidly illuminated by Neil Coughlin, *Young John Dewey: An Essay in American Intellectual History* (Chicago, 1975).

9. Kuklick, *Rise of American Philosophy.*

10. James B. Gilbert, *Work without Salvation: America's Intellectuals and Industrial Alienation, 1880–1910* (Baltimore, 1977), 197–211.

11. Fowler's chapter on "Pragmatic 'Realism' " can be read as a study of the political uses to which the vocabulary of the pragmatist philosophers was put in the anti-utopian climate of the two decades following World War II. See Robert Fowler, *Believing Skeptics: American Political Intellectuals, 1945–1964* (Westport, Conn., 1978), 121–148. See also the discussion of the interwar era's debate over the absolute or relative character of political values in Edward A. Purcell, Jr., *The Crisis of Democratic Theory: Scientific Naturalism and the Problem of Value* (Lexington, Ky., 1973). Pragmatism also figures in the examination of the idea of progress as it informed the work of James, Dewey, and Charles Beard in David W. Marcell, *Progress and Pragmatism: James, Dewey, Beard, and the American Idea of Progress* (Westport, Conn., 1974), and in Jean B. Quandt, *From the Small Town to the Great Community: The Social Thought of Progressive Intellectuals* (New Brunswick, N.J., 1970). See also John P. Diggins, "Flirtation with Fascism: American Pragmatic Liberals and Mussolini's Italy," *American Historical Review* LXXI (January 1966), 487–506.

12. Darnell Rucker, *The Chicago Pragmatists* (Minneapolis, 1969); Morton G. White, *Social Thought in America: The Revolt against Formalism* (New York, 1949). It is interesting that of the works in this genre more narrowly defined than White's, one of the finest dates also from more than twenty years ago. See Cushing Strout, *The Pragmatic Revolt in American History: Carl Becker and Charles Beard* (New Haven, Conn., 1958).

13. John Dewey, "Science as Subject-Matter and as Method," *Science* XXXVI (January 28, 1910), 127.

14. It is quoted without specific citation, for example, as the epigram to Leo E. Saidla and Warren E. Gibbs, eds., *Science and the Scientific Mind* (New York, 1930).

15. John Dewey, *The Influence of Darwin on Philosophy: And Other Essays in Contemporary Thought* (New York, 1910), 8–9, 19, 55–57, 70–72; John Dewey, *Reconstruction in Philosophy* (New York, 1920), 40, 54, 60–61, 67, 175–177; John Dewey, *The Quest for Certainty: A Study of the Relation of Knowledge and Action* (New York, 1929), 99–101, 192–194, 228, 251, 296; John Dewey, *A Common Faith* (New Haven, Conn., 1934), 26, 32–33, 39.

16. William James, *The Will to Believe and Other Essays in Popular Philosophy* (New York, 1897), 54.

17. Ibid., x, xii–xiii, 7–10, 14, 18–19, 52–54, 323–327.

18. Ibid., 299–327.

19. Walter Lippmann, "An Open Mind: William James," *Everybody's Magazine,* XXIII (December 1910), 800–801; Robert H. Lowie, "Science," in *Civilization in the United States: An Inquiry by Thirty Americans,* ed. Harold E. Stearns (New York, 1922), 152–153; T. V. Smith, "The Scientific Way of Life with William James as Guide," in T. V. Smith, *The Philosophic Way of Life* (New York, 1934), 69–110.

20. For an interesting discussion of this problem in Peirce, see Nicholas Rescher, *Peirce's Philosophy of Science: Critical Studies in His Philosophy of Induction and Scientific Method* (Notre Dame, 1978), 19–39.

21. *Collected Papers of Charles Sanders Peirce*, ed. Charles Hartshorne, Paul Weiss, and Arthur W. Burks (8 vols., Cambridge, Mass., 1931–58), 1. 116–120 (this refers to paragraphs 116–120 of Volume I of *Collected Papers*, which, in Peirce scholarship, is always cited by paragraph instead of page).

22. This is emphatically stated in ibid., 1. 135.

23. Ibid., 5.311. This aspect of Peirce has been helpfully called to the attention of historians by R. Jackson Wilson's essay, "Charles Sanders Peirce: The Community of Inquiry," in R. Jackson Wilson, *In Quest of Community: Social Philosophy in the United States, 1860–1920* (New York, 1968), 32–59. Cf. Jakob Liszka, "Community in C. S. Peirce: Science as a Means and as an End," *Transactions of the Charles S. Peirce Society* XIV (Fall 1978), 305–321.

24. Josiah Royce, *The Problem of Christianity*, ed. John E. Smith (New York, 1968), 404–405. Peirce's direct influence on this crucial work of Royce's is clarified by Bruce Kuklick, *Josiah Royce: An Intellectual Biography* (Indianapolis, 1972), esp. 214–215, 235.

25. William James, "Philosophical Conceptions and Practical Results," in William James, *Collected Essays and Reviews* (New York, 1920), 406–437, esp. 410.

26. *Collected Papers*, ed. Hartshorne, Weiss, and Burks, 5. 403.

27. According to H. S. Thayer, Peirce's maxim "is probably the unclearest recommendation for how to make our ideas clear in the history of philosophy." Thayer, *Meaning and Action*, 87. See also Morris, *Pragmatic Movement*, 20–23; Smith, *Purpose and Thought*, 18–32, 35; Elizabeth Flower and Murray G. Murphey, *A History of Philosophy in America* (2 vols., New York, 1977), II, 590.

28. For a useful chronology of the development of pragmatism as a movement and a sketch of steps antecedent to this development, see Max H. Fisch, "American Pragmatism before and after 1898," *American Philosophy from Edwards to Quine*, ed. Robert W. Shahan and Kenneth R. Merrill (Norman, Okla., 1977), 78–110.

29. William James, *Pragmatism: A New Name for Some Old Ways of Thinking* (New York, 1907), 48, 51–54.

30. Ibid., 55–58, 67, 197–236.

31. Less publicized among nonphilosophers, this depiction is very much the stuff of debate among philosophers assessing the pragmatists. Peirce's relevant texts include *Collected Papers*, ed. Hartshorne, Weiss, and Burks, 5. 407, 565.

32. James, *Pragmatism*, 201. See also William James, *The Meaning of Truth: A Sequel to 'Pragmatism'* (New York, 1909), v–vi. For help in sorting out the various versions of the pragmatic theory of truth, see Gertrude Ezorsky, "Pragmatic Theory of Truth," in *Encyclopedia of Philosophy*, ed. Paul Edwards (8 vols., New York, 1967), VI, 427–430; H. S. Thayer, "Introduction," in William James, *The Meaning of Truth* (Cambridge, Mass., 1975), xi–xlvi; Smith, *Purpose and Thought*, 32–33, 50–77.

33. John Dewey, "The Need for a Recovery of Philosophy," in John Dewey et al., *Creative Intelligence: Essays in the Pragmatic Attitude* (New York, 1917), 48–50; Dewey, *Reconstruction in Philosophy*, 112–113, 121–122, 177; Dewey, *Quest for Certainty*, 3, 24–25, 85–86, 103–105, 204–205.

34. John Dewey, *Logic: The Theory of Inquiry* (New York, 1938). How differently the history of pragmatism looks to a historian from the way it looks to a philosopher is shown by the eagerness of philosophers to overlook the forty years of mushy work Dewey did in this area in order to focus on his most rigorous, climactic work. See Thayer, *Meaning and*

Action, 190–199, and Smith, *Purpose and Thought,* 96–112. This approach is understandable if one's aim is to recover the completed structure of Dewey's philosophy; the approach makes less sense if one wants to understand the living tradition that Dewey had built before his *Logic* appeared.

35. The connection is emphasized by White, *Social Thought in America;* Eric F. Goldman, *Rendezvous with Destiny: A History of Modern American Reform* (New York, 1952), 119–124; and most of the references to pragmatism that still appear in survey textbooks of American history.

36. William James, *The Principles of Psychology* (2 vols., New York, 1890). See also the discussion of this work in John Wild, *The Radical Empiricism of William James* (Garden City, N.Y., 1969), 1–262.

37. James, *Will to Believe,* 21, 92–93, 130.

38. Bertrand Russell, "Dewey's New Logic," in *The Philosophy of John Dewey,* ed. Paul Arthur Schilpp (Evanston, Ill., 1939), 143–156.

39. James, *Pragmatism,* 43–81.

40. Dewey, *Reconstruction in Philosophy,* 161–186; Dewey, *Quest for Certainty,* 254–286; James, *Pragmatism,* 75–76.

41. John B. Watson, *Behaviorism* (New York, 1924).

42. This was particularly true in the 1930s, when Dewey himself sometimes supported socialist candidates for public office.

43. Bertrand Russell, *Mysticism and Logic and Other Essays* (New York, 1917), 46–57.

44. Sinclair Lewis, *Arrowsmith* (New York, 1925).

45. Robert A. Millikan, *Science and the New Civilization* (New York, 1930).

46. See, for example, Henry S. Pritchett, "Science (1857–1907)," *Atlantic Monthly* C (November 1907), 613–625.

47. See, for example, the numerous publications during the 1920s of Edwin E. Slosson, including Edwin E. Slosson, *Chats on Science* (New York, 1924).

48. Oliver Wendell Holmes, Jr., *Collected Legal Papers* (New York, 1920). Holmes was often claimed as a prophet of the pragmatist tradition, and it is a mark of the strength of this tradition that such claims went unchallenged for so long. Of the many warm accounts of Holmes as a "liberal" and as a "pragmatist," the most eloquent is Commager, *American Mind,* 385–390. For a reading of Holmes more representative of the scholarship of the last twenty years, see Yosal Rogat, "The Judge as Spectator," *University of Chicago Law Review* 31 (Winter 1964), 213–256. See also G. Edward White, "The Rise and Fall of Justice Holmes," ibid. (Fall 1971), 51–77.

49. The recognition that Peirce, James, and Dewey shared something important philosophically was first promoted by James himself, and it was acknowledged almost as readily by Dewey as it was resisted by Peirce. This much is often said in histories of pragmatism; what deserves more attention is the process by which the idea of a single "American Pragmatism" was kept alive after James's death, especially during the 1920s and 1930s. Dewey and Dewey's followers played a very large role in this process and helped to persuade most Americans who took an interest in the matter that Dewey's work was the logical culmination of the pragmatism of Peirce and of James. So it is that one can responsibly analyze "pragmatism" as a presence in American intellectual life without taking up the texts of C. I. Lewis or of the later Royce; elements in their work that a discerning historian *of philosophy* might call "pragmatic" simply were not assimilated into the tradition constructed by American intellectuals under the dominating influence of Dewey. For a document of Dewey's that is representative of the process, see "The De-

velopment of American Pragmatism," in John Dewey, *Philosophy and Civilization* (New York, 1931), 13–35.

50. Lucid, brief analyses of C. I. Lewis and George Herbert Mead in the context of the work of Peirce, James, and Dewey can be found in Thayer, *Meaning and Action*. Although Mead has recently enjoyed a considerable vogue in several of the human sciences, he was not widely known beyond philosophy prior to his death in 1931, except in the circles of "Chicago social science." For Mead in that setting, see Rucker, *Chicago Pragmatists*. Lewis was very much a philosopher's philosopher from the onset of his career in the 1910s through his death in 1964; his role as an examplar of professionalism in philosophy is discussed ably in Kuklick, *Rise of American Philosophy*. For a cogent and illuminating account of Lewis's philosophic work, see ibid., 533–562. Cf. Flower and Murphey, *History of Philosophy in America*, II, 891–958.

51. Joseph Ratner, "Introduction to John Dewey's Philosophy," in *Intelligence in the Modern World: John Dewey's Philosophy*, ed. Joseph Ratner (New York, 1939), 5, 57, 61, 115, 187, 227, 241.

52. Horace M. Kallen began writing articles about James and about pragmatism in 1910, contributed in 1917 to Dewey's pivotal anthology, *Creative Intelligence*, edited in 1925 the Modern Library edition of James's writings, and was involved in numerous symposia, *Festschriften*, and commemorative volumes honoring James and Dewey in later years. See Dewey et al., *Creative Intelligence*, 409–467; *The Philosophy of William James: Drawn from His Work*, ed. Horace M. Kallen (New York, 1925), 1–55; Horace M. Kallen, "John Dewey and the Spirit of Pragmatism," *John Dewey: Philosopher of Science and Freedom*, ed. Sidney Hook (New York, 1950), 3–46. *Festschriften* for Kallen himself were meeting grounds for keepers of the pragmatist flame. See, for example, Sidney Ratner, ed., *Vision and Action: Essays in Honor of Horace M. Kallen on His 70th Birthday* (New Brunswick, N.J., 1953). Sidney Hook's operations began with Sidney Hook, *The Metaphysics of Pragmatism* (Chicago, 1927). His other writings included *John Dewey: An Intellectual Portrait* (New York, 1939). Hook also had a tour of duty similar to Kallen's on the symposia-*Festschrift* circuit of the 1940s and 1950s. For a good example of Hook's writings as they consolidate and interpret the pragmatist tradition, see "The Centrality of Method," in *The American Pragmatists: Selected Writings*, ed. Milton R. Konvitz and Gail Kennedy (Cleveland, 1960), 360–379. The essay begins with an epigram from Kallen. Kallen, who was widely known also for his exposition of "cultural pluralism," died in 1974; Hook remains to this day one of the pragmatist tradition's most forceful, capable, and visible defenders.

53. Horace M. Kallen, "Pragmatism," *Encyclopaedia of the Social Sciences*, ed. Edwin R. A. Seligman and Alvin Johnson (15 vols., New York, 1930–35), XII, 307–311.

54. Charles Forcey, *The Crossroads of Liberalism: Croly, Weyl, Lippmann, and the Progressive Era, 1900–1925* (New York, 1961).

55. Walter Lippmann, *Drift and Mastery: An Attempt to Diagnose the Current Unrest* (New York, 1914). For a recent effort to determine this text's historical significance, see David A. Hollinger, "Science and Anarchy: Walter Lippmann's *Drift and Mastery*," *American Quarterly* XXIX (Winter 1977), 463–475, and chapter 3 of this book.

56. Frederick Barry, *The Scientific Habit of Thought: An Informal Discussion of the Source and Character of Dependable Knowledge* (New York, 1927); James Harvey Robinson, *The Mind in the Making: The Relation of Intelligence to Social Reform* (New York, 1921); Paul H. Douglas, "The Absolute, the Experimental Method, and Horace Kallen," in Ratner, ed., *Vision and Action*, 39–55; Lyman Bryson, *The New Prometheus* (New York, 1941); Lyman Bryson, *Science and Freedom* (New York, 1947).

57. For William Heard Kilpatrick's career at Teachers College, see Lawrence A. Cremin, *The Transformation of the School: Progressivism in American Education, 1876–1957* (New York, 1961), 215–224. Another work, although presented as in part a history, is richly revealing as a statement of the "progressive" educational philosophy inspired by Dewey. John L. Childs, *American Pragmatism and Education: An Interpretation and Criticism* (New York, 1956).

58. Papini's aphorisms about pragmatism, published in Italian, became known to Americans primarily through James's own rendering of them. See William James, "G. Papini and the Pragmatist Movement in Italy," *Journal of Philosophy, Psychology and Scientific Methods* III (June 21, 1906), 337–341.

59. Of the many accounts of the rise of this ideal, the most discussed is Robert H. Wiebe, *The Search for Order, 1877–1920* (New York, 1967), 133–163. See also William E. Nelson, "Officeholding and Powerwielding: An Analysis of the Relationship between Structure and Style in American Administrative History," *Law and Society Review* 10 (Winter 1976), 188–233.

60. R. G. Tugwell, *The Brains Trust* (New York, 1968), 93–105. The New Deal is perhaps the most noticed of many instances in the history of pragmatic rhetoric in which the use of that rhetoric seems to have concealed from its users the unarticulated assumptions that guided their own experimentation. See especially Thurman W. Arnold, *The Symbols of Government* (New Haven, 1935), and Thurman W. Arnold, *The Folklore of Capitalism* (New Haven, 1937). See also the critique of Arnold by Sidney Hook, "The Folklore of Capitalism: The Politician's Handbook—A Review" *University of Chicago Law Review* 5 (April 1938), 341–349.

61. Richard Rorty, "Dewey's Metaphysics," in *New Studies in the Philosophy of John Dewey*, ed. Steven M. Cahn (Hanover, N.H., 1977), 45–74. Cf. the different interest in Dewey manifest in the work of W. V. Quine, *Ontological Relativity and Other Essays* (New York, 1969), 26–29.

62. Louis Hartz, *The Liberal Tradition in America: An Interpretation of American Political Thought since the Revolution* (New York, 1955); Daniel J. Boorstin, *The Genius of American Politics* (Chicago, 1953). Of the many works purporting to find "pragmatic" continuities throughout American history, these two still repay the effort to come to grips with them critically.

3. SCIENCE AND ANARCHY: WALTER LIPPMAN'S *DRIFT AND MASTERY*

1. Numbers in parenthesis refer to pages in Walter Lippmann, *Drift and Mastery: An Attempt to Diagnose the Current Unrest*, William E. Leuchtenburg, ed. (Englewood Cliffs, N.J., 1961), the edition now most readily available. The book was originally published in 1914 in New York by Mitchell Kinnerley.

2. The most widely discussed explorations of this insight are Robert H. Wiebe, *The Search for Order, 1877–1920* (New York, 1967), John Higham, *From Boundlessness to Consolidation* (Ann Arbor, Mich.: William M. Clements Library, 1969), R. Jackson Wilson, *In Quest of Community, 1860–1920* (New York, 1968), and George M. Fredrickson, *The Inner Civil War: Northern Intellectuals and the Crisis of the Union* (New York, 1965). An especially cogent analysis is Richard M. Abrams, "The Failure of Progressivism," in Abrams and Lawrence W. Levine, eds., *The Shaping of Twentieth Century America*, 2nd ed. (Boston, 1971), 207–224.

3. Matthew Arnold, *Culture and Anarchy*, J. Dover Wilson, ed. (Cambridge, England, 1932), 16. *Culture and Anarchy* first appeared in 1869.

4. Ibid., 12, 14, 22.

5. Ibid., 72ff.

6. Ibid., 6, 10, 12.

7. This bill sought to repeal the prohibition in Great Britain of marriages between a man and the sister of his deceased wife. Arnold scorned it in *Culture and Anarchy*, 180–184.

8. For a sensitive portrait of the Nonconformist subculture caricatured by Arnold, see J. D. Y. Peel, *Herbert Spencer, The Evolution of a Sociologist* (New York, 1971), 33–55.

9. This interest in spontaneity, which was not always acknowledged by Arnold's critics, was a major concern of *Culture and Anarchy*, e.g., 132, 146.

10. E.g., Huxley's address of 1880, "Science and Culture," in T. H. Huxley, *Collected Essays*, 3 (London, 1893), 134–159.

11. William James, *The Will to Believe* (New York, 1896), 1–31, esp. 8–25.

12. E.g., Robert E. Kohler, "The Management of Science: The Experience of Warren Weaver and the Rockefeller Foundation Programme in Molecular Biology," *Minerva* 14 (1976), 305.

13. Theodore Roosevelt, "Two Noteworthy Books on Democracy," *Outlook* 108 (November 18, 1914), 648–651; Randolph Bourne to Dorothy Teall, June 14, 1915, Bourne Papers, Columbia University, quoted by Paul F. Bourke, "The Status of Politics, 1909–1919: *The New Republic*, Randolph Bourne and Van Wyck Brooks," *Journal of American Studies* 8 (1974), 197.

14. Louis Untermeyer, "The First Few Books," *Masses* (March 1915), 21. Dozens of newspaper and magazine reviews of *Drift and Mastery*—including all of those known to me—are conveniently available in the Walter Lippmann Papers, Yale University Library (Division VII, Box 42).

15. See, e.g., *Detroit News Tribune*, April 4, 1915; *Living Age*, April 17, 1915; *Chicago Tribune*, January 2, 1915; *Chicago Evening Post*, March 12, 1915; *Boston Herald*, January 16, 1915; *Indianapolis News*, March 13, 1915; *Los Angeles Graphic*, December 12, 1914; *Nation* 100 (January 7, 1915), 21–22.

16. [Horace Traubel], review of *Drift and Mastery*, in *The Conservator* (October 1914), 120–121.

17. *American Hebrew*, May 21, 1915.

18. Louis H. Wetmore, "The Ignorance of the Past," *America* 12 (November 28, 1914), 173.

19. *New York Times Book Review*, August 1, 1915; cf. Margaret C. Anderson, "Our First Year," *Little Review* 1 (February 1915), 4–5.

20. For a straightforward depiction of human beings as mere objects for the reception of "stimuli," preferably "constant," "uniform," and derived from a single political source, see L. L. Bernard, "The Transition to an Objective Standard of Social Control," *American Journal of Sociology* 16 (1910–11), 523, 528–531.

21. E.g., Paul F. Bourke, "The Pluralist Reading of James Madison's Tenth *Federalist*," *Perspectives in American History* 9 (1975), 277, 280–281.

22. Among American commentators, especially by the reviewer for the *Nation* 100 (January 7, 1915), 21–22. This failing was criticized sharply by the *British* critic "J. A. H." [J. A. Hobson] in *Nation* (London), December 19, 1914, 379–380. Cf. the complaints about vagueness in two other British reviews, *New Age*, December 3, 1914, 127, and S. K. Ratcliffe, undated and unidentified periodical, clipping in Walter Lippmann Papers, Division VII, Box 42, Yale University Library.

23. *A Preface to Politics* (New York, 1913), had already established Lippmann as a

critic, although that book remained aloof from the enthusiasm about organization and science that marked *Drift and Mastery*. This abrupt shift in Lippmann's outlook has been widely discussed, and is generally attributed to the influence of Graham Wallas. See esp. Charles Forcey, *The Crossroads of Liberalism: Croly, Weyl, Lippmann, and the Progressive Era, 1900–1925* (New York, 1961), 109–118, 166–167, and Leuchtenburg, "Introduction" to the Prentice-Hall edition, 5. Cf. Charles Wellborn, *Twentieth Century Pilgrimage: Walter Lippmann and the Public Philosophy* (Baton Rouge, La., 1969), 25–27; and Hari N. Dam, *The Intellectual Odyssey of Walter Lippmann* (New York, 1973), 19.

24. The contrast between *Drift and Mastery's* dependence upon a positive view of science and the ambivalence toward science in Lippmann's later works, especially *A Preface to Morals* (New York, 1929), has been widely acknowledged, but not extensively analyzed. Since the present concern is with the place of *Drift and Mastery* in American intellectual history, and not with its place in Lippmann's own career, a brief clarification of the relationship between *Drift and Mastery* and *Preface to Morals* will suffice. The two books agree that the essence of the modern problem is finding a stable and fulfilling life in the absence of traditional authorities, and they share the sense that science is a Promethean and experimental enterprise grounded in the insight that we live in a radically contingent world. The 1929 volume laments the failure of apparently all fashionable efforts to deal with the modern problem, and specifically doubts the viability of science as a social and spiritual ideal. In *Preface to Morals*, "humanism" and "maturity" function much in the same way that "the discipline of science" and "mastery" did in the 1914 text. These new (for Lippmann) terms are used to express a larger measure of resignation than *Drift and Mastery* would endorse, as well as a more tolerant attitude toward asceticism, and a greater willingness to attribute to human experience a stable moral structure which "the progress of science cannot upset" (*Preface to Morals,* 327). In 1929 Lippmann stressed the difficulty, rather than the ease, with which the gap between science and the everyday life of the layman could be bridged, and, finally, Lippmann associated his own efforts as a critic not with the methods of science, but with the spirit of classical philosophy.

25. Paul F. Bourke, "The Social Critics and the End of American Innocence: 1907–1921," *Journal of American Studies* 3 (1969), 57–72. Cf. Christopher Lasch, *The New Radicalism in America, 1889–1963: The Intellectual as a Social Type* (New York, 1965).

26. Lippmann's most well-known attack on "collectivism" in the 1930s was *The Good Society* (Boston, 1936).

27. Leuchtenburg, "Introduction," 12. For a competent but conventional reading of *Drift and Mastery* in the categories of political thought, see Benjamin F. Wright, *Five Public Philosophies of Walter Lippmann* (Austin, Texas, 1973), 26–37.

28. This, the most legendary of all the phases of the young Lippmann's life, has been frequently described and assessed; see, in addition to Leuchtenburg's "Introduction," the following: Heinz Eulau, "Mover and Shaker: Walter Lippmann as a Young Man," *Antioch Review* 11 (1951), 291–312; Wellborn, *Pilgrimage,* 20–24; Forcey, *Crossroads,* 88–118; Henry F. May, *The End of American Innocence* (New York, 1959), 318–322.

29. Leuchtenburg, "Introduction," 11, 13.

30. The "emancipation of women" was among the chief preoccupations of Lippmann's brief introduction (16–17). The chapter devoted to the "Woman's Movement" (123–134) confirmed that his fascination with it was its novelty; it stood as a metaphor for the sharp breaks with the past Lippmann saw throughout American life. Similarly, he endorsed feminism not only as an advance for women, but as an expression of true democracy. When Lippmann got specific, however, he spoke mostly about the more efficient housework and healthy family life that would result from the triumph of feminism; Lippmann was gently

chided for this narrowness of focus by Winnifred Harper Cooley, "The Feminism of a Man," unidentified clipping, Box 42, Division VII, Walter Lippmann Papers, For *Drift and Mastery's* vision of consumer power, see esp. 52–56.

31. Morton G. White, *Social Thought in America: The Revolt Against Formalism* (New York, 1949); Wiebe, *Search for Order*.

4. ETHNIC DIVERSITY, COSMOPOLITANISM, AND THE EMERGENCE OF THE AMERICAN LIBERAL INTELLIGENTSIA

1. Randolph Bourne, "Trans-National America," *Atlantic* 118 (1916), 86–97, rpt. Carl Resek, ed., *War and the Intellectuals: Essays by Randolph Bourne, 1915–1919* (New York, 1964), 107–123. Since Bourne was destined to become a cultural hero to so many intellectuals, his advocacy of this view is especially pertinent to an inquiry into the development of the intelligentsia. A handful of other writers, less well-known, expressed similar views in the 1910s, e.g., Horace J. Bridges, *On Becoming an American: Some Meditations of A Newly Naturalized Immigrant* (Boston, 1919), esp. 117–121, 135–149. Ironically, the British immigrant Bridges used the term "cosmopolitanism" to denote exactly the view that he and Bourne were against, the eradication of cultural differences in the interest of a narrowly homogeneous society. Bridges was aware of the semantical problem, and proposed "Internationalism" as a more appropriate term for the overcoming of provincialism in the interests of merging many cultures "into a distinctive American civilization which shall transcend them all" (see esp. 120, 148).

2. On nativism in the 1910s, see John Higham, *Strangers in the Land: Patterns of American Nativism, 1860–1925* (New Brunswick, 1955), 158–193. The editor of the *Atlantic* was shocked by Bourne's lack of allegiance to the "English instinct" and the "Anglo-Saxon ideal," but decided to publish the "utterly mistaken" article because it seemed "the ablest and certainly the most interesting" thing that his protégé, Bourne, had written; Ellery Sedgwick to Bourne, March 30, 1916, Bourne MSS, Columbia University Special Collections.

3. The term "intelligentsia," it could be argued, ought to be reserved to distinguish radical literati from "mandarins." This usage would be true to the word's most conventional association, with the Russian intellectuals of the mid-nineteenth century. Yet the term has developed a broader meaning in recent years, especially in the United States. The Webster-Merriam *Third International Dictionary* counts as an *intelligentsia* any "class of well-educated, articulate persons constituting a distinct, recognized, and self-conscious stratum within a nation and claiming or assuming for itself the guiding role of an intellectual, social, or political vanguard."

4. For a representative and widely read example of this presumption, see "The Intellectual: Alienation and Conformity," the final chapter of Richard Hofstadter's *Anti-Intellectualism in American Life* (New York, 1963), 393–432, esp. 394.

5. For an attempt to pursue this question in detail, and to discover who are the "top 70" American intellectuals, see the amusing, but seriously intended book by the sociologist Charles Kadushin, *The American Intellectual Elite* (Boston, 1974), esp. 28–30.

6. Milton Gordon, *Assimilation in American Life* (New York, 1964), 224–232, and "Marginality and the Jewish Intellectual," in Peter I. Rose, ed., *The Ghetto and Beyond* (New York, 1969), 477–491.

7. Certainly, there were a number of prominent intellectuals whose origins were neither Jewish nor Protestant Anglo-Saxon, including, for example, the Yugoslavian immigrant Louis Adamic, the black James Baldwin, and such Catholics (or one-time

Catholics) as James Burnham, C. Wright Mills, and James Agee. Yet there is no doubt that the bulk of the intelligentsia descended from either the Jewish immigration from Eastern Europe or the older American "WASP" tradition.

8. Randolph Bourne, "The Jew and Trans-National America," *Menorah Journal* 2 (1916), 277–284, rpt. Resek, 124–133. Cf. Bourne's references to Lippmann, Frankfurter, and Harold Laski in his letter to Alyse Gregory, November 10, 1916, Bourne MSS. Cf. to Bourne, Thorstein Veblen, "The Intellectual Preeminence of Jews in Modern Europe," *Political Science Quarterly* XXXIV (1919), 33–42.

9. Floyd Dell, *Homecoming* (New York, 1933), esp. 121, 170, 192.

10. Alvin Johnson, *Pioneer's Progress: An Autobiography* (New York, 1952), 11, 127.

11. Lincoln Steffens, *Autobiography* (New York, 1931), 318.

12. Hutchins Hapgood, *The Spirit of the Ghetto* (New York, 1909; rpt. 1965), esp. 47–52. Cf. Hapgood, *A Victorian in the Modern World* (New York, 1939), esp. 144–145. That Hapgood's revealing *Spirit of the Ghetto* has not been more thoroughly analyzed and absorbed into the canon of American cultural history is an index of the extent to which scholarly writing about the relations of Gentiles and Jews has been dominated by the question of anti-Semitism. On the tendency of scholarship to overlook manifestations of cordiality in relations between ethnic groups, see Rudolph J. Vecoli, "European Americans: From Immigrants to Ethnics," *International Migration Review* 6 (1972), 414, 416, 434.

13. Edmund Wilson, *Classics and Commercials* (New York, 1950), 503–505.

14. Daniel Aaron, *Writers on the Left* (New York, 1961); Christopher Lasch, *The New Radicalism in America, 1889–1963: The Intellectual as a Social Type* (New York, 1965); Henry F. May, ed., *The Discontent of the Intellectuals* (Chicago, 1963); Frederick J. Hoffman, *The Twenties: American Writing in the Postwar Decade* (New York, 1955); John P. Diggins, *The American Left in the Twentieth Century* (New York, 1973); and Hofstadter, *Anti-Intellectualism.* These historians are not always oblivious to the cosmopolitan impulse; for example, Henry F. May's *The End of American Innocence: A Study of the First Years of Our Own Time, 1912–1917* (New York, 1959), although it is couched in other terms, offers a very helpful exploration of this impulse in Bourne's generation (see esp. 279–301).

15. Ezra Pound, "Provincialism the Enemy," *New Age* 22 (1917), 269, 289, 309.

16. For a helpful overview of the cosmopolitan aspirations within the genteel tradition, see Howard Mumford Jones, *The Age of Energy: Varieties of American Experience, 1865–1915* (New York, 1971), 259–300 For James in this context, see esp. *The Portrait of a Lady* (New York, 1881).

17. For the tradition of "cosmopolitan nationalism" and its decline, see Higham, *Strangers,* 20–23, 63, 97, 110, 120, 124, 251, 304. For James's reaction to the Yiddish ghetto, see Henry James, *The American Scene* (New York, 1907), 131–135.

18. [Van Wyck Brooks,] "Where Are Our Intellectuals," *Freeman* 2 (1920), 53–54; Harold Stearns, "America and the Young Intellectuals," *Bookman* 3 (1921), 42–48; Lewis Mumford, "The American Intelligentsia," *World Tomorrow* 8 (1925), 200–201; Mumford, conversation with author, Amenia, New York, June 21, 1974. Cf. Susan J. Turner, *A History of The Freeman: Literary Landmark of the Early Twenties* (New York, 1963), esp. 25, 62–67; and Floyd Dell, *Intellectual Vagabondage: An Apology for the Intelligentsia* (New York, 1926).

19. H. L. Mencken, *Prejudices: Third Series* (New York, 1922), 35–36.

20. E.g., Allen Guttmann, *The Jewish Writer in America: Assimilation and the Crisis of Identity* (New York, 1971).

21. Indeed the concept of the "cosmopolitan Jew" has long been a stereotype of adulation (e.g., Isaac Deutscher, *The Non-Jewish Jew* [New York, 1968], 24–41) and of anti-Semitism (e.g., the writings of G. K. Chesterton).

22. E.g., Morris R. Cohen, *A Dreamer's Journey* (New York, 1949), 74, 85–86, 94–99, 166–167; Joseph Epstein, *Let There Be Sculpture* (New York, 1940), esp. 8–13; cf. Moses Rischin, *The Promised City: New York's Jews, 1870–1914* (Cambridge, Mass., 1962), esp. 130–131, 209.

23. Morris R. Cohen, "The East Side," *Alliance Review* 2 (1902), 451–454; Cohen, *Journey*, 98.

24. E.g., the use of this phrase by Morris Friedman, "The Jewish College Student; New Model," in Elliot Cohen, ed., *Commentary on the American Scene* (New York, 1953), 282.

25. Bourne, "Jew and Trans-National America," 133; "The Holmes-Cohen Correspondence," in Leonora Cohen Rosenfield, *Portrait of A Philosopher: Morris R. Cohen in Life and Letters* (New York, 1962), 313–360; John Herman Randall, Jr., "Annual Meeting of the Eastern Division of the American Philosophical Association," *Journal of Philosophy* 23 (1926), 37–38.

26. E.g., Gilbert Seldes, "The Demoniac in the American Theatre," *Dial* 75 (1923), 303–308.

27. Joseph Freeman, *An American Testament: A Narrative of Rebels and Romantics* (New York, 1936), esp. 28, 49, 61, 65, 160–161, 246.

28. James Oppenheim, "The Story of the *Seven Arts*," *American Mercury* 20 (1930), 156–164, esp. 158. On the background of Lippmann and Weyl, see Charles Forcey, *Crossroads of Liberalism* (New York, 1961), 56–58 and 91–93. For the marginally "foreign" perspective of the chief *New Republic* editor, Herbert Croly, see Forcey, 12.

29. Sherman Paul, "Introduction" to Paul Rosenfeld, *Port of New York* (Urbana, Ill., 1961), ix. *Port of New York*, a collection of essays, was originally published in 1924.

30. Paul Rosenfeld, "Randolph Bourne," *Dial* 75 (1923), 546, 552, 555.

31. Rosenfeld, *Port of New York*, 20, 47–48, 62.

32. Horace Kallen, "Democracy Versus the Melting Pot," in *Culture and Democracy in the United States* (New York, 1924), 67–125. The essay appeared originally in the *Nation* 100 (1915), 191–194, 217–220.

33. The figure of the "melting pot" was used in support of radically contrasting social policies concerning immigrants, some of which were very close to the "cultural pluralism" Kallen viewed an antithetical to the "melting pot." These ambiguities are very helpfully discussed by Philip Gleason, "The Melting Pot: Symbol of Fusion or Confusion?" *American Quarterly* 16 (1964), 20–46.

34. E.g., Kallen, *Culture and Democracy*, 124–125. See also the exchange over Zionism between Morris R. Cohen and Kallen: Cohen, "Zionism: Tribalism or Liberalism," *New Republic* 18 (1919), 182–183; Kallen, "Zionism: Democracy or Prussianism," *New Republic* 18 (1919), 311–313.

35. Alfred Kazin, *Starting Out in the Thirties* (Boston, 1965), 5, 136–137.

36. Lionel Trilling, *A Gathering of Fugitives* (Boston, 1956), 49–51. Cf. Irving Howe's characterization of Wilson in "The New York Intellectuals: A Chronicle and A Critique," *Commentary* 46 (1968), 31; and James Burkhart Gilbert's account of Wilson's influence on Phillip Rahv and William Phillips, in Gilbert's *Writers and Partisans: A History of Literary Radicalism in America* (New York, 1968), 99. Cf. also, Kazin's description of how Malcolm Cowley appeared to him in 1934; *Thirties*, 15–17.

37. Alfred Kazin, "Under Forty: A Symposium on American Literature and the Younger Generation of American Jews," *Contemporary Jewish Record* 7 (1944), 12; Kazin, *Thirties*, 86.

38. Lionel Trilling, "Under Forty," 15–17; Trilling, "Introduction" to Robert Warshow, *The Immediate Experience* (New York, 1962), 14 (to associate with a "Jewish" magazine would be, for Trilling, a "posture and a falsehood"). Cf. Trilling, "Afterword" to Tess Slesinger, *The Unpossessed* (New York, 1934; reprint edition with Trilling's comments, New York, 1967), 316–324.

39. As representative of the recent reassessment of Trilling, see Roger Sale, "Lionel Trilling," *Hudson Review* 25 (1973), 241–247.

40. Leslie Fiedler, *To the Gentiles* (New York, 1972), 183. Cf. Howe, "New York Intellectuals," 30–31, and David T. Bazelon, "A Writer Between Generations," in Bazelon, *Nothing But a Fine Tooth Comb* (New York, 1969), 17–47, esp. 18–22.

41. On the attraction of intellectuals of Jewish origin to the Communist movement, see the essay by Daniel Aaron, "The Jewish Writer and Communism," *Salmagundi* 1 (1965), 23–36. This piece is an important supplement to Aaron's more general study of the appeal of Communism, *Writers on the Left*. The essay is reprinted in Rose, ed., *Ghetto and Beyond*, 253–269.

42. Trilling, "Afterword" to *Unpossessed*, 324.

43. An especially vivid memoir is in Dwight Macdonald, *Politics Past: Essays in Political Criticism* (New York, 1970), 9–14. Cf. Gilbert, *Writers and Partisans*, 155–233, and Richard H. Pells, *Radical Visions and American Dreams: Culture and Social Thought in the Depression Years* (New York, 1973), 334–346.

44. Harold Rosenberg, "The Fall of Paris," *Partisan Review* 7 (1940), 440–448; reprinted in Rosenberg, *The Tradition of the New* (New York, 1960), 209–220. Cf. F. W. Dupee, "The Americanization of Van Wyck Brooks," *Partisan Review* 6 (Summer 1939), 69–85, esp. 76–77, 81, 83, 85. On cosmopolitanism as a factor in Dupee's inability to work with the *New Masses*, where he had been before switching to the *Partisan Review*, see Gilbert, *Writers and Partisans*, 174.

45. On the need for a cultural capital of some kind, and the relation of this need to American expatriation to Paris, see the illuminating essay by Warren Susman, "The Expatriate Image," in Cushing Strout, ed., *Intellectual History in America* (New York, 1968), 2:145–157.

46. Kazin, *On Native Grounds* (New York, 1942; abr. ed., 1956), 380.

47. See Donald Fleming and Bernard Bailyn, eds., *The Intellectual Migration, 1930–1960* (Cambridge, Mass., 1969).

48. Kazin, *On Native Grounds*, 380.

49. James Agee and Walker Evans, *Let Us Now Praise Famous Men* (Boston, 1941).

50. Alfred Kazin, *A Walker in the City* (New York, 1951). On the generation of "Jewish intellectuals" who began their careers in the mid-1940s, there are two especially revealing memoirs: Bazelon, "A Writer Between Generations," and Norman Podhoretz, *Making It* (New York, 1967), 83–102.

51. Ben Hecht, *A Guide for the Bedeviled* (New York, 1944), esp. 3, 44, 60, 64, 78–79; Ben Hecht, *A Child of the Century* (New York, 1954).

52. Norman Podhoretz, "Jewish Culture and the Intellectuals," in Irving Malin and Irwin Stark, eds., *Breakthrough: A Treasury of Contemporary Jewish-American Literature* (Philadelphia, 1964), 301–311.

53. Christopher Lasch, *The Agony of the American Left* (New York, 1969), esp. 58, criticizes the intelligentsia in precisely this way.

54. Hannah Arendt, *Eichmann in Jerusalem* (New York, 1964).

55. Dwight Macdonald, "Hannah Arendt and the Jewish Establishment," *Partisan Review* XXXI (1964), 262–269.

56. Of the various attempts to provide an overview of the "split" in the intelligentsia reflected in the outlook of these two journals, Peter Steinfels, "The Cooling of the Intellectuals: The Case of *Commentary* and *The New York Review of Books,*" *Commonweal* 94 (May 21, 1971), 255–261, is especially cogent.

57. E.g., the exchange between Robert Alter and George Steiner in *Commentary* 49 (1970), 4–14.

58. Irving Howe, "Thinking the Unthinkable about Israel," *New York Magazine* (December 24, 1973), 44–45, 48–52.

59. Michael Novak, *The Rise of the Unmeltable Ethnics* (New York, 1971); Harold Cruse, *The Crisis of the Negro Intellectual* (New York, 1967).

60. The same obligation was felt in the 1930s when some intellectuals did go beyond the "more-cosmopolitan-than-thou" frame of argument to repudiate the cosmopolitan ideal itself. This repudiation was most common among those willing to accept the discipline of the Communist Party, as in the case of Michael Gold, author of the *locus classicus* of the anticosmopolitan strain in the 1930s, "Wilder: Prophet of the Genteel Christ," *New Republic* 64 (1930), 266–267.

61. This preoccupation informs, and has an unfortunately constricting effect on, even *Radical Visions and American Dreams,* the recent learned study of the intelligentsia in the 1930s by Richard Pells, whose findings are nevertheless compatible with the argument of this essay.

62. Malcolm Cowley, *Exile's Return* (New York, 1934; rev. ed., New York, 1951). Cf. one of the latest examples of the genre, William Barrett, "The Truants: 'Partisan Review' in the 40's," *Commentary* 57 (June 1974), 48–54, esp. 53–54.

63. Lasch's *New Radicalism* considerably advanced the study of the intelligentsia, but the book is weakened by its highly abstract aim: to chart the growth of a collectivity of *individuals* who manifest the general social characteristics (e.g., detachment, reliance upon the mind in work and play) that presumably distinguish "an intellectual" from other individuals (see esp. ix–xi). At times, Lasch's account of the experience of particular intellectuals can be read as a commentary on certain value conflicts within a community of discourse, but the authenticity of these conflicts and of the community divided by them is muted by Lasch's tendency to depict these arguments merely as occasions for the triumph of a single and generic "social type."

5. The Canon and Its Keepers: Modernism and
Mid-Twentieth-Century American Intellectuals

1. R. P. Blackmur, "A Burden for Critics," *Hudson Review* I (1948), 174, 177.

2. Blackmur, "Burden," 178, 180–181, 184. See also Blackmur's Library of Congress Lectures for 1956 in which he addresses at greater length the unique significance of modern literature and of its critical study: Blackmur, *Anni Mirabiles, 1921–1925: Reason in the Madness of Letters* (Washington, 1956).

3. Robert Penn Warren, *All the King's Men* (New York, 1946), 464.

4. A recent example is Grant Webster, *Republic of Letters: A History of Postwar American Literary Opinion* (Baltimore, 1979), which sharply divides the critics of the 1940s and 1950s into traditions defined by methods of criticism. Although Webster is more

concerned than most historians of criticism have been with the *historical development of distinctive practices* of criticism, he shares the methodological preoccupations that have informed most studies of the subject. These preoccupations defined the widely noted, early study by Stanley Edgar Hyman, *The Armed Vision: A Study in the Methods of Modern Literary Criticism* (New York, 1948).

5. There is an extensive literature on Blackmur, written almost entirely by fellow critics, and written with the polemicism characteristic of critics writing about other critics. For the relevant bibliography, see Webster, *Republic,* 340–341. One of the more sympathetic of these pieces is a sound starting point for the study of Blackmur: Joseph Frank, "R. P. Blackmur: The Later Phase," in Frank's *The Widening Gyre: Crisis and Mastery in Modern Literature* (New Brunswick, N.J., 1963), 229–251. More recently, Russell Fraser has published a biographical study, *A Mingled Yarn* (New York, 1982).

6. The most indispensable book for the study of literary modernism is Malcolm Bradbury and James McFarlane, eds., *Modernism, 1890–1930* (London, 1976).

7. Pound's "insanity" is now known to have been a fraud by means of which Pound avoided being prosecuted for treason, a charge on which he was indicted in 1945. See the excellent treatment of this episode in Stanley I. Kutler, *The American Inquisition: Justice and Injustice in the Cold War* (New York, 1982), 59–88.

8. Morton Dauwen Zabel, "Editor's Introduction," *The Portable Conrad* (New York, 1947), 26, 40, 47. See also R. W. Stallman, "The Reputation of Joseph Conrad," in Stallman, ed., *Joseph Conrad: A Critical Symposium* (East Lansing, Mich., 1960), xvii, xix.

9. Marshall Berman, " 'All That Is Solid Melts into Air': Marx, Modernism, and Modernization," *Dissent* XXV (Winter 1978), 54–55.

10. Edmund Wilson, *Axel's Castle: A Study in the Imaginative Literature of 1870–1930* (New York, 1931). Eliot's most influential essays included "Tradition and the Individual Talent," in his *The Sacred Wood* (London, 1920), 42–53, and "The Metaphysical Poets," in his *Selected Essays* (London, 1934), 281–291. On Leavis and his circle, see Francis Mulhern, *The Moment of 'Scrutiny'* (London, 1979).

11. Cleanth Brooks, *Modern Poetry and the Tradition* (Chapel Hill, N.C., 1939), esp. 219–244. See also the famous textbook edited by Brooks and Robert Penn Warren, *Understanding Poetry* (New York, 1938). Brooks has recently reminisced about the writing and reception of these books; see "An Interview with Cleanth Brooks," *Humanities Report* IV (January 1982), 4–11. Brooks's early career is an interesting commentary on the changing use of the term "modernism" in the 1930s. When Brooks wrote "The Christianity of Modernism," *American Review* VI (1935–36), he took it for granted that this term denoted the liberal Protestantism Brooks then attacked (see esp. 437). Brooks's views on religion had not changed appreciably when he published *Modern Poetry and the Tradition,* but "modernism" had so quickly come to be associated with Eliot and other "modern" writers that Brooks's book was reviewed by his friend Ransom as "An Apologia for Modernism," *Kenyon Review* II (1940), 247–251.

12. Critics devoted to authors outside this perimeter sometimes sounded defensive notes. Howard Mumford Jones, who admitted in 1948 to being attracted to "the sunny humanity" of such out-group authors as Burns, Dickens, and Turgenev, went on to complain about "the exploitation of a small shelf of books and the elimination of the rest of world's vast library." See Jones, *The Theory of American Literature* (Ithaca, N.Y., 1948), 2–3.

13. Both the reality of the canon and the difficulties in spelling out the processes by which it is maintained and revised are addressed candidly in Frank Kermode, "Institutional Control of Interpretation," *Salmagundi* #43 (1979), 72–86, esp. 80–83.

14. Donald A. Stauffer, "The Modern Myth of the Modern Myth," in *English Institute Essays—1947* (New York, 1948), 46–49.

15. Blackmur, "Anni Mirabiles," 10.

16. Lionel Trilling, "On the Modern Element in Modern Literature," *Partisan Review* XXVIII (1961); as reprinted in Trilling, *Beyond Culture: Essays on Literature and Learning* (New York, 1965), 7–9, 13, 26, 28. Trilling's guarded attitude toward modernism is sensitively analyzed throughout William Chace, *Lionel Trilling: Criticism and Politics* (Stanford, Calif., 1980).

17. Important examples include Harry Levin, "What Was Modernism?" *Massachusetts Review* I (1960), 609–630; Paul de Man, "What is Modern?" *New York Review of Books* V (August 26, 1965), 10–13; Irving Howe, "The Culture of Modernism," *Commentary* (November 1967), 48–59; and the essays by two British critics with extensive followings in America, Frank Kermode, "The Modern," in Kermode, *Modern Essays* (London, 1971), 39–70; and A. Alvarez, *Beyond All This Fiddle* (London, 1968), 3–21. More recently, see Robert M. Adams, "What Was Modernism," *Hudson Review* XXV (1978), 19–33, and the thirty-four essays, mostly by British scholars, in Bradbury and McFarlane, *Modernism*.

18. Richard Ellmann and Charles Feidelson, Jr., *The Modern Tradition: Backgrounds of Modern Literature* (New York, 1965).

19. Zabel, "Editor's Introduction," 40.

20. Brooks, *Modern Poetry*, 11, 15, 17.

21. Joseph Frank, "Spatial Form in Modern Literature," *Sewanee Review* LIII (1945), 652–563.

22. Perhaps the most forthright and historically informed effort to deal with the apparent link between the term "modernism" and a set of specific ideas is Bradbury and McFarlane's "The Name and Nature of Modernism," in their *Modernism*, 19–55.

23. Common ground—and to some extent common texts—between existentialist philosophy and literary modernism came to be more widely acknowledged in the 1950s when Nietzsche's work was added to the canon. The recognition was registered in, and reinforced by, two books that were popular on American campuses; Walter Kauffman, ed., *Existentialism from Dostoevsky to Sartre* (New York, 1956); and William Barrett, *Irrational Man: A Study in Existential Philosophy* (New York, 1958), esp. 37–58.

24. E.g., Kermode, "Modern," 66.

25. Of the many works addressed to the political activities of the artist-heroes, and to the political implications of their work, one is particularly judicious: William Chace, *The Political Identities of Ezra Pound & T. S. Eliot* (Stanford, Calif., 1973).

26. Blackmur, "Burden," 180–181, 184.

27. The number of doctoral degrees in English granted per year in the United States almost doubled between 1940 (172) and 1955 (328). See National Academy of Sciences, *Doctorate Production in United States Universities* (Washington, 1963), 10–11.

28. Randall Jarrell, "The Age of Criticism," *Partisan Review* XIX (1952), 185–201. See also the comments of Norman Podhoretz, *Making It* (New York, 1967), 29: This was an era when someone asking a youth "what do you want to be when you grow up," might expect the answer, *"a literary critic"!*

29. The connection between the Moscow Trials and the interest of the editors of the *Partisan Review* in modern literature is discussed by James Burkhart Gilbert, *Writers and Partisans: A History of Literary Radicalism in America* (New York, 1968), 205–221.

30. For an overview of these developments, see my "Ethnic Diversity, Cosmopolitanism, and the Emergence of the American Liberal Intelligentsia," *American Quarterly* XXVII (1975), 133–151, and chapter 4 of this book.

31. T. S. Eliot, *After Strange Gods: A Primer of Modern Heresy* (London, 1934), 19–20. Eliot made these soon-to-be famous remarks in lectures at the University of Virginia. Eliot praised the agrarian manifesto of 1930, *I'll Take My Stand,* and defended the ideal of a racially homogeneous, "particular" people grounded in "a particular place."

32. Delmore Schwartz, "T. S. Eliot as the International Hero," *Partisan Review* XII (1945), 199–206, esp. 201, 206. Schwartz's later obsession with Eliot's anti-Semitism, is dealt with in James Atlas's splendid *Delmore Schwartz: The Life of an American Poet* (New York, 1977), 287.

33. See, for example, Webster, *Republic,* 106. Webster's determination to present the 1940s in terms of two, virtually monolithic traditions is surprising in view of the very extensive evidence he presents, in passing, of shared interests and experiences of the "tory-formalists" and the "New York intellectuals." Webster's book is decidedly the most thorough, informative, and historically rigorous contribution to the study of American literary criticism during the mid-century decades. Its strength is sadly diminished by the rigidity of its classification of its sources, and also by the jejune and irrelevant judgments of its author, examples of which have been cited and effectively criticized by Denis Donoghue, *Times Literary Supplement,* July 11, 1980.

34. As early as 1939 Philip Rahv wrote on Kafka in the first volume of John Crowe Ransom's *Kenyon Review,* the chief organ of "tory-formalism." As early as 1940 and 1941 the *Partisan Review* (VII, 181–187; VIII, 174–180) published new poetry by T. S. Eliot himself: two of the *Four Quartets.*

35. The *Hudson's* sense of superiority to the *Partisan* was expressed in its fourth issue; William Arrowsmith, "Partisan Review and American Writing," *Hudson Review* I (1948), 526–536.

36. See, e.g., Marshall Berman, *All That Is Solid Melts Into Air: The Experience of Modernity* (New York, 1981), esp. 16–17.

6. DEMOCRACY AND THE MELTING POT RECONSIDERED

1. Nathan Glazer and Daniel Patrick Moynihan, *Beyond the Melting Pot* (Cambridge, Mass., 1963); Horace Kallen, "Democracy Versus the Melting Pot," *Nation* 100 (1915) 191–194, 217–220. For a helpful study of the various uses to which the symbol of the melting pot has been put, see Philip Gleason, "The Melting Pot: Symbol of Fusion or Confusion?" *American Quarterly* XVI (1964), 20–46.

2. Michael Novak, *The Rise of the Unmeltable Ethnics* (New York, 1971); Peter Schrag, *The Decline of the WASP* (New York, 1971).

3. For a more carefully written and well-informed popular history of the problem of identity in America, see Arthur Mann, *The One and the Many: Reflections on the American Identity* (Chicago, 1979).

4. The extent to which "voluntary" immigration from Europe was produced by the impact of American capitalist expansion on Eastern Europe has been helpfully explored by Gabriel Kolko, *Main Currents in American History* (New York, 1976), 67–79, esp. 67–72.

7. T. S. KUHN'S THEORY OF SCIENCE AND ITS IMPLICATIONS FOR HISTORY

1. R. G. Collingwood, *The Idea of History* (New York, 1946); Thomas S. Kuhn, *The Structure of Scientific Revolutions* (Chicago, 1962; 2d ed. 1970), 1.

2. Collingwood, *Idea of History,* 205–334.

3. See, as examples, the references to Kuhn in Arthur Koestler and J. R. Smythies, eds., *Beyond Reductionism* (Boston, 1970), esp. 228, and in Jean Piaget, *Structuralism*

(London, 1971), 132. Cf. Karl W. Deutsch et al., "Conditions Favoring Major Advances in Social Science," *Science* 171 (1971), 450–459.

4. David H. Fischer, *Historian's Fallacies: Toward a Logic of Historical Thought* (New York, 1970), 162; J. G. A. Pocock, *Politics, Language and Time* (New York, 1971), 15; George W. Stocking, Jr., *Race, Culture, and Evolution* (New York, 1968), 302; Harry W. Paul, "In Quest of Kerygma: Catholic Intellectual Life in Nineteenth-Century France," *American Historical Review* (hereafter *AHR*) 75 (1969–70), 423; Arthur M. Schlesinger, jr., essay review of Robert A. Skotheim, *American Intellectual History and Historians,* in *History and Theory* 7 (1968), 219–221; Hayden V. White, "The Tasks of Intellectual History," *Monist* 53 (1969), 619.

5. E.g., James S. Ackerman, "The Demise of the Avante Garde: Notes on the Sociology of Recent American Art," *Comparative Studies in Society and History* 11 (1969), esp. 372; Murray G. Murphey, "On the Relation Between Science and Religion," *American Quarterly* 20 (1968), 275–295; Pocock, *Politics,* 13–41; Sheldon S. Wolin, "Paradigms and Political Theories," in Preston King and B. C. Parekh, eds., *Politics and Experience: Essays Presented to Professor Michael Oakeshott on the Occasion of His Retirement* (Cambridge, Mass., 1968), 125–152; Reba N. Soffer, "The Revolution in English Social Thought," *AHR* 75 (1969–70), 1938–1964; Bruce Kuklick, "History as a Way of Learning," *American Quarterly* 22 (1970), 609–628. Two examples of Kuhn's use in the history of social science are of special interest to historiography generally: Stocking, *Race,* esp. 7–8, 70, 111–12, 232, 237, 302–303; Nathan G. Hale, Jr., *Freud and the Americans: The Beginnings of Psychoanalysis in the United States, 1876–1917* (New York, 1971), esp. 71–115. This article is not concerned with the applicability of Kuhn's work to the field for which it was designed, the historiography of the developed sciences, but historians outside that field should be aware of the skepticism expressed by some historians of science. See, for example, John C. Greene, "The Kuhnian Paradigm and the Darwinian Revolution," in Duane H. D. Roller, ed., *Perspectives in the History of Science and Technology* (Norman, Okla., 1971), 3–25, but compare the persuasive defense of Kuhn by Leonard G. Wilson, "Commentary on the Paper of John C. Greene," ibid., 31–37.

6. Kuhn, "Postscript" to 2d ed. of *Structure,* 208; Kuhn, "Comment" [on the relation between art and science], *Comparative Studies in Society and History* 11 (1969), 409.

7. Pocock, *Politics,* 13–41; Sheldon S. Wolin, "Paradigms and Political Theories," 125–152.

8. Kuklick, "History," 621.

9. Pocock, *Politics,* 13–41, is without question the most sophisticated and successful contribution to this effort yet to appear. Cf. the interesting essay by Randolph Starn, "Historians and 'Crisis,'" *Past and Present,* no. 52 (August 1971), 3–22, esp. 17–18.

10. One ostensibly friendly reader claimed to find twenty-one meanings for this word in *The Structure of Scientific Revolutions:* Margaret Masterman, "The Nature of a Paradigm," in Imre Lakatos and Alan Musgrave, eds., *Criticism and the Growth of Knowledge* (Cambridge, Mass., 1970), 59–89. Kuhn has subsequently distinguished between two senses of "paradigm": (1) the "disciplinary matrix" consists of "the entire constellation of beliefs, values, techniques, and so on shared by the members of a given community," including (2) "exemplars," the specific, "concrete puzzle-solutions which, employed as models or examples, can replace explicit rules as a basis for the solution of the remaining puzzles of normal science." See "Postscript," 175, 182, 187.

11. Kuhn's concentration on this one factor is species-specific to *The Structure of Scientific Revolutions* and follows from the relative insulation of scientific communities from contingent social conditions external to the traditions of the community.

12. E.g., Guy E. Swanson, *Social Change* (Glenview, Ill., 1971), 119–122; Isaac Kramnick, "Reflections on Revolution: Definitions and Explanation in Recent Scholarship," *History and Theory* 11 (1972), 26–63; Robert A. Nisbet, *Social Change and History: Aspects of the Western Theory of Development* (New York, 1969), esp. 324; and the attempt by the editors of *Comparative Studies in Society and History* to make Kuhn central to a discussion of "A General Theory of Innovation" 11 (1969), 369–432, esp. 369.

13. Bruce Mazlish, *The Riddle of History: The Great Speculators From Vico to Freud* (New York, 1966); Nisbet, *Social Change and History,* esp. 303–304.

14. Kramnick, "Reflections on Revolution," 48, whose discussion of functionalism I have found helpful.

15. On the role of theoretical "generalizations" as opposed to "laws" in historical inquiry, see Carey B. Joynt and Nicholas Rescher, "The Problem of Uniqueness in History," *History and Theory* 1 (1961), 150–162; Maurice Mandelbaum, "Historical Explanation: The Problem of 'Covering Laws,'" ibid., 229–242; C. J. Arthur, "On the Historical Understanding," ibid., 7 (1968), 203–216; and Rudolph Weingartner, essay review of Morton White, *Foundations of Historical Knowledge,* in *History and Theory* 7 (1968), 240–256, esp. 255.

16. Gordon S. Wood, "Rhetoric and Reality in the American Revolution," *William and Mary Quarterly,* 3d ser., 26 (1966), 23.

17. See especially Quentin Skinner, "Meaning and Understanding in the History of Ideas," *History and Theory* 8 (1969), 3–53, which is offered as an attempt to apply to the history of ideas a "set of concepts" similar to that applied to the history of science by Kuhn and to the history of art by E. H. Gombrich, *Art and Illusion* (Princeton, 1960); Skinner, 7. Cf. John Dunn, *John Locke* (Cambridge, 1968); Stocking, *Race,* 1–12. Stocking discusses *The Structure of Scientific Revolutions* along with another contextualist classic, Joseph R. Levenson, *Confucian China and Its Modern Fate* (Berkeley, 1958–65).

18. But cf. Pocock, *Politics,* 14.

19. Winthrop D. Jordan, *White over Black: American Attitudes toward the Negro, 1550–1812* (Chapel Hill, 1968), 3–98.

20. Representative examples include Gene Wise, "Implicit Irony in Perry Miller's *New England Mind,*" *Journal of the History of Ideas* 29 (1968), especially 579–581, and papers given on December 28, 1968, at the meeting of the American Historical Association in Boston: Gene Wise, "Paradigm Formulation in Recent American Studies," and J. Rogers Hollingsworth, "A Paradigm for the Study of Political History." C. Vann Woodward interpreted the paradigm concept more strictly in his presidential address in 1969, when he observed that history, unlike the sciences, had never been endowed with a ruling paradigm: "The Future of the Past," *AHR* 75 (1969–70), 726. Cf. John Higham's careful use of the term in his *Writing American History* (Bloomington, Ind., 1970), 172.

21. John Higham et al., *History* (Englewood Cliffs, N. J., 1965).

22. E.g., J. H. Hexter, "The Rhetoric of History," *History and Theory* 6 (1967), 12–13, and Schlesinger, review of Skotheim, 219–221.

23. Not all the social scientists who use Kuhn can be accused of simply wrapping themselves in "true science." An interesting example of restraint is Robert I. Watson, "Psychology: A Prescriptive Science," *American Psychologist* 22 (1967), 436–440. Cf. David Truman, "Disillusion and Regeneration: The Quest for a Discipline," *American Political Science Review* 59 (1965), esp. 865–866. Yet even Truman, in his final paragraph (873), seems to lean in the direction of the caricature of Kuhnian social scientists offered by Paul Feyerabend, "Consolations for the Specialist," in Lakatos and Musgrave, *Growth,* 198. Cf., as examples without Truman's restraint, Gabriel Almond, "Political Theory and Political

Science," *American Political Science Review* 60 (1966), esp. 869, 875; and Robert T. Holt, "Comparative Studies Look Outward," in Fred W. Riggs, ed., *International Studies: Present Status and Future Prospects* (Philadelphia, 1971), esp. 134–136.

24. E.g., Dudley Shapere, "The Paradigm Concept," *Science* 172 (1971), 706; Israel Sheffler, *Science and Subjectivity* (Indianapolis, 1967); Karl Popper, "Normal Science and Its Dangers," in Lakatos and Musgrave, *Growth*, 56–57; Imre Lakatos, "Falsification and the Methodology of Scientific Research Programmes," in ibid., esp. 93, 115, 178–179. Cf. Alan Ryan, *The Philosophy of the Social Sciences* (London, 1970), esp. 233–235, and Peter Munz, essay review of Robert W. Friedrichs, *A Sociology of Sociology,* in *History and Theory* 10 (1971), esp. 364.

25. This paragraph is based primarily on Kuhn, "Reflections on My Critics," in Lakatos and Musgrave, *Growth,* especially 238, 247, 254, 261–264. Cf. Kuhn, *Structure,* esp. 144–159; and Kuhn, "Postscript," 198–200, 209–210.

26. Kuhn, "Reflections," 244–245.

27. For an especially willful expression of these fears, see Feyerabend, "Consolations," 198–199. Feyerabend's essay, incidentally, is one of the most trenchant critiques of Kuhn yet written. It and Margaret Masterman's "The Nature of a Paradigm" (59–89) are the most readable and interesting contributions to the Lakatos and Musgrave volume, which is a symposium on Kuhn's work and its relation to Karl Popper's philosophy of science. For a lively analysis of this volume and of its place in contemporary philosophy of science, see Joseph Agassi, "Tristram Shandy, Pierre Menard, and All That," *Inquiry* 14 (1971), 152–164. The most reliable guide to the differences between Kuhn and the Popperians, however, is David Bloor, "Two Paradigms for Scientific Knowledge?" *Science Studies* 1 (1971), 101–115. Bloor's sensitive analysis of how the Popperians, especially Lakatos, have revised their position to meet Kuhn's challenge helps to correct the popular misconception that it is only Kuhn who has been led to reformulate some of his claims since 1962.

28. Kuhn, "Reflections," esp. 245, where attention is directed only at the development of disciplines that seek to predict the behavior of natural phenomena and thereby attain "maturity."

29. Feyerabend, "Consolations," 201; Kuhn, "Reflections," 245.

30. Kuhn does make these prescriptions, of course, for the disciplines he practices, or is close to; see not only *Structure,* passim, but also "The Relations between History and History of Science," *Daedalus* 100 (1971), 271–304.

31. Rudolph Weingartner, "The Quarrel about Historical Explanation," in Ronald H. Nash, ed., *Ideas of History* (New York, 1969), 2: 140–157.

32. An excellent summary of what has been conventional wisdon for historians during the past twenty years is found in Higham, et al., *History,* 135–144, esp. 136 (since the 1950s the emphasis has been on "the positive opportunities of the historian's observational position").

33. Kuhn has not been alone in these efforts, as he acknowledges in *Structure,* especially 2–3, and in "History of Science," *International Encyclopedia of the Social Sciences* (New York, 1968), 14: 74–83. Cf. Kuhn, "The Relations between History and History of Science," 288–291. Cf. also two very helpful accounts of recent developments in the history and philosophy of science: Arnold Thackray, "Science: Has Its Present Past a Future?" in Roger H. Steuwer, ed., *Historical and Philosophical Perspectives of Science* (Minneapolis, 1970), 112–127; and Stephen Toulmin, "Rediscovering History: New Directions in Philosophy of Science," *Encounter,* January 1971, 53–64.

34. For Holmes and his intellectual environment, see Morton G. White, *Social*

Thought in America: The Revolt Against Formalism (New York, 1949), 59–75. The comparison of Kuhn to Holmes is also made in an essay I read only after this paper was well advanced, M. D. King, "Reason, Tradition, and the Progressiveness of Science," *History and Theory* 10 (1971), 24–25.

35. Wilfrid E. Rumble, Jr., *American Legal Realism: Skepticism, Reform, and the Judicial Process* (Ithaca, N.Y., 1968).

36. E.g., W. I. Thompson, "Alternative Realities," *The New York Times Book Review*, February 13, 1972, where the view that scientific discoveries are made by those "working outside the containers [of knowledge] in the dark of the unknown . . ." is misleadingly attributed to Kuhn. Cf. the equally dubious attempt to link Kuhn with the socioeconomic determinism of Engels and J. D. Bernal: James E. Hansen, "An Historical Critique of Empiricism," in David H. DeGrood et al., *Radical Currents in Contemporary Philosophy* (St. Louis, 1971), 44, 48.

37. Kuhn, *Structure*, 171–172.

38. Ibid., 170.

39. This continuity of basic aims (see ibid., 168) is what I take Kuhn to be clarifying by his recent references to the "paramount" values of scientific communities. Kuhn, "Logic of Discovery or Psychology of Research?" in Lakatos and Musgrave, *Growth*, 21; "Postscript," esp. 184–185; "Reflections," 262. These clarifications have been interpreted by some as an important change in Kuhn's position. E.g., King, "Progressiveness of Science," 29. In any case, further research on what scientific communities value, tolerate, and disdain is Kuhn's own chief desideratum. See "Reflections," 238.

40. Kuhn, *Structure*, 173.

41. Karl Popper, "Normal Science and Its Dangers," in Lakatos and Musgrave, *Growth*, 53; cf. Herbert Feigl, "Beyond Peaceful Coexistence," in Stuewer, *Perspectives*, 7.

42. Levenson, *Confucian China*, 3: 89.

43. The phrase is Kuhn's. *Structure*, 172.

44. See, as examples of the formulation and use of this distinction, Herbert Feigl, "Philosophy of Science," in Roderick M. Chisholm, et al., *Philosophy* (Englewood Cliffs, N. J., 1964), 472; and Popper, "Normal Science and Its Dangers," 56–58.

45. E.g., Bernard Barber, "The Sociology of Science," *International Encyclopedia of the Social Sciences* (New York, 1968), 14: 92–100; cf. Stephen Cotgrove, "The Sociology of Science and Technology," *British Journal of Sociology* 21 (1970), 1–15.

46. Kuhn, *Structure*, v, 160–173; Kuhn, "Reflections," 236.

47. Two very important contributions to the controversy appeared just when this article was being completed, Stephen Toulmin, *Human Understanding: The Collective Use and Evolution of Concepts* (Princeton, N. J., 1972); and Jerome R. Ravetz, *Scientific Knowledge and Its Social Problems* (Oxford, England, 1972).

8. HISTORIANS AND THE DISCOURSE OF INTELLECTUALS

1. R. G. Collingwood, *An Autobiography* (Oxford, England, 1939), 31.

2. I have in mind particularly John Dunn, "The Identity of the History of Ideas," *Philosophy* 43 (April 1968), 85–104; Quentin Skinner, "Meaning and Understanding in the History of Ideas," *History and Theory* 8 (1969), 3–53; J. G. A. Pocock, *Politics, Language, and Time: Essays on Political Thought and History* (New York: Atheneum, 1971), esp. 3–41. Pocock is closest to the second enterprise on 24 and 25 and 28 and 29, but he manifests throughout this important essay a tendency to return always to the particular "speech act" as the unit of study. An intelligent discussion of these three methodologists

from the perspective, again, of strictly "political thought," is Charles D. Tarlton's "Historicity, Meaning, and Revisionism in the Study of Political Thought," *History and Theory* 12 (1973), 307–328. Skinner's most recent writings are refreshingly more explicit in promoting the investigation of entire political languages, including the asking of how they interact with and gain predominance over one another; see especially his "Political Language and the Explanation of Political Action" (Paper presented to the Annual Meeting of the American Political Science Association, Washington, D.C., September 1977).

3. A number of methodological treatises on intellectual history were written between twenty and thirty years ago, when the field was becoming established in the curricula of American universities. A number of contributions to this earlier literature made sound observations, especially John C. Greene's "Objectives and Methods in Intellectual History," *Mississippi Valley Historical Review* 44 (June 1957), 58–74, which, if read without a mean-spirited eagerness to find Hegel between the lines, remains one of the most sensible articles in the field.

4. On this concept, see the helpful remarks of David L. Hull, "Central Subjects and Historical Narratives," *History and Theory* 14 (1975), 253–274.

5. William J. Bouwsma, *Venice and the Defense of Republican Liberty: Renaissance Values in the Age of the Counter Reformation* (Berkeley, Calif., 1968); Charles Coulston Gillispie, *Genesis and Geology: A Study in the Relations of Scientific Thought, Natural Theology, and Social Opinion in Great Britain, 1790–1850* (Cambridge, Mass., 1951); Perry Miller, *The New England Mind: The Seventeenth Century* (New York, 1939); Perry Miller, *The New England Mind: From Colony to Province* (Cambridge, Mass., 1953).

6. See also Robert Young, "Malthus and the Evolutionists: The Common Context of Biological and Social Theory," *Past and Present,* no. 43 (May 1969), 109–145.

7. Miller, *Seventeenth Century,* x. Compare with Miller the references to "discourse," "dialogue," and "cultural conversation" in the introduction to another classic work in American intellectual history, R. W. B. Lewis, *The American Adam: Innocence, Tragedy and Tradition in the Nineteenth Century* (Chicago, 1955), 1–3.

8. Clifford Geertz, *The Interpretation of Cultures* (New York, 1973), esp. 3–30.

9. Arthur O. Lovejoy, *The Great Chain of Being: A Study of the History of an Idea* (Cambridge, Mass., 1936), 14. Although an extensive literature exists on Lovejoy, one recent contribution is especially helpful: Thomas Bredsdorff, "Lovejoy's Idea of Idea," *New Literary History* 8 (1977), 195–211. See also Daniel J. Wilson, "Arthur O. Lovejoy: An Intellectual Biography" (Ph.D. diss., The Johns Hopkins University, 1975).

10. Lovejoy, *Chain,* 3.

11. Theodore Dwight Bozeman, *Protestants in an Age of Science: The Baconian Ideal and Antebellum American Religious Thought* (Chapel Hill, N.C., 1977).

12. Representative examples from 1975, 1976, and 1977 imprints in American history include the following: Mary O. Furner, *Advocacy and Objectivity: A Crisis in the Professionalization of American Social Science, 1865–1905* (Lexington, Ky., 1975); William R. Hutchison, *The Modernist Impulse in American Protestantism* (Cambridge, Mass., 1976); Thomas L. Haskell, *The Emergence of Professional Social Science: The American Social Science Association and the Nineteenth-Century Crisis of Authority* (Urbana, Ill., 1977); Bruce Kuklick, *The Rise of American Philosophy: Cambridge, Massachusetts, 1860–1930* (New Haven, Conn., 1977). One intellectual biography designed explicitly as a study of the functions performed by a single career in the overlapping communities of discourse of an American academic generation is David A. Hollinger, *Morris R. Cohen and the Scientific Ideal* (Cambridge, Mass., 1975).

13. Ronald G. Walters, *The Antislavery Appeal: American Abolitionism After 1830* (Baltimore, Md., 1976), xiii.

14. On this problem, see E. H. Gombrich, *In Search of Cultural History* (Oxford, England, 1969).

15. John F. Kasson, *Civilizing the Machine: Technology and Republican Values in America, 1776–1900* (New York, 1976).

16. I am thinking here even of the important essays of Quentin Skinner, above all, "Meaning and Understanding," by far his most widely quoted and influential article. Skinner's focus on texts is somewhat less pronounced in a more carefully wrought article that is, unfortunately, read by all too few historians, "Some Problems in the Analysis of Political Thought and Action," *Political Theory* 2 (August 1974), 277–303, but even here "the recovery of the historical meaning of a text" is for Skinner "obviously the main question" (283). Closer to my concerns are his unpublished paper, "Political Language and the Explanation of Political Action," and his *The Foundation of Modern Political Thought*, 2 vols. (Cambridge, England, 1978).

17. Joseph Wood Krutch, *The Modern Temper* (New York, 1929).

18. This extremely common phenomenon might be called, with apologies to Robert K. Merton, the "unanticipated consequences of purposive intellectual acts." A recent and well-known case involves Thomas S. Kuhn, *The Structure of Scientific Revolutions*, rev. ed. (1962; Chicago, 1970). An inquiry into this book's intentions and an inquiry into the questions it was used to answer by many of its readers, especially in the social sciences and the humanities, would produce very different results. Less common, perhaps, but equally interesting is the opposite phenomenon, the obliviousness of the discourse of an author's generation to work that a later generation makes integral to its own discourse, and in relation exactly to the questions the author aimed to answer; classic examples of this involve Spinoza and Mendel.

19. An example of a yet different kind is Daniel Walker Howe, "American Victorianism as a Culture," *American Quarterly* 27 (1975), 507–532, which takes one of the more notorious and amorphous "isms" of nineteenth-century intellectual history and gives it definition as both a "communication system" and a "value system."

20. Kuhn, *Structure;* George W. Stocking, Jr., "On the Limits of 'Presentism' and 'Historicism' in the Historiography of the Behavioral Sciences," *Journal of the History of the Behavioral Sciences* 1 (1965), 211–218; idem, *Race, Culture, and Evolution: Essays in the History of Anthropology* (New York, 1968); Skinner, "Meaning and Understanding." The extent to which Kuhn's theory of scientific change is rooted in traditional historiography is emphasized in David A. Hollinger "T. S. Kuhn's Theory of Science and Its Implications for History," *American Historical Review* 78 (April 1973), 370–393, and chapter 7 of this book.

21. Henry Nash Smith, *Virgin Land: The American West as Symbol and Myth* (Cambridge, Mass., 1950). Frustrating as is its lack of exactness, *Virgin Land* remains one of the most informative contributions ever made to the study of American intellectual history.

22. John William Ward, *Andrew Jackson: Symbol for an Age* (New York, 1955).

23. One sharply drawn critique of this school is effective chiefly as a demonstration of the inadequacy of the theoretical efforts its members have offered as commentaries on their own enterprise: Bruce Kuklick, "Myth and Symbol in American Studies," *American Quarterly* 24 (1972), 435–450.

24. Christopher Lasch, *The New Radicalism in America, 1889–1963: The Emergence of the Intellectual as a Social Type* (New York: 1965).

25. For a more explicitly discourse-based view of the development of an intellectual "class" in America, see David A. Hollinger, "Ethnic Diversity, Cosmopolitanism, and the Emergence of the American Liberal Intelligentsia," *American Quarterly* 28 (1975), 133–151, and chapter 4 of this book.

26. See the suggestions made in papers at the Wingspread Conference and published in John Higham and Paul Conkin, eds., *New Directions in American Intellectual History* (Baltimore, 1979), by Thomas Bender and Murray Murphey. Another pertinent paper was presented at Wingspread by Michael Fellman, "Approaching Popular Ideology in Nineteenth-Century America." See also Howe, "Victorianism."

27. The *OED* entry begins with "Onward course; process or succession of time, events, actions, etc." and with the ancient association between the word "discourse" and "running to and fro."

28. For a hint of Foucault's awareness of this problem, see his *The Archaeology of Knowledge* (New York, 1976), 200.

29. For example, "Foreword to the English edition," Michel Foucault, *The Order of Things: An Archaeology of the Human Sciences* (New York, 1971), and Foucault, *Archaeology of Knowledge,* passim. I find it a general rule in Foucault that whenever the name of "the history of ideas" is invoked, something particularly wrongheaded and unhelpful is about to follow.

30. A cogent discussion can be found in Hayden V. White, "Foucault Decoded: Notes from the Underground," *History and Theory* 12 (1973), 23–54. White is more sympathetic than I am to Foucault's entire program. Practitioners of American history have written remarkably little about Foucault, whose *The Archaeology of Knowledge* is surely one of the most ambitious and intelligent theoretical essays on intellectual history. A partial exception to this silence—partial since the piece remains unpublished—is Robert F. Berkhofer, Jr., "Does History Have a Future? The Challenge of New Ways of Understanding Past Human Behavior for Traditional Historical Analysis" (Paper delivered at the Annual Meeting of the Organization of American Historians, Denver, Colorado, April 1974). This paper is the liveliest of recent discussions, by Americanists, of methodological issues in intellectual history. A helpful piece more directly on Foucault is Alexander N. Block, "Archaeological Analysis and Historiography" (Seminar paper, Department of History, State University of New York at Buffalo, 1974).

31. Foucault, *Archaeology of Knowledge,* esp. 22–26.

32. Since this essay has an essentially affirmative tone regarding American intellectual history, I want to acknowledge that I share the widespread conviction that the subdiscipline has not been living up to its potential in recent years. My complaints, however, are not at all the ones that have been the most loudly proclaimed (for example, the field is elitist, excessively fascinated by ambiguity and complexity, idealist, oblivious to the social origins of ideas, and too literary). Four of the most keenly felt of my own disappointments are these: (1) Our books and articles often are not sufficiently rigorous in clarifying the questions they ask about the American past; (2) Our field has been slow to come to grips with natural knowledge as produced by scientists and as differentially assimilated and employed by various individuals and groups in the twentieth century; (3) We remain too concerned—despite some exemplary repudiations of this limitation—with the uniqueness of American history and not enough with the place of American intellectual history in the history of the West, side-by-side with the national cultures of England, Germany, France, etc.; (4) We have failed to make as clear as we might have that our subject is often the history of the discourse of intellectuals. This fourth complaint alone is a basis for the present essay.

9. PERRY MILLER AND PHILOSOPHICAL HISTORY

1. Edmund S. Morgan, "Perry Miller and the Historians," *Proceedings of the American Antiquarian Society* 74 (1964), 18. Heimert suggests that Miller was implicitly referring to his own work as well as that of Brooks Adams when he quoted, sympathetically, Adams's

claim to have written "not a history of Massachusetts but a metaphysical and philosophical inquiry as to the action of the human mind in the progress of civilization." Alan Heimert, "Perry Miller: An Appreciation," *Harvard Review* 2 (Winter-Spring 1964), 30.

2. The entire oeuvre as it appears in book form, in order of publication, with abbreviations I shall use in notes, is as follows: *Orthodoxy in Massachusetts* (Cambridge, 1933; Boston, 1959); *The New England Mind: The Seventeenth Century* (New York, 1939; Cambridge, 1954; Boston, 1961), *NEM:17; Society and Literature in America* (Leiden, 1949), *SL; Jonathan Edwards* (New York, 1949, 1959), *JE; The New England Mind: From Colony to Province* (Cambridge, 1953; Boston, 1961), *NEM:CP; Roger Williams: His Contribution to the American Tradition* (Indianapolis, 1953; New York, 1962); *Errand into the Wilderness* (Cambridge, 1956; New York, 1964); *EW; The Raven and the Whale* (New York, 1956); *Consciousness in Concord* (Boston, 1958), *CC; The Life of the Mind in America: From the Revolution to the Civil War* (New York, 1965, posthumous), *LMA; Nature's Nation* (Cambridge, 1967, posthumous), *NN*.

3. *JE*, 98. All this may make Miller sound too much like the young Joseph Wood Krutch, but it is clear that Miller confronted the problem with utter seriousness. Such crude materialism as that which defines "the Mechanical" is now out of fashion (although it continues to influence historical writing), but in defense of Miller's sophistication, it should be pointed out that as late as 1949, Gilbert Ryle published *The Concept of Mind;* moreover, the behaviorist, stimulus-response psychology of B. F. Skinner was formidable far into the 1950s.

4. *JE*, 180.

5. *JE*, 148; cf. *JE*, 72, 98, 292, 296–297.

6. *JE*, 73; cf. *JE*, xiii.

7. *JE*, 149; cf. *JE*, 156, 262.

8. *JE*, 148. Many critics have condemned Miller for making Edwards "too modern"; see especially Vincent Tomas, "The Modernity of Jonathan Edwards," *New England Quarterly* 25 (March 1952), 60–84. Although Tomas is literal-minded to a fault, his essay is useful because it demonstrates how a scholar not engaged by the tensions which gripped Miller can define "modernity" so differently, can even fail to grasp the unity of Miller's interpretation of Edwards. Peter Gay is even less successful in attempting to join issue with Miller; see his *A Loss of Mastery: Puritan Historians in Colonial America* (Berkeley, Calif., 1966), 154.

9. *CC*, 127.

10. *CC*, 126.

11. *CC*, 105 (Miller's phrasing); cf *CC*, 79, and, for Thoreau's similar language, a letter quoted in *CC*, 73.

12. *CC*, 55; cf *CC*, 34, 63 and *JE*, 124. The tension between "the Conscious" and "the Mechanical" is less central in Miller's treatment of Roger Williams and Brooks Adams, but the language of two passages is too striking to ignore. Williams's use of typology, an archaic method of reading Scripture, "enabled him to step aside from the juggernaut of historical continuity. . . . It is a plea for an awareness of the infinite depths of consciousness." *The Complete Writings of Roger Williams*, VII, Perry Miller, ed. (New York, 1963), 24. Miller insisted that "no thinking or responsive mind" could now disagree with Adams's gloomy view of the future if mankind fails to attain "a balance between mind and matter." Introduction to Brooks Adams, *The Emancipation of Massachusetts* (Boston, 1962), xxxv.

13. *NEM:17*, 194; cf. *NEM:17*, 155–161, 184–194, 268–279.

14. *NEM:17*, 398–399; cf. *NEM:17*, 484.

15. Perry Miller, "The Responsibility of Mind in a Civilization of Machines," *American Scholar* 31 (Winter 1961–62), 58, 64, 67, 69; cf. *NN*, 160.

16. *NEM:CP*, preface to the Beacon Press edition.

17. *NEM:CP*, x; cf. *NEM:17*, viii–ix.

18. *EW*, 1.

19. *EW*, 2.

20. *EW*, 2; cf. *EW*, 210; *NN*, 160.

21. *LMA*, 293.

22. *EW*, 153.

23. *NN*, 7.

24. *EW*, 1.

25. *NN*, 12; cf. *EW*, 187.

26. *NN*, 13.

27. *EW*, ix.

28. *JE*, 193; cf. *JE*, 190, 260.

29. *NEM:17*, 8.

30. *NEM:17*, 10; cf. *NEM:17*, 20–21.

31. *NEM:17*, 487.

32. *NEM:17*, 157.

33. *NEM:17*, 485–486; cf. *NEM:17*, esp. 397, 430, 462, 489.

34. *NEM:17*, 372–373; cf. *EW*, 184–203.

35. Perry Miller, "Morris Cohen's Philosophy of History," *Nation* 166 (May 15, 1948), 553.

36. *JE*, 245; *NN*, 159; Perry Miller, "The Influence of Reinhold Niebuhr," *Reporter* 18 (May 1958), 39–40; Perry Miller, review of *Faith and History* by Reinhold Niebuhr, *Nation* 169 (August 6, 1949), 138–139.

37. *NN*, 133; cf. *NN*, 161.

38. *JE*, esp. xiii, 271.

39. Miller, "Responsibility," 52–55; *NN*, 118–119; Perry Miller, introduction to the John Harvard Library edition of Philip Schaff, *America* (Cambridge, 1961).

40. *EW*, 101.

41. *NN*, 102.

42. See esp. *SL*, 8–9.

43. J. H. Hexter, "The Rhetoric of History," *History and Theory* 6 (1967), 3–13; David Levin, *In Defense of Historical Literature* (New York, 1967), chapter 1.

44. *JE*, 304–305.

45. *JE*, 311.

46. *JE*, 312; cf. *JE*, 290, 297, 330.

47. *NEM:17*, 47, is perhaps the boldest example.

48. Stephen Toulmin and June Goodfield, *The Discovery of Time* (New York, 1965), 269.

49. F. Scott Fitzgerald, "The Crack-Up," in Edmund Wilson, ed., *The Crack-Up* (New York, 1956), 69.

50. *JE*, 195.

10. The Voice of Intellectual History in the Conversation of Mankind: A Note on Richard Rorty

1. Princeton, N. J., 1980.

2. Michael Oakeshott, "The Voice of Poetry in the Conversation of Mankind," in Oakeshott, *Rationalism and Politics* (London, 1962), 197–247.

3. See, for two guarded responses to Rorty, the commentaries by Ian Hacking and Jaegwon Kim in *The Journal of Philosophy* LXXVII (1980), 579–597.

4. Rorty, "A Reply to Dreyfus and Taylor," *Review of Metaphysics* XXXIV (1980), 39.

5. This is the most interesting follow-up on Rorty's book that I have seen. Dreyfus's "Holism and Hermeneutics" and Taylor's "Understanding in Human Science" are followed by Rorty's "Reply," and by the transcript of a three-way debate. See also David Couzens Hoy, "Hermeneutics," *Social Research* XLIX (1980), 649–671.

6. See, for example, Barry Barnes, *Interests and the Growth of Knowledge* (London, 1977).

7. To bring this heritage to mind, it ought to be sufficient to list here the names of Auerbach, Lovejoy, Miller, Cassirer, H. N. Smith, and Kristeller.

8. Dominick LaCapra, "Rethinking Intellectual History and Reading Texts," *History and Theory* XIX (1980), 275–276.

9. This phrase was offered by Taylor ("Human Science," 26) as a characterization of a popular misconception spread by, among other people, Mary Hesse, in her Academy Lecture, "In Defense of Objectivity," *Proceedings of the British Academy* XVIII (1972), 275–292. Rorty ("Reply," 39) springs to Hesse's side, and to the defense of the charming hyperbole.

10. Rorty, "Reply," 53.

11. AMERICAN INTELLECTUAL HISTORY: SOME ISSUES FOR THE 1980s

1. Morton White, *Social Thought in America: The Revolt Against Formalism,* 3rd ed. (New York, 1976; originally published in 1949); Henry F. May, *The End of American Innocence* (New York, 1959); Ralph Gabriel, *The Course of American Democratic Thought* (New York, 1940); Merle Curti, *The Growth of American Thought* (New York, 1943); Stow Persons, *American Minds* (New York, 1958); Perry Miller, ed., *American Thought: Civil War to World War I* (New York, 1954).

2. William J. Bouwsma, "Intellectual History in the 1980s: From History of Ideas to History of Meaning," *Journal of Interdisciplinary History* 12 (1981), 280.

3. K. M. Minogue, "Method in Intellectual History: Quentin Skinner's Foundations," *Philosophy* 56 (1981), 542.

4. Bernard Bailyn, "The Challenge of Modern Historiography," *American Historical Review* 87 (1982), 22.

5. Bouwsma, "History of Meaning," 283, 287–288.

6. Two helpful reassessments of Miller and his critics, each correcting many popular misconceptions, have just appeared: James Hoopes, "Art as History: Perry Miller's *New England Mind,*" *American Quarterly* 34 (1982), 3–25; Francis T. Butts, "The Myth of Perry Miller," *American Historical Review* 87 (1982) 665–694.

7. Laurence Veysey, "Intellectual History and the New Social History," in *New Directions in American Intellectual History,* eds. John Higham and Paul K. Conkin (Baltimore, 1979), 9.

8. Gordon Wood, "Intellectual History and the Social Sciences," in Higham and Conkin, *New Directions,* 32–33.

9. J. G. A. Pocock, *Politics, Language, and Time: Essays on Political Thought and History* (New York, 1971), esp. 3–41; Quentin Skinner, "Some Problems in the Analysis

of Political Thought and Action," *Political Theory* 2 (1974): 277–303. See also Pocock, "*The Machiavellian Moment* Revisited: A Study in History and Ideology," *Journal of Modern History* 53 (1981), 49–72, esp. 52–53.

10. Veysey, "Intellectual History," esp. 11, 13, 17. See also Veysey, "The New Social History in the Context of American Historical Writing," *Reviews in American History* 7 (1979), 1–12. Although I disagree with much of what Veysey says in these two essays, they do articulate very effectively the whole range of complaints recently made about intellectual history, especially but not exclusively in the name of social history.

11. Richard Rorty, *Philosophy and the Mirror of Nature* (Princeton, N. J., 1980), 394. This book criticizes the epistemological preoccupations of modern philosophy and entreats the contemporary learned world to view its practices with the historical self-awareness that the study of intellectual history has traditionally sought to provide. For a more extensive discussion of this book, see my "The Voice of Intellectual History in the Conversation of Mankind: A Note on Rorty's *Philosophy and the Mirror of Nature*," *Newsletter of the Intellectual History Group* (Spring 1982), 23–28, and chapter 10 of this book.

12. The extent to which even the beliefs that constitute scientific knowledge are to be explained with reference to such "external" conditions as the national and class interests of scientists is now a matter of animated controversy among students of the sociology, history, and philosophy of science. I allude to the controversy here because it has attracted very little notice among American historians, yet has generated some fairly rigorous methodological arguments about an enterprise basic to many projects in American intellectual history: the explanation of belief. See, for example, Larry Laudan, *Progress and Its Problems: Toward a Theory of Scientific Growth* (Berkeley, Calif., 1977), esp. the chapter on "The History of Ideas," 171–195, and the extended exchange between Laudan and two critics: Barry Barnes, "Vicissitudes of Belief," *Social Studies of Science* 9 (1979), 247–263; Laudan, "The Pseudo-Science of Science," *Philosophy of Social Sciences* 11 (1981), 173–198; David Bloor, "The Strengths of the Strong Programme," *Philosophy of Social Sciences* 11 (1981), 199–213; and Laudan, "More on Bloor," *Philosophy of Social Sciences* 12 (1982), 71–74. Although the participants in this exchange are too stubborn to acknowledge common ground, and delight too much in scoring debater's points against one another, the exchange brings out the relevant methodological issues with a sharpness rarely found in the considerable body of literature devoted to the aims and methods of intellectual history generally.

13. See, for example, the very sensible essay by Norman S. Fiering, "Early American Philosophy vs. Philosophy in Early America," *Transactions of the Charles S. Peirce Society* 13 (1977), 216–237.

14. Two such episodes have been studied with admirable sensitivity by Henry F. May, *The Enlightenment in America* (New York, 1976), and Fred H. Matthews, *Quest for an American Sociology: Robert E. Park and the Chicago School* (Montreal, Quebec, 1977).

15. Sacvan Bercovitch, *The Puritan Origins of the American Self* (New Haven, Conn., 1975).

16. Ian Hacking, "Wittgenstein the Psychologist," *New York Review of Books* (April 1, 1982), 42.

17. This presumption and the prospects for its critical renewal are discussed in my "Historians and the Discourse of Intellectuals," in Higham and Conkin, *New Directions,* 42–63, and chapter 8 of this book.

18. Keith Michael Baker, "Enlightenment and Revolution in France: Old Problems, Renewed Approaches," *Journal of Modern History* 53 (1981), 303. See also Wood, "Social Sciences," 32.

19. Pocock, *Politics, Language, and Time,* 38.

INDEX